Nations in Medieval Britain

NATIONS
IN MEDIEVAL
BRITAIN

edited by
HIROKAZU TSURUSHIMA

SHAUN TYAS
DONINGTON
2010

© The Contributors
Published in 2010 by
SHAUN TYAS
(an imprint of 'Paul Watkins')
1 High Street
Donington
Lincolnshire
PE11 4TA

ISBN paperback
1-900289-06-7 (ten digits)
978-1-900289-06-1 (thirteen digits)

ISBN hardback
1-900289-08-3 (ten digits)
978-1-900289-08-5 (thirteen digits)

Typeset and designed from the discs of the authors
by Shaun Tyas

Printed and bound by the MPG Book Group of Bodmin and King's Lynn

CONTENTS

LIST OF CONTRIBUTORS

Hirokazu Tsurushima, FSA, FRHistS, has taught world history at Kumamoto University since 1986. At present he is a member of the councils of the Haskins Society and of the Historical Society of Japan (Shigakukai). He is the editor and translator in chief of *The Oxford Short History of the British Isles*. Recent publications include 'The Eleventh Century in England through Fish-Eyes: Salmon, Herring, Oyster, and 1066', *Anglo-Norman Studies* 29, 2007, 193–213'; *Medieval Documents in Japan and England,* ed. with Associate-Professor Haruki, Tokyo: Nihon Keizai Hyouronsya, 2008.

Ann Williams, FSA, FRHistS, taught early medieval history at the Polytechnic of North London from 1965 to 1988. Since retiring she has lectured and researched in the same field, and in 1997 received an honorary fellowship at the University of East Anglia. Recent publications include *Kingship and Government in Pre-Conquest England*, London: Macmillan, 1999; *Æthelred the Unready: the Ill-counselled King,* London: Hambledon and London, 2003; *The World Before Domesday: the English Aristocracy, 870–1066*, London: Continuum, 2008.

David Roffe, FSA, FRHistS, has worked widely in archaeological units and more recently as a research fellow in the University of Sheffield. His research interests include the Danelaw, landscape history, church history, and insanity in the Middle Ages. Much of his work, however, has focused on the inquest as an instrument of government and Domesday Book. Recent publications include *Domesday: the Inquest and the Book*, Oxford: OUP, 2000; *Decoding Domesday*, Woodbridge: The Boydell Press, 2007, and *The Origins of the Borough of Wallingford: Archaeological and Historical Perspectives*, co-edited with K. S. B. Keats-Rohan, British Archaeological Reports, British Series 494, 2009.

William M. Aird, FRHistS, lectures in Medieval History in the School of History and Archaeology at Cardiff University. His publications include *Robert 'Curthose', Duke of Normandy,* Woodbridge: The Boydell Press, 2008, and *St Cuthbert and the Normans: The Church of Durham, 1071–1153*, Woodbridge: Boydell & Brewer, 1998.

Emily Albu is associate professor of Classics at the University of California at Davis. Recent publications include *The Normans in Their Histories: Propaganda, Myth, and Subversion,* Woodbridge: Boydell & Brewer, 2001; 'Probing the Passions of a Norman on Crusade', *Anglo-Norman Studies* 2005; and 'Bohemond and the Rooster: Byzantines, Normans, and the Artful Ruse', in *Anna Komnene and Her Times*, ed. Thalia Gouma-Peterson, Garland, 2000.

Bronagh Ní Chonaill is a lecturer in the Departments of History, Celtic and Gaelic at the University of Glasgow since 2002. Her research interests include medieval Irish and Welsh law and legal traditions, the medieval life-cycle, and the growth of the medieval town. Recent publications include: 'Child-centred Law in Medieval Ireland', in *The Empty Throne*, eds R. Davis and J. Dunne, Cambridge: CUP, forthcoming; 'Flying Kites with the Children of Hiberno-Norse Dublin', in *Medieval Dublin*, eds J. Bradley, A. J. Fletcher and A. Simms, Dublin: Four Courts, 2008; and 'Impotence, Disclosure and Outcome', Glasgow: Centre of Scottish and Celtic Studies (e-article), 2008.

Dauvit Broun has taught medieval Scottish History at the University of Glasgow since 1990. In 2009 he was appointed to the Chair of Scottish History at Glasgow in succession to Prof. Edward J. Cowan. He is Principal Investigator of the AHRC-funded project, the 'Paradox of Medieval Scotland 1093–1286: Social Relationships and Identities before the Wars of Independence', in collaboration with King's College London and the University of Edinburgh. Recent publications include *Scottish Independence and the Idea of Britain from the Picts to Alexander III*, Edinburgh: EUP, 2007; *The Chronicle of Melrose Abbey*, vol. i, *Introduction and Facsimile Edition* (with Julian Harrison), Woodbridge: Boydell and Brewer and the Scottish History Society, 2007; and *Mìorun Mòr nan Gall: 'the Great Ill-Will of the Lowlander?' Lowland Perceptions of the Highlands, Medieval and Modern* (ed. with Martin MacGregor), Glasgow: Centre of Scottish and Celtic Studies, 2009 (e-book, 2007).

Marie Therese Flanagan is professor of medieval history at the Queen's University of Belfast. She is the author of books and articles on twelfth-century Ireland before and after the intrusion of English settlers, including *Irish Society, Anglo-Norman Settlers, Angevin Kingship: Interactions in Ireland in the Late Twelfth Century*, Oxford, 1989, and *Irish Royal Charters: Texts and Contexts*, Oxford, 2005. Her forthcoming book is on the transformation of the twelfth-century Irish church.

PREFACE AND ACKNOWLEDGEMENTS

This book could not have been written without the research grants from the Japanese Society for the Promotion of Science in 2006 and 2007, the Scientific Research Fund of the Daiwa Anglo-Japanese Foundation in 2006, and the publication itself has been supported by the Kumamoto University research aid for publications fund in 2009. These grants made it possible for me to invite seven specialists from the United Kingdom and the United States of America, and to hold two symposia concerned with 'Nations in Medieval Britain' (the British Isles and Ireland). On the 19th of November, 2006, I held the first symposium on 'The Early Medieval Nations in England' at Tohoku University, with Dr Ann Williams and Dr David Roffe from England, Dr William Aird from Wales, and Professor Emily Albu from the United States. Its proceedings have already been published in Japanese with English summaries without notes, in *Seiyoshi Kenkyu (Studies in Western History)* 36, 2007, 144–222. The second symposium was concerned with the 'Celtic districts' of Wales, Scotland and Ireland, with Dr Bronagh Ní Chonaill, Professor Dauvit Broun, and Professor Marie-Therese Flanagan. It was held at Keio University on the 19th of May, 2007. Other papers by the same scholars read in Kumamoto University at the time were translated and published as 'Identities and Historical Sources in the Medieval Celtic Area', *The Western History Essays, Kansai University* 11, 2008, 34–83.

However, this book is not just the proceedings of two symposia. Since then, all the contributors have revised their original papers with additional thoughts and footnotes. The editor has written a new introduction to highlight the relevant subjects for the discussion of medieval nationhood in Britain. I hope that I have accomplished this purpose in some small degree. As a subject of historical research, however, the idea of the nation is quite problematic, and the topic is too important to be subject to sentimental arguments rather than scientific research.

No nation could be born without mutual relations with its neighbours; the idea of a nation developing from within, in isolation from the outside, is a 'castle in the air'. In this collection I and all the other contributors consider the formation of nations as sincerely and as objectively as we can. Even so, it is inevitable that there will be a lot of criticism, in particular against my introduction, which may be too stereotypical and theoretical in its approach. This, however, is partly a result of the tradition of education I have received in the Japanese university system since 1972. I was born in Hokkaido, on the northern fringe of Japan, educated in

Tohoku, the northern semi-peripheral country, and found a post in Kumamoto, the southern semi-peripheral country. I am, therefore, conscious of being a frontiersman; indeed I take some small pride in this fact.

It has been my great honour and privilege to edit this book, since all the contributors are leading historians in this subject in the Anglo-American world. When I first came to Britain in 1977, I was a vulnerable Japanese student. Thirty-three years have passed since then. How many, and how great the changes which have happened since! I cannot edit this book without being influenced by these political and cultural changes, over more than one generation; I have also been influenced by the kind and serious help of many people in Japan, Britain and Ireland, and the United Sates; in addition to my honourable contributors, I thank Professor Kenji Yoshitake, Professor Hideyuki Arimitsu, Professor Nobuyo Tsunemi, Professor Shigeru Akita, and my colleagues at Kumamoto University, Dr Kenji Nishioka, Dr Miho Tanaka and Dr Hiroko Yanagawa. Professor John Gillingham helped me when I read my first paper in the Institute for Historical Research, London, in 1978 (though he may not remember it); Dr Marjorie Chibnall kindly invited me to the Battle Conference on Anglo-Norman Studies, accepting me into an academic fraternity; and Dr Susan Reynolds sharpened my interests in historical research and especially historical dispute (how often I can hear her saying 'nonsense!'). Another friend from the Anglo-Norman conference was the late Ian Pierce, who helped me (and many others) to spend a wonderful time in Battle.

Shaun Tyas, our publisher, has shown me his endurance and tolerance, since he received a final paper, final final paper, absolutely final paper and then a new final paper of my introduction; and the contributors Ann Williams and David Roffe have helped me considerably with the editing of the book.

If we consider the last, miserable war between us, from 1941 to 1945, we now stand at a commanding height, which we could not have imagined before, from where we can think about what nations were, are and will be. If this book contributes, even in a small degree, to the development of such research, it will surpass all my dreams.

Lastly it is my dearest wish to express my thanks to Etsuko within whose hand I have danced.

Hirokazu Tsurushima, 14th March, 2010
Kanade IHR, Mashiki-Kumamoto, Japan

LIST OF ABBREVIATIONS

AI	*Annals of Inisfallen*, ed. S. Mac Airt, Dublin Institute for Advanced Studies, Dublin 1951
AU	*Annals of Ulster (to A.D. 1131)*, ed. Gearóid Mac Niocaill, Dublin Institute for Advanced Studies, Dublin 1983
ANS	*Anglo-Norman Studies*
ASC	*The Anglo-Saxon Chronicle: a Revised Translation* ed. D. Whitelock, D. C. Douglas and Susie Tucker, London 1969
ASC, Swanton	*The Anglo-Saxon Chronicle,* trans. and ed. Michael Swanton, London 1996
ASE	*Anglo-Saxon England*
BAR	British Archaeological Reports
EHD	*English Historical Documents* i, *500-1042* ed. D. Whitelock, London 1955
EHR	*English Historical Review*
fo, ff	folio, folios
GDB	*Great Domesday Book: Library Edition,* ed. Ann Williams, R. W. H. Erskine and G. H. Martin, 6 vols, London, 1986–92
Gesta Regum	*William of Malmesbury, Gesta Regum Anglorum*, ed. R. A. B. Mynors, R. M. Thomson and M. Winterbottom, 2 vols, OMT, 1998–9
HE	*Bede's Ecclesiastical History of the English People*, ed. B. Colgrave and R. A. B. Mynors, OMT, 1969
Historia de Sancto Cuthberto	*Historia de Sancto Cuthberto: a History of Saint Cuthbert and a Record of his Patrimony,* ed. Ted Johnson-South, Woodbridge 2002

Historia Regum	in *Symeonis Monachi Opera Omnia*, ed. Thomas Arnold, Rolls Series, 2 vols, London 1882–85, vol. II
John of Worcester	*The Chronicle of John of Worcester*, ed. R. R. Darlington and P. McGurk, 2 vols, Oxford 1995–8
LDB	*Little Domesday,* ed. Ann Williams and G. H. Martin, 6 vols, London 2000.
ModE	Modern English
ModWelsh	Modern Welsh
OB	Brittonic
ODNB	*Oxford Dictionary of National Biography (New Dictionary of National Biography),* Oxford, 2004
OE	Old English
Orderic	*Orderic Vitalis Historia Ecclesiastica*, ed. M. Chibnall, OMT, 1969-80
s.a.	*sub anno*
Scottish Annals	*Scottish Annals from English Chroniclers AD 500–1286*, ed. A. O. Anderson, London 1908; corrected edn, Stamford 1991
SHR	*Scottish Historical Review*
Symeon, *Libellus*	*Libellus de Exordio atque procursu istius, hoc est Dunhelmensis ecclesie: Tract on the Origins and Progress of this, the Church of Durham,* ed. D. W. Rollason, OMT, 2000
Symeonis	*Symeonis monachi opera omnia*, ed. T. Arnold, Rolls Series, 2 vols, London 1882–85

What Do We Mean by 'Nations' in Early Medieval Britain?

HIROKAZU TSURUSHIMA

As a teacher of world history[1] in the faculty of Kumamoto University, I frequently ask my students when the name of Japan first appeared. Most of them fail to give me a correct answer, though they are not less able students for that. However, they cannot even imagine that the name 'Japan' was invented when the high-king of Yamato entitled himself *Ten-nou* (emperor) in the latter part of the seventh century. This was after the defeat of Hakusuki-no-e-no-tatakai ('Battle of the White Village River', or the 'Battle of the Paekchon River') against the combined fleet of the Tang Empire and the Silla Kingdom in 663,[2] when the Yamato Imperial court changed its policy and decided to pursue the conquest of the North-East (Emishi and Ezo) and South (Kumaso, or more precisely Hayato) parts of the Islands. They aimed to make a small empire in the East Sea, following the Chinese example.[3] The names of both the state, Nippon, that is Japan, which means 'the place where the sun rises', and of its ruler, the emperor, were created at this time.[4] The name Nippon itself was an ideological symbol for this policy of making a small eastern empire in the Chinese world, because it is not from the point of view of Japan itself but from that of China that the Japanese islands are the place where the sun rises. It is, of course, anachronistic to maintain that the Japanese state *and* the Japanese nation were firmly formed at this time; this is a belief and not a historical fact. In the seventh century, the word 'Japan' did not mean the same as it does in modern times. Even if the name itself is the same, the fabric of state and nation have continued to be constructed and deconstructed up to the present date. But as far as the idea of the nationhood is concerned, there is more to it than that. People,

[1] As a high-school subject, world history was introduced into Japan after the Second World War, under the influence of the United States. One modern text book says simply that 'in 1066 Duke William of Normandy conquered England and established a line of Norman kings. Afterwards, feudal institutions were introduced into England and the lords who had come from Northern France dominated the Anglo-Saxons'; *World History B*, Teikoku-shyoin 2009, 87. Nevertheless, the events of 1066 are also famous in Japan. See Emily Albu, 'Normans and the kingdom of the English, below, pp. 61–70.

[2] Bruce L. Batten, *Gateway to Japan: Hakata in War and Peace, 500–1300*, University of Hawaii Press 2006, 23–25.

[3] T. Yoshida, *The Birth of Japan*, Iwanami 1997 (written in Japanese).

[4] Y. Amino, *What is Japan?*, Koudanshya 2000 (written in Japanese).

especially nationalists, easily believe in the eternal existence of the nation. When you open the text books of Japanese history, you will find palaeolithic men in the first chapter, but in what sense were they Japanese? Frequently the concept of nationality is a matter of doctrine rather than science. But the only point I wish to highlight here is that the Japanese nation in the seventh century, which arguably only included the ruling group, developed within the Chinese world (using the term 'the world' in the sense of a broad society sharing such cultural values as a common calendar). Seventh-century Japan, located on the fringes of this world, tried to be a small empire in its own right by expanding its immediate borders,[5] although it still derived its culture from China.

This book consists of the proceedings of two symposia, following the inspiration of an earlier symposium organised by Dr Susan Reynolds at Kumamoto University in 1997, entitled 'Nationalism and the Idea of Nation: Modern or Pre-Modern?' The two symposia were held at Kumamoto in 2006 and 2007 and were concerned with the medieval nations in the British Isles.[6] The purpose of the book is to show the formative processes of nations in early medieval Britain. The term 'early medieval' here means the period from the fifth century, when imperial power dissolved in the western part of the Roman Empire, to the eleventh and twelfth centuries, when European secular kingdoms, which were partial prototypes of modern nation-states, came on the scene. The concept of 'Britain' might be unacceptable to modern Irish people, like the term 'Celtic fringe', which has frequently been used derogatorily. However, 'Ptolemy's usage justifies our lumping Britain and Ireland together as "the British Isles"'.[7]

The concept of a 'nation' is problematic and difficult to define, since it does not necessarily reflect the innate characteristics of actual human communities.

[5] The Kumaso, the peoples in the southern part of Kyushyu, had already been subjected to Yamato in the fifth century, and the central government regarded the peoples to the north of them as barbarians. Of these, the Emishi in the north-east of the main island were assimiliated in about the twelfth century, leaving only the Yezo in Hokkaido. The Yezo were also called Ainu (originally meaning 'good human-beings'), but they called themselves Utari, a term analogous to Cymry. See Ann Williams, 'Why are the English not Welsh?', below, pp. 19–31.

[6] For the 1997 symposium see *The Review of History* 84, 1998, 5–22 (written in Japanese). The two recent symposia have been published in Japanese with English summaries without notes, *Seiyoshi Kenkyu (Studies in Western History)* 36, 2007, 144–222.

[7] E. James, *Britain in the First Millennium,* London 2001, 8. The term 'Celtic fringe' is also used geopolitically: 'Hence the radicalism dominant behind Gladstone was that of districts hitherto in the background, and particularly of Wales and Scotland. Over and above its alliance with the Irish, the liberal party came very visibly to depend on the "Celtic fringe"' (R. C. K. Ensor, *England 1870–1914*, Oxford History of England 14, Oxford 1936, 207); and from the point of view of cultural ethnicity, see Michael Hechter, *International Colonialism: the Celtic Fringe in British National Development 1536–1966,* London 1978, and Laura O'Connor, *Haunted English: The Celtic Fringe, the British Empire, and De-Anglicization*, Baltimore 2006.

The word 'nation' as it will be used here means people who had built a state,[8] or had a strong intention of state-building, and whose ruling group had (or was believed to have) shared common memories of culture and history with the various communities over which it had established unification. According to this definition, the forms and structures of nations could vary from time to time, but always embodied the idea of a political community with a common culture.[9] This community, however, may change its characteristics from time to time, according to fluctuations in political structures through the ages. The same is true of the more recent concept of 'ethnicity'. Originally this was used for non-Christian communities, and then for ethnological groups with their own cultural, religious or linguistic characteristics. However, even these elements may have changed, gradually or drastically, through the ages. As for the early middle ages, although it may be said that an ethnic group is a sort of cultural community, it cannot be maintained that this community coincided with the nation governed by the ruling group. Just as the idea of a medieval Anglo-Saxon nation-state is anachronistic if it is defined as a secular state with self-determination, so ideas of medieval ethnicity may also carry a faint aroma of anachronism.[10]

The nations which are discussed here were born during the process which forged the European world into Latin Christendom. The formation of nations in Britain had a long history, in the course of which many peoples interacted with each other, conquering or being conquered, repeatedly meeting and parting, changing their own and others' identities. The crucial period was 'the long eleventh-century' (c.970–1135).[11] The tenth- and eleventh-century kingdoms of

[8]   There was no equivalent word for 'state' in the period concerned. Susan Reynolds maintains that this was a matter of language rather than reality, and regards it as an analytical concept; Sarah Foot, however, takes it as designating a real difference, perhaps from the view-point of historiography rather than the concepts in the sources. See Susan Reynolds, 'The historiography of the medieval state', in *Companion to Historiography*, ed. Michael Bently, London 1997, 117–138; Sarah Foot, 'The historiography of the Anglo-Saxon "nation" state', in *Power and the Nation in European History*, ed. Len Scales and Oliver Zimmer, Cambridge 2005, 125–142, at 128–129. A close study of the concept 'state' is not necessary for our present concern. The point I want to make here is simply that we cannot examine pre-modern polities from the point of view of the modern state *a priori*.

[9]   Susan Reynolds, 'The idea of the nation as a political community', in *Power and the Nation in European History*, ed. Scales and Zimmer, 54–66. I do not think that we need to over-use other working concepts like ethnicity to designate this kind of political group, though we must consider the potential of a new nation for creating ethnicity. William Aird suggests that 'Englishness' does not refer to a single ethnicity, but, rather to a combination of ethnicities; see William Aird, 'Northumbria and the making of the kingdom of the English', below, p. 60. See also Anthony D. Smith, *The Ethnic Origins of Nations*, Oxford 1986; Hugh M. Thomas, *The English and the Normans,* Oxford 2003.

[10]   Foot, 'The historiography of the Anglo-Saxon "nation" state, 125–142.

[11]   Cf. John Gillingham, *The English in the Twelfth Century,* Woodbridge 2000, 163.

England and Alba (later Scotland), as well as the smaller kingdoms of Wales and Ireland, were the result of such processes. These kingdoms and districts, which experienced in different degrees Roman occupations (or at least Roman cultural influences), missions of the Roman church, Germanic and Danish invasions, and Norman conquests, must all, because of their mutual inter-relationships, be understood as the object of British history.

The work of Benedict Anderson has been very influential in the study of the nation as a concept.[12] Anderson sees two elements as absolutely crucial for the development of a concept of nationalism: a kingdom and a religious community. The structures of kingdoms and churches in medieval Britain may thus be considered for discussion as two co-ordinate axes. As Anderson suggests, a 'nation' was an imagined community. We need a flexible interpretation of medieval European nations, for those 'nations' which are described in contemporary documents were not realities but constructs, heavily influenced by the world of the Old Testament. It is also relevant to consider not only what happened but what did not happen, so aborted or extinct nations such as the Hwicce, Mercians, Northambrians, Danes, Normans, and so on, are also of interest.[13]

In Britain the starting point of research into nations must be the *Ecclesiastical History of English People*, written by the eighth-century Northumbrian monk, the venerable Bede. He followed concepts introduced in the Torah when he divided the nations of Britain into five language groups, the Britons, the Picts, the Irish, the English, and the Latin-speakers (*HE* i, 1).[14] After the Romans retreated, the Britons retained a consciousness of being heirs of the Roman heritage.[15] In the

[12] Benedict Anderson, *Imagined Communities: Reflections on the Origins and Spread of Nationalism*, London, 2nd edn 1991.

[13] Is it possible to interpret the history of Japan not from the points view of Tokyo or Kyoto, but from Kumamoto or Sapporo? So might English history be seen 'not from Winchester, but from Durham'? (Foot, 'The historiography of the Anglo-Saxon "nation" state, 138). See William Aird, 'Northumbria and the making of the kingdom of the English', below, p. 47, who asks a serious question: 'we might move away from the West Saxon "master-narrative" and question the assumption that the region was predestined to be included in the kingdom of England'. There is, of course, no 'if' in history, but if we use the terms 'imperialism', 'Celtic fringe', 'conquest' or 'hegemony of England', we should also take into consideration the conquered, the absorbed, integrated and resisting sides. In the tenth, eleventh and early twelfth centuries, for example, there was still some potentiality for the incorporation of Northumbria into an enlarged Scottish kingdom. The last attempt to create a 'Scoto- Northumbrian realm' was in 1216–17, when Alexander II took Carlisle and received the homage of the barons of Northumberland and some of the barons of Yorkshire (Professor Broun's sugesstion). This book attempts to give the subject a thorough grounding by considering these different perspectives.

[14] When we read Bede's work, we must remember his hostility and prejudice against the British people. See Ann Williams, 'Why are the English not Welsh?', below, pp. 26–7.

[15] T. M. Charles-Edwards, 'The making of nations in Britain and Ireland in the early mid-

4

eighth century, however, language was not the criterion for defining the nation, although we cannot underestimate the 'constructive power of language and its application in a political sphere'.[16] On the contrary, it might often have been the case that a political unit established its own language. It was the Romans who actually divided the Britons from the Picts by describing only those who accepted the *pax Romana* as 'Britons', though the language of the Picts was related to that of the Britons. Political, not linguistic, situations therefore defined the division between Picts and Britons.[17]

The nations of the Saxons and Angles built their own kingdoms. However, we must remember that there may have been 'a degree of rapprochement at the top level of society' in the cultural accommodation and assimilation of the British people.[18] Political relations with the continental kingdoms should also be taken into account.[19] These 'Germanic' people must have consolidated their own identities as 'Saxons' and 'Angles' only after settlement, so that Saxon and Anglian provinces were a reality, but they were not linguistic but political units. Both Angles and Saxons belonged to the same English-speaking people, although they had their own dialects.[20] We may be sure that English, as the normative language,

---

dle ages', in *Lordship and Learning: Studies in Memory of Trevor Aston*, ed. R. Evans, Woodbridge 2004, 11–37. Cf. R. R. Davis, 'The peoples of Britain and Ireland, 1100– 1400', *TRHS* ser. 6, 4–7 1994–1997, 1–20; 1–20; 1–23; 1–24.

[16] Foot, 'The historiography of the Anglo-Saxon 'nation' state', 126.

[17] Charles-Edwards, 'The making of nations in Britain and Ireland in the early middle ages', 28. It was in the time of Constantius Chlorus, the father of Constantine the Great, that the word 'Pict' first appeared; therefore it is 'not of great antiquity and may have been bestowed by Roman writers around the turn of the fourth century to describe a new coalition of peoples (Caledonians, Maeatae and the various other northern tribes) whose earlier recorded names appear to be of British origin'; *A Companion to the Early Middle Ages*, ed. Pauline Stafford, Oxford 2009, 47. Gildas had some sense that the Britons were a part of a wider community of the Roman empire, so for him the Picts were among the invaders of Britain; James, *Britain in the First Millennium*, 36–37.

[18] See Ann Williams, 'Why are the English not Welsh?', below, p. 23. The monolingualism of the English shows the assimilation of the British people into the Germanic groups, although we can never know whether they called themselves English or British. The early medieval nations were depicted through the words of the ruler or the conqueror. The nation was composed of many ethnic groups, which were not usually noticed in written records. Thus ethnicity is a difficult subject to research (see above, note 9). It may well be that an individual could belong to more than one nation, if he was the subject of more than one ruler, and might therefore adopt a particular 'nationality' according to varying political situations. One's 'nation' might sometimes thus be a matter of choice. See Ann Williams, 'Why are the English not Welsh?', below.

[19] See Ann Williams, 'Why are the English not Welsh?', below, p. 25. On the close connections of Kent and Frankia, see Barbara Yorke, *Kings and Kingdoms of Early Anglo-Saxon England*, London 1997, 38–42.

[20] See Ann Williams, 'Why are the English not Welsh?', below, p. 28.

was created in the area now called England (*Engla lond*).[21] As for the Britons, in the sixth century they spoke both British and (probably) Latin, but these languages were not a hallmark of their identity. Only in the process of Germanic immigration did the British language gradually come to be a standard of national consciousness. It was as a result of military confrontation with the English that 'Britishness' came to depend more and more on linguistic characteristics, while, at the same time, the English language came to be the norm for the Germanic peoples. In the time of Bede, many Britons spoke English and were assimilated into English political units. In the south and east the British language seems to have completely disappeared and Old English certainly came to be the dominant language throughout most of Britain east of the Severn.[22] A new sense of Britishness was generated as a contrast to the dominance of the English.

In his biography of *Gerald of Wales*,[23] Robert Bartlett maintains that self-consciousness is created in a mutual relationship with others. A nation was not a natural and given entity, but was made in the course of relations with neighbouring peoples. In a polemical paper ('Bede, the *bretwaldas* and the origins of the *gens Anglorum*'), Patrick Wormald widened our view of this subject.[24] In the course of his demolition of the 'Bretwalda theory',[25] which saw secular politics as the origin

[21] According to the Oxford English Dictionary (2nd edn 1989), 'England' originally meant the territory of the Angles as distinguished from that of the Saxons. It was in the eleventh century that the word *Engla-lond* was first used as it is today; see Patrick Wormald, '*Engla lond*: the making of an allegiance', *Journal of Historical Sociology* 7, 1994, 1–24, at 10. During the reign of King Alfred, both in his writings and in the *Anglo-Saxon Chronicle*, the word *Ange-cynn* (Bede's *gens Anglorum*) is used to denote collectively all the so-called Germanic peoples in Britain: 'when Alfred united the men of Kent, Wessex and Mercia and received their submission to his rule in 886, his court promoted a new word to define that imagined community: *Angelcynn*' (Foot, 'The historiography of the Anglo-Saxon "nation" state', 19 and cf. Sarah Foot, 'The making of *Angelcynn*: English identity before the Norman Conquest', *TRHS* 6th ser. 6, 1996, 25–49). It is in the process of unifying the kingdom and with the appearance of a single king of the English (*rex Anglorum*) that England came to be seen as the territory governed by that king.

[22] J. Hines, 'The beginning of the English: identity, material culture and language in early Anglo-Saxon England', *Anglo-Saxon Studies in Archaeology and History* 7, 1994, 49–59.

[23] Robert Bartlett, *Gerald of Wales*, Oxford 1982, 10.

[24] Patrick Wormald, 'Bede, the *bretwaldas* and the origins of the *gens Anglorum*', in *Ideal and Reality in Frankish and Anglo-Saxon Society: Essays Presented to J. M. Wallace-Hadrill,* ed. Patrick Wormald, D. A. Bullough and R. Collins, Oxford 1983, 99–129.

[25] Wormald, 'Bede, the *bretwaldas* and the origins of the *gens Anglorum*', 105. The term 'bretwalda', meaning 'ruler of Britain', first appears in the 'A' recension of the Anglo-Saxon Chronicle for 829, which says that Ecgberht of Wessex was the eighth king to be so styled. However, other recensions of the Chronicle, such as 'E', have 'brytenwalda', which means 'wide ruler'. There is much dispute over the correct term, which is not important for this historical survey. Although this term seems to have only meant 'high-

of the English nation, he laid especial emphasis on the role of the Roman Church. It was, he suggested, as a result of Bede's vision that the English came to see themselves as a single people, united under the jurisdiction of the archbishop of Canterbury. From the ninth and tenth centuries, the religious element in the coronation of the king became the main distinguishing feature of this 'official kingdom', approved by the pope in Rome as a unit of Latin Christendom, as opposed to the personal rule of self-proclaimed kings, local chieftains or powerful leaders. It was the archbishop who anointed and crowned the king, and thus the existence and primacy of the archbishop came to be the crucial point for the formation of the nation.

The invasion of the Danes 'brought about the unification of the English kingdom, and aided in the unification of the kingdom of Scotland'.[26] Dr David Roffe here discusses their impact on the making of the kingdom of English. Their activity also nipped in the bud the making of the kingdom of the Northumbrians, the subject of Dr William Aird's contribution.[27] The Norman Conquest inextricably tied the medieval English kingdom into the politics of France, yet by the 1130s the union of Normans and English had created a new, profoundly English people. Dr Emily Albu discusses the problem of Norman and English identities. Though it was the Normans who through their invasion made British history by tying together England, Wales, Scotland and Ireland, we, as modern historians, still live in the shadow of the Norman myth when we use the invented phrase 'Anglo-Norman', because 'there is no extant evidence that anyone in the eleventh or twelfth centuries ever used the term "Anglo-Norman" [and] in the absence of some such term, it is clearly not easy to argue for the existence of an Anglo-Norman nationality'.[28] Although the Normans maintained at least some sense of Norman identity through the twelfth century, R. H. C. Davis identified the unity of land and people as 'a most important part of the Norman myth', and once they had left Normandy behind, it was not easy for Normans to resist assimilation into the nationalities of those they conquered. In the end, their origin-legend was the product 'not of

---

king', or 'overlord', it has always been understood in the context of Bede's own statement that seven kings had *imperium* over much or all of Britain (*HE* ii. 5, 148–150). Some modern historians based the 'Bretwalda theory' on the term 'bretwalda' and Bede's statement. It has a whiggish characteristic, suggesting some sort of eternal life and destiny for the English polity, comparable to the concept of the 're-Conquest of the Danelaw'(see, for example, F. M. Stenton, *Anglo-Saxon England*, Oxford, 3rd edn 1971, 34–5). See Aird, 'Northumbria and the Making of the Kingdom of the English', below, pp. 46, 59.

[26] James, *Britain in the First Millennium,*, 2.

[27] However, he requires us to reconsider the extent and nature of the Scandinavian settlement even in the North. See William Aird, 'Northumbria and the Making of the Kingdom of the English', below, pp. 47–8.

[28] Gillingham, *The English in the Twelfth Century*, 124.

blood, but of history', as opposed to the legend of 'Míl of Spain', which envisaged a group bound by common descent.[29]

Making the Nation: Religious Communities

Bearing all this in mind, let us examine the roles of Anderson's two axes of nation-hood, religious communities and kingdoms, in the emergence of the nations of Britain. To take the religious aspect first, we may start by reading Bede's *Ecclesiastical History*. His chief words for peoples are *gens, populus,* and *natio*, among which *gens* is the most frequently employed; possibly because it is also used in the famous phrase of *Matthew* 28: 19: 'go ye therefore and teach all nations (*gentes* in the Vulgate)'.[30] Although all three terms may have meant the nation as a political community, it is worthwhile exploring Bede's usage of *natio*, which is the direct ancestor of the word nation. Since the British church survived in the west and influenced the conversion of the local English settlers in the region, the underlying purpose of Bede's book was to maintain the orthodoxy of the Roman and English (*Anglus*) church, in the course of which he expresses both animosity and disdain towards the church of the Britons. *Anglus* in this context did not denote the Northumbrian people to which Bede belonged, nor even the Angles, the group of peoples which included the Northumbrians and others, but all those people in Britain who later came to be known as the English (Saxons and Jutes as well as Angles), a christianized people and a spiritual community loosely unified by a common language and ecclesiastical structure, although politically there were many kings and kingdoms diverse in dimensions and characteristics.[31] In the eighth century an English nation in the political sense was an imagined construct, but Bede's vision had already provided the sense of a unified church, centred on the archiepiscopal church of Canterbury, bound to wider Christendom through Rome since the time of Augustine's mission.[32]

[29] See Emily Albu, 'Normans and the kingdom of the English, below, p. 62, and Marie-Therese Flanagan, 'Strategies of distinction: defining nations in medieval Ireland', below, pp. 107–8.

[30] *HE* iii 8, 158; iv 19, 392, quoting *Matthew* 28:20 whose first sentence continues from the second sentence of 28:19. See further Marie-Therese Flanagan, 'Strategies of distinction: defining nations in medieval Ireland below, p. 106.

[31] 'This presupposes some fusion of the concepts of national and spiritual identity'; J. M. Wallace-Hadrill, *Bede's Ecclesiastical History of the English People, A Historical Commentary*, Oxford 1988, 67.

[32] There were probably some Christians, remnants of the Romano-British population, in Kent before Augustine's mission. The missionary party was augmented by Frankish priests at Gregory's request, and the kingdom of Kent itself was under Frankish influence. King Æthelberht, who had married a Christian princess named Bertha, a daughter of Charibert I, one of the Merovingian kings of the Franks, was at that moment a leading ruler and held a dominant position in south-eastern Britain. See H. Mayr-Harting, *The Coming of Christianity to Anglo-Saxon England*, London, 3rd edn 1991, 32–33; N. Brooks, *The Early History of the Church of Canterbury*, Leicester 1984, 4–7.

Bede used the word *natio* not just for the English, but also, separately, for the Picts, the Britons, the Scots and (before their conversion) for the Mercians. The following citations show how the word *natio* might mean the people to be converted and incorporated into the religious community: 'if they would preach the way of life to the English nation: *si nationi Anglorum noluissent uiam uitae praedicare*' (*HE* ii, 2, 140); 'the archbishop [Honorius] sent him [Felix] to preach the word of life to this nation of the Angles: *misit eum ad praedicandum uerbum uitae praefatae nationi Anglorum*' (*HE* ii, 15, 190); 'the southern Picts who lived on this side of the mountains had, so it is said, long ago given up the errors of their idolatry and received the true faith through the preaching of the Word by that reverend and holy man Bishop Ninian, a Briton [*uiro de natione Brettonum*] who had received orthodox instruction at Rome in the faith and the mysteries of the truth' (*HE* iii, 4, 222); 'King Penda did not forbid the preaching of the Word even in his own people that is the Mercian [*in sua, hoc est Merciorum, natione*] if any wished to hear it'(*HE* iii, 21, 280); 'Egbert, an Englishman [*de natione Anglorum*], came to them [the Irish] … and brought them to observe the true and canonical Easter Day (*HE* iii, 4, 224) … and brought much blessing both to his own race [*genti suae*] and to those among whom he lived in exile, the Irish and the Picts [*nationibus Scottorum siue Pictorum*], by example of his life, the earnestness of his teaching'(*HE* iii, 27, 314). The table on the following page reviews Bede's use of eight key words for different groups in the British Isles.

In Ireland, the church system differed between north and south, as Bede reveals: 'the northern province of the Irish and the whole nation of the Picts [*omnis natio Pictorum*] were still celebrating Easter Sunday according to this rule [to celebrate Easter Sunday between the fourteenth and twentieth day of the moon] right up to that time … But the Irish people who lived in the southern part of Ireland [*gentes Scottorum, quae in australibus Hiberniae insulae partibus morabantur: HE* iii. 3, 218 and n.3] had long before learned to observe Easter according to canonical custom, through the teaching of the pope' (since c.633).

The division between north and south went back a long way. It was not surprising that Pope Celestine should choose to send Palladius as a bishop to Ireland, as part of the campaign against Pelagianism. This mission might have produced a new Irish church, confined to the province of Leinster.[33] In any case, it probably affected the Irish Christians who lived in the south and the east in the second half of the fifth century. It was not, however, Palladius, but St Patrick who established Christianity in the west and north of Ireland, in association with Connachta led by the Ui Neil dynasty. Did the rise of Connachta reform the political geography of Ireland and bring about the difference in customs between the churches of the south and north in seventh-century Ireland?

[33]   James, *Britain in the First Millennium*, 80; *After Rome*, ed. Thomas Charles-Edwards, Short Oxford History of the British Isles 2, Oxford 2003, 104.

	gens	populus	natio	rex	regnum	provincia	regio	lingua
1. Angles & English	o	o	o	o	o	o		o
2. Angles East	o			o	o			o
3. Angles Middle						o		
4. Northumbria						o	o	
5. Transhumbrana	o							
6. Bernicia	o			o	o	o		
7. Deira				o	o	o		
8. Mercia	o		o	o	o	o		
9. Hwicce						o		
10. Saxons								o
11. East Saxons	o				o	o		
12. South Saxons				o		o		
13. West Saxons	o			o	o			o
14. Kentish people	o			o	o	o		
15. Latin								o
16. Picts (North/South)	o		o	o				o
17. Britons	o		o	o				o
18. Scots	o		o			o		o

Table 1: Bede's terminology in *The Ecclesiastical History*.

So, in the end it was St Patrick, not Palladius, who was celebrated as the apostle of the Irish nation. We can already perceive the idea of a nation being present in the work of Patrick's hagiographer Muirchú, who described the Irish as a people included among the *omnes gentes* of the evangelist Matthew.[34] Though there were many political powers competing with one another in Ireland, they were sufficiently, if loosely, consolidated by a common culture for the birth of a national consciousness. The expression *Fir hÉrend*, the Irish, appeared as early as the ninth century. This may also have been influenced by Ireland's geographical condition as an island,[35] but the idea of the nation as an ecclesiastical community had also been formed by the development of church organizations between the eighth and ninth centuries.

The concept I have been discussing is not simply that of the nation but a Christian nation, a political entity within Christendom, and one having official episcopal sees approved by the papacy. In this respect there were differences between the English and the Irish. Missionary work to the English began with the strong initiative of Pope Gregory I and continued into the seventh century, by which time the bishops of Rome were establishing their position as leaders and arbiters of Western Christendom. The propagation of the faith in Ireland started in the fifth century, partly as a reation to Pelagianism, at a time before Roman leadership was consolidated, when local churches could still establish relative independence.

[34] See Marie-Therese Flanagan, 'Strategies of distinction: defining nations in medieval Ireland', below, p. 107, note 9. For Muirchu's life of Patrick, see *Muirchú moccu Mactbéni's 'Vita Sancti Patricii': Life of Saint Patrick*, ed. David Howlett, Dublin 2006.

[35] *The Patrician Texts in the Book of Armagh*, ed. Ludwig Bieler, Scriptores Latini Hiberniae, Dublin 1979, 184–91.

Moreover, it was not the legitimate mission of Palladius sent by the pope but the individual initiative of Patrick that was memorialized by Irish Christians. The different physical distances from the papacy and the political geography of the two peoples might also have affected the formation of their respective nations. Nevertheless, from the seventh century onward, the concept of a Christian nation had been created both in Britain and in Ireland. In the earlier period, we should pay particular attention to the saints who played a role in the making of a Christian nation.[36] In order to make it easier to integrate the Northumbrians into his kingdom, for instance, King Æthelstan adopted the northern saint, Cuthbert, and became patron of St Cuthbert's community.[37] In England, however, the concept of the nation came to be more secular and systematic; around 1020, facing the crisis of the Danish Conquest, Archbishop Wulfstan of York issued a manifesto emphasizing the roles and responsibilities of both laity and ecclesiastics within a Christian nation (*christener theode*).[38]

Making the Nation: Kingdoms

We now turn to the second axis of nationhood, the kingdom, here defined as a body politic which occupied an accepted place in Latin Christendom, in which legitimacy was conferred on one 'lawful' king, established by rules of succession through rituals of coronation and unction celebrated by a pope, an archbishop or an authorized bishop. In the tenth century, the unified kingdom of England was such an official polity, authenticated by the church. It was different from a tribal-kingdom comprising a high-king and some sub-kings or sub-kingdoms. England was the first such unified kingdom to emerge in Britain and once it had appeared,

---

[36] *After Rome*, ed. Charles-Edwards, 261; Wormald, 'Engla lond', 13. This is especially true in Ireland, where Muirchú, in about 690, wrote that it was St Patrick who baptized the Irish *gens*, 'greater than the individual dynastic, or political, groupings'. He thus regarded Patrick as the apostle of the whole people. Marie-Therese Flanagan maintains that 'Muirchú therefore fashioned a unifying Christian identity that could operate in the secular world as an alternative to competing dynasties and population groups, and even offered the Irish a collective destiny in the Afterlife'; see Flanagan, 'Strategies of distinction: defining nations in medieval Ireland', below, p. 107. The saint appeared as the representative of his own nation not only in the earthly world but also in heaven.

[37] See William Aird, 'Northumbria and the Making of the Kingdom of the English', below, p. 47.

[38] *Wulfstan's Institutes of Polity* (ed. K. Jost, Bern 1959), translated in Michael Swanton, *Anglo-Saxon Prose*, London 1975, 125–138, at 126–127; Wormald, 'Engla lond', 13. In this context we should also consider the Benedictine reform, introduced into England in the reign of Edgar, and in Durham in 1083. See William Aird, 'Northumbria and the making of the kingdom of the English', below, pp. 58–9. Cf. Hirokazu Tsurushima, 'The Church and State in tenth- and eleventh-century England', *The Structure and Developments of the Unified Powers in Europe*, ed. Ikuo Ato, Soubun-shya, Tokyo 1994, 125–243 (written in Japanese).

the rest of Britain (and from the twelfth century, Ireland) was brought under its political and ecclesiastical pressure.

By the late seventh century the Saxons in Britain were divided into the East Saxons, the West Saxons and the South Saxons. These names clearly date from after the settlement, and roughly correspond to the bishoprics of London, Winchester and Selsey. The two bishoprics in Kent, Canterbury and Rochester, share with these a probable correspondence with the old Roman *civitas* system, and a similar pattern occurs among the Anglian peoples north of the Thames.[39] The movement towards integration was launched by King Alfred of the West Saxons, whose authority was recognised in Anglian Mercia as well as Wessex, and whose regnal styles included 'king of the West Saxons', 'king of the Angles and Saxons', and 'king of the English'. It has long been common practice to apply the term 'Anglo-Saxon' to the whole period from the Roman retreat to 1066, and to call the inhabitants of England during those years 'Anglo-Saxons'. It is instructive, however, to ask what the phrase 'Anglo-Saxon', which was invented in the sixteenth century, actually means. In the 'Anglo-Saxon' period, it was used only temporarily, during the years when the West Saxon kings were also acknowledged by the Anglian Mercians, to denote two tribal kingdoms under one ruler.[40]

In the time of Alfred's son Edward, who consolidated the unification of Wessex and Mercia, including the areas overrun by the Danes, the usual royal title was 'king of the Anglo-Saxons'. Edward's son Æthelstan, who achieved a (temporary) conquest of the Danish kingdom in York, used on a massive scale the title *rex Anglorum* which his grandfather and father had employed more modestly.[41] Æthelstan also used titles expressing his claim to rulership of all Britain and dropped the title *rex Saxonum* (king of the Saxons), the usage of which decreased in inverse proportion. In the tenth century, the term 'Saxons' itself disappeared from English usage (though it was still used in Welsh and Irish sources) and use of the title of 'king of the Anglo-Saxons' also drastically decreased in favour of *rex Anglorum* and similar expressions. *Angli* in this context no longer designates the tribal name but the Christian *gens Anglorum*, the nation first envisaged by Bede. It was in the reign of King Edgar, Edward's grandson, who not only used the title

[39] Nicholas Brooks, 'The creation and early structure of the kingdom of Kent', in *Origins of Anglo-Saxon Kingdoms,* ed. S. Bassett, Studies in the Early History of Britain, Leicester 1989, 55–74.

[40] S. Reynolds, 'What do we mean by 'Anglo-Saxon' and 'Anglo-Saxons'?', *Journal of British Studies* 24, 1985, 395–414; H. R. Loyn, 'The imperial style of the tenth-century Anglo-Saxon kings', *History* 40, 1955; H. Tsurushima, '*Rex Anglorum*: Anglo-Saxon or Anglo-English? the structure of a unified kingdom in tenth-century England, *Studies for the Occidental History*, new ser. 19, 1990, 146–159 (written in Japanese).

[41] On the ideology of Æthelstan's kingship, see Michael Wood, 'The making of King Æthelstan's Empire: an English Charlemagne?', in *Ideal and Reality in Frankish and Anglo-Saxon Society*, ed. Womald *et al.*, Oxford 1983, 250–271.

	Alfred	Edward	Æthelstan
King	13% (2)	4% (1)	2% (1)
King of the Saxons	20% (3)	4% (1)	
King of the West Saxons	13% (2)	4% (1)	
King of the Angles and Saxons	41% (6)	71% (17)	6% (4)
King of the English	13% (2)	17% (4)	69% (44)
King of Britain			23% (15)

Note: King: *rex*. King of the Saxons: *rex Saxonum*. King of the West Saxons: *rex Occidentalium Saxonum*. King of the Angles and Saxons: *rex Anglorum et Saxonum*; *rex Angul-Sexna & North(an)hymbra imperator*. King of the English: *rex (basileus) Anglorum (et...)*. King of Britain: *rex (basileus) Brittanniae*; *rex Albionis*.

Table 2: Regnal styles of the West Saxon kings, 870–939 [42]

'king of the English' but who also described himself as 'governor', 'rector', 'king' and even 'emperor' of all Britain,[43] that this unified kingdom finally appeared as a fully-conceptualised Christian community, symbolised most clearly in the coronation of Edgar performed by Archbishop Dunstan of Canterbury in 973. On the analogy of the formation of Japan in the shadow of China (see above), it might be seen as the institution of a small western insular empire, peripheral to the construction of the 'Holy German Empire' by King Otto I in 961.

The unified kingdom which appeared in tenth-century England became the first official polity in Britain, whose principle of integration was that of a Romano-Christian community. Its primary position and 'quasi-caesarism' affected the other nations in Britain, and, as a result of the strengthening of its royal authority after the Norman Conquest, the whole of England shared a common political destiny. The title 'king of the English' was used until the latter part of the twelfth century. To be English meant to be a member of the English church and a subject of the English king, and it was in this context that Archbishop Lanfranc called himself 'a new Englishman' (*novus Anglicus*).[44] By the 1130s, all the immigrant Normans were integrated with the native English into a new English people.[45]

In what later became Scotland and Wales, two factors held back the formation of the idea of a Christian nation, one of which was the slow development of

[42] This is based on the texts in Walter de Gray Birch, *Cartularium Saxonicum*, 3 vols and index, London 1885–1899. It shows only a general tendency.

[43] S. 698 (961): *ego Eadgar tocius Brittannie gubernator et rector*; S. 723 (963): *ego Eadgar rex tocius Brittanniæ Christi favente gratia sublimates*; S. 730 (963): *ego Adgar rex Anglorum ceterarumque gencium in circuitu persistencium gubernator et rector*; S. 789 (970): *ego Ædgarus totius Brittanniæ basileus*; S. 793 (973): *ego Edgar annuente altitrono Anglorum basileus ceterarumque gentium triviatim persistentium gubernator et rector.*

[44] *The Letters of Lanfranc Archbishop of Canterbury*, ed. Helen Glover and Margaret Gibson, Oxford Medieval Texts 1979, 40–41.

[45] Gillingham, *The English in the Twelfth Century*, 84–5.

ecclesiastical institutions. In both cases, however, the cause of this was political; for the two English archbishoprics, Canterbury and York, consistently attempted to extend their jurisdictions over the Welsh and Scottish sees, thus constantly interfering in the making of their respective nations. Though Hywel Dda (the Good, c.880–950) ruled much of Wales at almost the same time as when Æthelstan was 'king of the English', he brought about no political integration, and Wales remained no more than an aggregation of British dynasties and regions whose borders frequently changed. A sort of territoriality was conceived, but there was no stable political power which could lead and maintain the integration process; Hywel himself seems to have been reconciled to the status of a sub-king to Æthelstan. Nor had any comprehensive system of bishoprics been developed throughout Wales. The plan to make St David's an archbishopric for all Wales, in which both the king of the English and the archbishop of Canterbury interfered, did not move from vision to reality. The Welsh people failed to establish any system to transform themselves into a fully-fledged Christian nation.

While Cornwall and Strathclyde, the other British areas, were absorbed into England and Scotland respectively, the British people in Wales as we know it today began to call themselves Cymry, an indigenous word denoting 'us', but by the 1130s, they had adopted, from English sources, the words 'Wales' and 'Welsh', adapted from Old English.[46] The formation of England and Wales from the tenth century onward made the borders, which came to be known as the March, a buffer area, whose inhabitants were compelled to choose their nationality, whether English or Welsh. As early as the 930s, Æthelstan made the Wye the boundary between the English and the Cymry, and the ordinance of the *Dunsaete*[47] divided a British people into two different communities who were, in the end, forced to live either as English or British.[48] In the 1160s, Owain Gwynedd (1100–1170), the ruler of North Wales, used the title *rex Wallie* in a letter addressed to Louis VII, king of France, and though it is a matter of fact that this title did not represent the actual political conditions which he faced, he nevertheless claimed an official status within the world of European politics. *Ad extremum,* however, the Welsh failed to produce even a document declaring the political legitimacy of their own

---

[46] H. Pryce, 'British or Welsh; national identity in twelfth-century Wales', *EHR* 116, 2001. Hywel was also the first ruler to use the title of prince of Wales (John Davies, *A History of Wales*, London 1991, 128).

[47] Margaret Gelling, *The West Midlands in the Early Middle Ages*, Leicester 1992, 114–18. Gelling identified the *Dunsaete* with the men of Archenfield (Ergyng), a British kingdom of sub-Roman and early medieval provenance. It lay mostly in what is now western Herefordshire in England, with its heartland between the River Monnow and River Wye, but also spread into modern Monmouthshire and east of the Wye, where sits the old Roman town of Ariconium (at Weston-under-Penyard). Presumably this was the first capital.

[48] See Ann Williams, 'Why are the English not Welsh?', below, pp. 30–31.

monarchy to the papacy, such as the Irish Remonstrance of 1317, or the Scottish declaration of Arbroath in 1320. Without a common sense of Christian nationhood and an official kingdom, the Welsh people maintained their identity only in their own law and language, in rivalry with the English Common Law and the English tongue. They kept their consciousness as a Welsh nation by memorializing Welsh law in the fourteenth century as that of King Hywel Dda.[49]

As for Scotland, its emergence as a nation was even more protracted than that of Wales. The old joke about the Picts who were Scots and the Scots who were Irish has some historical foundations, for in the time of Bede the term *Scotti* denoted the Irish, a group of whom were established in Dalriada, in the western part of what became Scotland.[50] In the ninth century these Dalriadic Scots integrated with the Picts to form the kingdom of Alba. Subsequent kings extended their kingdom southward, expanding its territory and incorporating many different peoples into what was known, by the thirteenth century, as Scotland. The historic core area of 'Scotland'[51] lay north of the Firth of Forth and therefore was less than the area under the control of the king. The diocesan system, moreover, was complicated and intricate, and the establishment of an archbishopric was delayed, partly because of pressure from the kings of the English and the archbishops of York, so that the formation of a Christian nation remained rudimentary. The eventual promotion of the bishoprics of St Andrews (1472) and of

[49] Bronagh Ní Chonaill, 'The Welsh, you know, are Welsh: the individual, the alien, and a legal tradition', below, pp. 75–6, 79; 'this corpus iuris (medieval Welsh Law, called Cyfraith Hywel, the Law of Hywel) is often described in scholarship as native, traditional or customary law, which reflects its deep roots in the community (as opposed to deriving from the legislative hand of a king)'. There was a big difference in finding and making law between England-Scotland and Wales-Ireland. In England and Scotland 'the king should be the source of all legal authority in relation to secular matters', and the common law (the customary law of the king's court) 'could engender a sense of the kingdom as a single country'. See Dauvit Broun, 'Becoming a nation: Scotland in the twelfth and thirteenth centuries', below, p. 97. In Wales and Ireland, on the other hand, law was rooted in the community, although there were experts in native law.

[50] Generally speaking the archaeologists express scepticism about the immigration theory. See E. Campbell, 'Were the Scots Irish?', *Antiquity* 75, 2001, 285–292, at 288. However, this is a very difficult subject. According to Professor Broun (personal correspondence), 'Alba' was used simply for 'Pictland'. In other words, the kingdom of Alba was 'Pictland' continued, but with Gaelic replacing Pictish as the dominant language. Also, there was an explicit idea of Alba/Pictland as the landmass north of the Forth no later than the 870s. This reflects the policy of Constantine, king of Fortriu (789–820), to extend his power from the north to the south (reflected in the palace of Forteviot). This would have been an attempt to create a unified kingdom.

[51] On the definition of 'Scotland', see Dauvit Broun, Becoming a nation: Scotland in the twelfth and thirteenth centuries, below, p. 87: "Scotland' (in any language) typically referred to only part of the kingdom. It was sometimes used as the name of the entire

15

Glasgow (1492) came only in the latter part of the fifteenth century, after nearly 300 years of status as a 'special daughter' of the papacy (*cum universi*), first proclaimed in 1192. Unlike the situation in Wales and Ireland, however, the political core, that is the king's court, of the integrated kingdom continued to survive. This historic core extended round the east coast all the way to Inverness (and, by 1200, reached parts of the south-west coast at Ayr and Dumfries). It only began to embrace the whole of Scotland in 1293, but this development was cut short by the Wars of Independence from 1296.[52]

Partly because of the delay in the formation of an integrated religious community in Scotland, as well as the political and military pressures from England, the Scottish nation was only created in the thirteenth century, as the various peoples in the kingdom, above all the peoples of the south who had disdained the Scots as barbarians, and the immigrant aristocracy from England, accepted a common Scottish identity. This Scottish nation was imagined as a community of the kingdom, sharing a common history different from that of England. In 1320, the Declaration of Arbroath appealed to Pope John XXII, urging Scotland's position as a kingdom independent from England, governed by Robert Bruce as an official and legitimate king among the rulers of Europe. The Declaration was issued in the names of thirty-nine individual aristocrats and the community of the realm, who shared the same history and a concept of a Scottish nation united by a single succession of 113 kings. The different origins of the inhabitants were thus eliminated. This appeal was successful. Before the time of David II, the kings had performed the ceremony of their traditional coronation with a poet on the Stone of Scone, but in 1329 the papacy approved a coronation and anointing presided over by the bishop of St Andrews. In the process of creating a Scottish nation, the Northumbrians, whose territory had once stretched from the Humber up to Edinburgh, were also forced to choose their nationhood, as the Anglo-Scottish border now divided Northumberland from Lothian.

The formation of the Irish nation followed a different course. Here we can see, in the early years, a movement towards the formation of a Christian nation and the establishment of a parochial system, just as happened in England. But we must take into consideration the differences between the two, such as the longer distance of Ireland from the papacy, both geographically and historically, and the interference from the archbishopric of Canterbury after the Norman Conquest. From 1070 at the latest, Canterbury proclaimed its primacy over the churches in Ireland, and established close connections there with the foundation of the Dublin

---

landmass north of the Firth of Forth, or more commonly to denote the region north of the Firth of Forth, east of Argyll and south of Moray'. Scotland itself is a problematic term and not easy to define. We can say that Scotland was forged in the reign of Alexander III, in particular around the 1260s.

[52] David Carpenter, *The Struggle for Mastery. Britain 1066–1284*, London 2003, 521–3.

bishopric. In 1152 the Synod of Kells approved the foundation of four archbishoprics, whose pallia were conferred by the Papal Legate, Cardinal Giovani Paparoni. The Irish Church was organized along Roman lines, and had a official seat within the Latin Christendom, though there remained a conflict between Armagh and Dublin over the primacy in Ireland.

Ireland might be conceived as a Christian nation, but there was no integrated official kingship. Tairrdelbach Ua Cibncgibair (1088–1156) approved the decrees of the Synod of Kells, but though he was both High King and king of Connacht, he was not the only king in Ireland. The concept of an Irish nation subject to a single Irish king never came to birth. The rule of the English king, Henry II, over Ireland was legitimised by the provisions of *Laudabiliter*, issued by the English Pope Hadrian IV in 1155. The potential for Ireland to become a legitimate kingdom from within was being lost, and the military invasion and immigration from England of English noblemen, knights, burgesses, and peasants in and after the reign of King Henry II could only have posed further major practical impediments to the making of an Irish kingdom.[53] The Remonstrance of 1317, which urged on the papacy the claim of an official Irish kingship, was probably completely ignored. It was too late for Ireland to establish an integrated kingdom in the face of the hegemony of the English kingship. Without such a kingdom, 'an imagined Irish nation' might have laid stress on ethnicity (in the modern sense), but it was not to be.

Pitfalls of the Idea of the Nation

In an earlier version of this essay, I maintained that even if we ascribe the social uniqueness of the 'Danelaw' to Danish ethnicity, this 'Danelaw' is still only a construct invented by modern historians.[54] Immediately, I was subject to criticism. I became acutely aware of the persistence of the idea of the nation. The term 'Danes' as used in England was and is ambiguous, for Scottish chronicles used the term 'Norsemen' for the same people who in the *Anglo-Saxon Chronicle* were called 'Danes'.[55] So who were the 'Danes'? The word 'Danelaw' is effectively defined for the first time in the *Leges Henrici Primi* in the early part of the twelfth century, which also speaks of the law of Mercia, though it is difficult to find evi-

[53] For this immigration, see Robert Bartlett, *The Making of Europe,* London 1993, 183, Map. 7.

[54] Hirokazu Tsurushima, 'England: its place in the period of making Europe', *Iwanami History of the world* 8, Tokyo 1998, 221–250 (written in Japanese); Dawn Hadley, *Early Medieval Social Structures: The Northern Danelaw, 800–1100,* Leicester 1996. It was not the ethnicity of the Danish people but their relations with the natives that made the diverse social structures in the Danelaw, as it came to be called in the twelfth century. 'The men of the Danelaw [probably] thought of themselves less as Danes than men of York, men of Lincoln, men of Nottingham'; see David Roffe, 'The Danes and the making of the kingdom of the English', below, p. 40.

[55] A suggestion from Professor Dauit Broun.

dence of the latter's existence.[56] It seems that the term 'Danelaw' had only a regional connotation. It is very easy for us to be so trapped in an ideology that we unconsciously read back into the past a belief in the eternal existence of the present nation, ignoring the fact that nations have changed over time.

Like 'Danelaw', the 'terms 'Anglo-Norman' and 'Anglo-Saxon' are convenient words to describe the periods concerned, so that modern historians use them frequently. However, they too are modern constructs. Likewise the terms 'Anglo-Scandinavian', 'Anglo-Scottish', or 'Anglo-Irish' are all convenient words whose invention was based on the belief in the eternal life of the nation. They are biased by modern political ideology. John Gillingham has said that 'there is no extant evidence that anyone in the eleventh and twelfth centuries ever used the term 'Anglo-Norman' [and] in the absence of some such term, it is clearly not easy to argue for the existence of an Anglo-Norman nationality'.[57]

Norman identity did not depend on notions of a Christian nation and Kingdom, but on the home-province of Normandy.[58] Once the Normans left Normandy, their identity as Normans seemed to fade away. At the court of Henry II 'Norman' might well mean someone belonging to a political group based in Normandy rather than in England. But were the large numbers of common people among the immigrants from the continent 'Anglo-Normans' or 'Normans'? The twelfth-century invaders of Ireland were called 'English' or 'Saxons' in Irish historical sources. Contemporary Irish people therefore recognised them as the English, but modern historians of Ireland call them 'Normans', or 'Anglo-Normans'.[59] Is it possible to maintain that a hundred years after the Norman Conquest the descendants of the conquerors were still 'Normans' or 'Anglo-Normans'?[60] Of course, modern historians know that the invaders were known to contemporaries as 'the English', and the modern usage of the terms 'Norman' and 'Anglo-Norman' perhaps reflects modern political considerations rather than those which prevailed in medieval times. Beyond that, there remains the potential of making the British Isles the unit for the writing of history.

[56] *Leges Henrici Primi*, ed. L. J. Downer, Oxford 1972.
[57] Gillingham, *The English in the Twelfth Century*, 124
[58] R. H. C. Davis, *The Normans and Their Myth*, London 1976; Hugh M. Thomas, *The English and the Normans: Ethnic Hostility, Assimilation, and Identity 1066–c.1220*, Oxford 2003.
[59] See Marie-Therese Flanagan, 'Strategies of distinction: defining nations in medieval Ireland', below, p. 109. See also Matthew Bennett, 'Stereotype Normans in Old French Vernacular Literature', *ANS* 9, 1987 for 1986, 25–42, at p. 34: 'so much seems to depend on the perspective of the author (or his characters) in drawing distinctions between Normans and the French in general'.
[60] See Marie-Therese Flanagan, 'Strategies of distinction: defining nations in medieval Ireland', below, pp. 109, 112.

Why are the English not Welsh?

ANN WILLIAMS

In the year 937, Æthelstan, king of the English, and his brother Edmund led their army to the still-unidentified place called *Brunanburh*, and there defeated a coalition of enemies led by Constantine, king of the Scots of Alba, and Olaf, king of the Dublin Norsemen. A specially-composed praise-poem was entered into the *Anglo-Saxon Chronicle* to commemorate this victory: its closing lines run as follows:

> Never yet in this island before this, by what books tell us and our ancient sages, was a greater slaughter of a host made by the edge of the sword, since the Angles and Saxons came hither from the east, invading Britain over the broad seas, and the proud assailants, warriors eager for glory, overcame the Welsh and won a country: *Engle and Seaxe up becoman ofer brad brimu Brytene sohton ... Wealas ofercoman ... eard begeatan.*[1]

A little earlier, an anonymous poet, probably working somewhere in South Wales, produced a poetic exhortation entitled *Armes Prydein Vawr*, 'The Prophecy of Great Britain', in which he called upon his countrymen (*Cymry*) to make a grand alliance with the other people of western Britain and Ireland:

> there will be reconciliation between the Cymry and the men of Dublin, the Irish of Ireland and Anglesey and Scotland, the men of Cornwall and of Strathclyde will be made welcome among us.[2]

The target of this union was the Saxons, 'the scavengers of Thanet', who had oppressed the Cymry with taxes and driven them from their land; now, with the making of the grand coalition, it was the Saxons who would be driven from the island of Britain.[3] The alliance, of course, was never achieved, and the 'Saxons' remain *in situ* to this day.

[1] *ASC, s.a.* 937. This paper was first read at the Nations of Britain Symposium, held at Tohoku University, Sendai, in November 2006, at the invitation of Professor Hirokazu Tsurushima, for whose unstinting hospitality I am forever grateful. Thanks are also due to Val Fallan for reading the text and providing both penetrating comments and invaluable references.

[2] *Armes Prydein*, ed. Ifor Williams, translated by Rachel Bronwich, Dublin 1972, lines 9–11.

[3] Though neither the Welsh nor the Cornishmen took part in the battle of *Brunanburh*, the poem may still be connected with the alliance of King Constantine, supported by

19

The 'Saxons' of *Armes Prydein* correspond to the 'Angles and Saxons' of *Brunanburh*, and *Brunanburh*'s 'Welsh' to the 'Cymry' of *Armes Prydein*; to this very day, the Welsh call themselves *Cymry*, and refer to the English as *sais*: 'Saxon'.[4] The picture painted by both poets is the same: long ago the Angles and Saxons came from the east into the island of Britain, drove the Britons into the west, and made a country for themselves in the vacated lands. This interpretation of the history of the fifth and sixth centuries continued to be held by generations of subsequent historians, right down to the nineteenth and even into the twentieth century; a mass immigration of Germanic peoples (the Angles and Saxons) conquered that part of Britain which eventually became 'England', and either killed the indigenous British population, or drove them out to seek refuge in Wales.

It was a satisfying explanation of an obscure and ill-recorded period of history, because it accounted for the hiatus between Roman Britain and Anglo-Saxon England, a hiatus which made English history so different from that of the other 'successor-states' established in Europe after the collapse of the western Roman Empire. In the late nineteenth century, Edward Augustus Freeman, Professor of History at Oxford, discussed the problem at length:

> Everywhere else the invaders gradually adopted the language and the religion of the conquered. If the conquerors were heathen at the time of their settlement, they gradually adopted Christianity ... Everywhere but in Britain the invaders gradually learned to speak some form, however corrupt, of the language of Rome ... everywhere but in Britain the invaders respected the laws and arts of Rome ... everywhere but in Britain the local divisions and nomenclature survived ... In Britain everything is different. The conquering English entered Britain as heathens, and ... they still retained the heathen worship of their fathers ... they also retained their language ... In Britain too the arts of Rome perished as utterly as the language and the religion of Rome ... the laws of Rome perished utterly ... the municipal institutions of the Roman towns in Britain utterly perished ... In England too the local nomenclature is everywhere essentially Teutonic. A few great cities and a few great natural objects, London on the Thames and Gloucester on the Severn, still retain names older than the English Conquest; but the great mass of the towns and villages of England bear names which were given them ... by the Angles and Saxons of the fifth and sixth centuries.

There was, Freeman concluded, only one explanation for all this:

> though the literal extirpation of a nation is an impossibility, there is every reason to believe that the Celtic (i.e., British) inhabitants of those parts of Britain which had become English at the end of the sixth century had been

the men of Strathclyde, and the Dublin Vikings; the poet seems to be voicing the opinions of those who objected to the current rapport between Hywel Dda, the dominant figure among the Welsh kings, and Æthelstan. For a survey of the evidence, see Wendy Davies, *Wales in the Early Middle Ages*, Leicester 1982, 112–20.
[4]   To the Scots, too, the English are *sassenach*: 'Saxons'.

as nearly extirpated as a nation can be. The women would doubtless be largely spared, but as far as the male sex is concerned, we may feel sure that death, emigration, or personal slavery were the only alternatives which the vanquished found at the hands of our fathers ... In short, everywhere but in Britain an intruding nation sat down by the side of an older nation, and gradually lost itself in its mass. In Britain, in so far as such a process is possible, the intruding nation altogether supplanted the elder nation.[5]

The century or so which has passed since Freeman wrote has seen much ink spilt by historians of the 'dark ages', and, perhaps more significantly, a great deal of both physical and intellectual effort on the part of archaeologists. Neither a mass migration of Anglo-Saxons from the continent, nor an extirpation (however partial) of the Britons, are much in vogue today, though the latter at least has received some support from the geneticists.[6] Yet it is still necessary to explain the differences between Italy, Spain, and France (especially France) on the one hand, and England on the other. In the Roman province of Gaul, the invading Germanic people, the *Franci,* and the indigenous Gallo-Romans combined into a single nation, known certainly by the Germanic-derived name of 'Frankia' (later France), but speaking a language (eventually to be known as 'French') which was based on the late Latin current in Roman Gaul.[7] In the Roman province of Britain we find quite another picture. Here the invading Germanic peoples, the 'Anglo-Saxons' as they are commonly known, did not merge with the indigenous Romano-Britons, and the eventual result was not one but two distinct nations, England and Wales, each with its own non-Latin vernacular: English, a branch of Low German related to Dutch, and Welsh, derived from the Britonnic tongue spoken since before the Roman, let alone the English conquest.

Though Freeman's views on early Anglo-British relations no longer command assent, he did in fact point to the solution of this conundrum. His observation that 'Roman laws, manners and arts' were already in considerable disarray

[5] E. A. Freeman, *The History of the Norman Conquest of England,* 6 vols, Oxford 1870–9, i, 13–18, 18–19 (excerpted). A. S. Esmonde Cleary expresses the difficulty more succinctly: 'compared with the Germanic successor-states in the rest of the western [Roman] empire, Anglo-Saxon England in its political and social institutions, its language and law, to say nothing of its material culture, owed little or nothing to Roman Britain': see *The Ending of Roman Britain,* London 1989, 200.

[6] Michael E. Weale, Deborah A. Weiss, Rolf F. Jager, Neil Bradman and Mark G. Thomas, 'Y Chromosome evidence for Anglo-Saxon mass migration' *Molecular Biology and Evolution* 19, 2002, 1008–21; I owe this reference to Val Fallan. For some of the more intemperate interpretations of this exercise, see the article by Helen Studd in *The Times,* July 1 2002 'How the Old English put all their Basques in one exit' (a truly dreadful pun), and the subsequent correspondence in the letter-pages of *The Times* on July 4 and July 11 2002.

[7] Early references to the vernacular tongue of west Frankia—roughly modern France—call it *romans*: 'Roman'. Only from the late twelfth century did it become 'French'.

among the Britons when the Germanic settlements began is one which has been tacitly adopted by recent research. The general view seems to be that what the Germanic incomers (irrespective of their numbers) encountered was not Roman but post-Roman Britain, which should be seen as 'a singular entity with its own defining characteristics, rather than as a prelude, a transition, or a problem'.[8] Though both the paucity of the surviving written sources and the patchy archaeological record make any certainties about the state of Britain in the fifth and sixth centuries impossible to determine, it is in this period that the roots of both English and Welsh identities must be sought.

One theory which seems to have retained general assent through all the changing fashions of interpretation is that the earliest Germanic incomers arrived, probably in the middle of the fifth century, at the invitation of the British. In his polemical tract 'The Ruin of Britain' (*De Excidio et Conquestu Britanniae*), the British cleric Gildas, writing in the mid sixth century, relates the heroic tale of the 'great tyrant', Vortigern, who first employed the mercenary forces of Hengest and Horsa, whom Gildas calls 'the ferocious Saxons ... hated by God and man'.[9] Gildas's story (though not to be taken literally) may reflect the employment by British authorities of what in Roman times would have been called *foederati*, federate troops, defined as military units, usually from beyond the Rhine, who enlisted under a treaty (*foedus*) to defend specific territories.[10] Some memory of this system may have remained among the invaders themselves; Bede, the Northumbrian chronicler of the English advance, tells us that the West Saxons had once been known as the *Gewisse*, a name which seems to mean something like 'the reliable ones', and since their earliest known home was in the Upper Thames basin, west of London, 'the expression might relate to the protective role of Germanic troops in the fifth century'.[11] Once settled, such troops were prone to demand more than their hosts could afford to give, and, if denied, to take lands for their own use. This is what seems to have happened in Britain; at some point, probably in the last years

[8] Christopher Snyder, *An Age of Tyrants: Britain and the Britons, AD 499–600*, Stroud 1998, 251. There is of course considerable difference on what post-Roman Britain was like. One school of thought holds that there was a general collapse of Roman institutions, economy and culture, and a reversion to indigenous customs at much the same cultural and economic level as that of the incoming 'Anglo-Saxons' (Esmonde Cleary, *Ending of Roman Britain*, 200). On the other hand, it has been has argued that 'fifth- and sixth-century British society and culture retained far more of the Late Roman past than has usually been supposed, and did so within a political framework inherited from the fourth century'; see Ken Dark, *Britain and the End of the Roman Empire*, Stroud 2000, 57.

[9] *Gildas: The Ruin of Britain and Other Works*, ed. and trans. Michael Winterbottom, Chichester 1978, 26, 97.

[10] There is some archaeological evidence that the earliest Germanic settlements were those of *foederati* (Dark, *Britain and the End of the Roman Empire*, 48–53).

[11] Dark, *Britain and the End of the Roman Empire*, 59.

of the fifth century, the Germanic mercenaries threw off British control, and established a series of independent communities in eastern Britain. Some British communities remained, interspersed among those of their former employees, but they were cut off from their brethren in the west. At this point, around 500, the British of the west seem to have gathered themselves together in a belated confederacy, which won a great victory against the Germanic settlers; Gildas calls the leader of the coalition Ambrosius Aurelianus, and says that his victory was achieved at *Mons Badonicus*, Badon Hill, the site of which has been bitterly disputed right down to the present day. Whatever the locality of the engagement, Ambrosius's success stopped the advance of the Saxons and ushered in a period of peace (or at least truce) which lasted until Gildas's own day, that is, the mid sixth century.

Though Gildas was not writing history, the picture that he paints seems to reflect the realities of the sixth century. In the year 500, much of the former province of Roman Britain was still under British control, even in the east, where the earliest Germanic settlements are attested.[12] It is clear that for about half a century at least, natives and incomers must have lived side by side, though the details of their interaction cannot now be reconstructed. The surviving written sources, most of them compiled much later than the events described, concentrate on warfare, accompanied by the flight or slaughter of the British, but this is to be understood by the context in which they were produced; the sixth-century annals in the *Anglo-Saxon Chronicle*, for instance, appear to be based on heroic legends, which concentrate on the ethos of conquest and glory.[13] Flight and slaughter certainly happened; large numbers of British refugees are recorded in the late fifth century in North Gaul, Brittany, and Spain.[14] There are, however, signs of more peaceable contact. Though the *Anglo-Saxon Chronicle* presents the origins of Wessex in terms of conquest and war, the eponymous founder of the West Saxon royal line, Cerdic, has a British name, Ceretic (OB Coroticus, ModW Caradoc), and similar names are found among his successors well into the seventh century.[15] This suggests a degree of rapprochement, at least at the top level of society, and when the historical record becomes clearer in the seventh century, intermarriage between

---

[12]   Dark, *Britain and the End of the Roman Empire*, 97–103; see especially figure 23, a map showing the limited distribution of 'Anglo-Saxon' burials in eastern Britain at the time.

[13]   'The written sources concentrate on the conflict because that was what the heroic ethos of society required. Peaceful intercourse was not appropriate material for relating' (Esmonde Cleary, *Ending of Roman Britain*, 201).

[14]   Esmonde Cleary, *Ending of Roman Britain*, 201–5. The Britons arrived in sufficient numbers to affect the local place-names; Armorica, in north-west Gaul, became (and still is) Brittany, while an area of north Spain was known as Britoña by the sixth century.

[15]   The same name, Ceretic, was born by the last ruler of the British kingdom of Elmet; see *HE* iv, 23; *Annales Cambriae*, ed. J. Williams ab Ithel, Rolls Series, London 1860, *s.a.*

British and English ruling families, though rare, is not unknown.[16] What such high-level marriages imply for the general population is another matter; it has been assumed that English men, at least, took British wives (though this view has recently been challenged), but the evidence for such unions is lacking.[17]

A degree of integration between the incomers and the natives is suggested by the fact that at least some of the Germanic settlers, while not forgetting their continental origins, began to identify themselves with their new homeland. According to Bede, both Kent, the Isle of Wight and south Hampshire were colonised by Jutes (from north Denmark), but when they emerge into the historical record, the Kentish settlers are known as the *Cantware*, 'those who live in Kent', a name derived from the Romano-British province of *Cantium*; similarly the Jutes of the Isle of Wight became the *Wihtware*, 'those who dwell in *Vectis*', the Romano-British name for the island.[18] Further north, the English kingdom of Lindsey took its name from *Lindum Colonia* (Roman Lincoln), and its inhabitants called themselves the *Lindissi*.[19] If, as seems likely, the settlers took more than the names of their new communities from the British, and 'the basic infrastructure of the early Anglo-Saxon kingdoms was inherited from late Roman or sub-Roman Britain', then cultural accommodation must have taken place at the political as well as the social level.[20] Indeed, some basic institutions of later English life may have been influenced by British customs: the English hall itself, so eloquently described by Bede, and so central to the heroic ethos of English poets during the whole period, may have been based on Roman and British models.[21]

---

616. The second element of the name of King Cenwealh of Wessex (643–72) means 'Briton, Welshman' (see further below), and King Cædwalla (685–9) has a wholly British name, an anglicized version of the name Cadwallon.

[16] See the marriage of the Northumbrian prince Oswiu and Riemmelt of Rheged, below.

[17] Dr Mark Thomas has recently suggested that the genetic make-up of the modern populations implies that intermarriage between the two communities, 'English' and British, was restricted, so that the former, being economically advantaged, outbred the latter (see *The Times*, July 29 2006, 'England's apartheid roots').

[18] The chief centre of Kent was Canterbury, *Cantwaraburh*, 'the fortified place of the people of Kent', which relates to its Romano-British name, *Durovernum Cantiacorum*, 'the alder-fort of the *Cantiaci*': see Nicholas Brooks, 'The creation and early structure of the kingdom of Kent', in *Origins of Anglo-Saxon Kingdoms*, ed. Steven Bassett, Leicester 1989, 57–8; A. L. F. Rivet and Colin Smith, *The Place-names of Roman Britain*, London 1979, 299, 353–4, 487–9.

[19] Rivet and Smith, *Place-names*, 393. The Northumbrian kingdoms of Deira and Bernicia have British names, though the etymologies are unclear.

[20] Barbara Yorke, *Kings and Kingdoms of Early Anglo-Saxon England*, London 1990, 7–8.

[21] Esmonde Cleary, *Ending of Roman Britain*, 201–5. On the continent, building-types fall into two main groups, the *Grubenhäuser*, small sunken-floored buildings perhaps used mainly for craft-work, and aisled houses, in which the living accommodation for the family was at one end and the byres for the cattle at the other. Sunken-floored

The comparatively peaceful co-existence of the early sixth century was not to last. Around the middle of the century, the balance between incomers and natives seems to have shifted, and a second phase of conflict led to the extinction of most of the independent British communities in lowland Britain.[22] By the year 600, they had been absorbed into the emergent English kingdoms documented at the end of the seventh century by the Northumbrian historian Bede. These kingdoms were formed by the westward expansion of the most powerful Germanic settlements, whose advantageous position allowed continued immigration from the continent; Kent, one of the earliest to emerge, was heavily influenced by its powerful continental neighbour Frankia, to an extent which made it one of the richest regions in Britain.[23] Throughout the seventh century the English kingdoms continued to grow in power and extent, absorbing any surviving British communities in the region which was later to become 'England'.[24] From the late seventh century onwards the Germanic newcomers, though politically divided, began to think of themselves as a single people; no longer were they just Angles, Saxons or Jutes, they were also 'English'. In the same period, the British communities in the west, likewise politically divided, also developed a common identity, often expressed as 'British', but increasingly as *Cumbri* or *Cymry*, a native word (*cumbrogi*) signifying men of the same nation (*bro*).[25] Cymru is today the 'Welsh' name for Wales, as *cymry* (singular *cymro*) is for the Welsh people, but the survival of the name Cumberland in north-west England is a reminder that the *Cymry* were once more widespread.

It is rarely possible to determine how the various British communities fell into English hands. Sometimes the process was violent. Soon after 616, King Edwin of Northumbria invaded and crushed the independent British kingdom of Elmet (the region around Leeds), and the savagery of his assault was remembered generations later, when Stephanus of Ripon, writing in the early eighth century, speaks of the British clergy 'fleeing from the hostile sword wielded by the warriors of own nation'.[26] In contrast, the Northumbrian absorption of Rheged (the Carlisle

---

buildings are also common in the English areas of Britain, but the aisled house does not appear; in its place are 'the rectangular structures with opposing doors in the middle of the long sides', found also in Romano-British and British contexts. For Bede's poetic description of the hall ('The flight of the sparrow') see *HE* ii.13.

[22] Dark, *Britain and the End of the Roman Empire*, 47, 103–4, 227–30.

[23] The earliest Kentish king of whom anything certain is known was Æthelberht, whose wife Bertha was daughter of Charibert, king of Paris.

[24] For the development of the early English kingdoms, see Yorke, *Kings and Kingdoms of Early Anglo-Saxon England,* D. P. Kirby, *The Earliest English Kings*, London 1991, and the various articles in *Origins of Anglo-Saxon Kingdoms*, ed. Bassett.

[25] Snyder, *Age of Tyrants*, 249–50.

[26] *The Life of Bishop Wilfrid by Eddius Stephanus*, ed. Bertram Colgrave, Cambridge 1927, 36–7, 164, and see Kenneth Jackson, 'On the northern British section in Nennius', in

region) may have been a consequence of the marriage in 635 of the Northumbrian prince Oswiu with Riemmelt, daughter of Rheged's last recorded king.[27] In the west midlands too, the survival of the British church and British clergy, to whom the conversion of the incoming English may reasonably be attributed, suggests a more peaceful scenario.[28]

The English takeover of lowland Britain was a protracted affair, marked by sporadic and often bitter warfare, against a stubborn and equally bitter British resistance. It was perhaps in this period that both 'English' and 'Welsh' developed those feelings of mutual hostility so evident in the *Brunanburh* poem and in *Armes Prydein*.[29] The earliest exponent of this institutionalized aversion (and perhaps its chief progenitor) is the Northumbrian monk Bede. The theme of his *Ecclesiastical History,* completed in 731, was the salvation of the English nation, and its emergence as a Christian people. This process Bede attributed to missionaries from outside Britain, from Ireland, from Frankia and pre-eminently from Rome itself. British Christians do not figure in Bede's account of the conversion of the English; indeed his hostility to all things British is attributed to their failure to attempt the salvation of the English, but the roots of his dislike may be as much political as religious.[30] The heroes of the earlier books of the *Ecclesiastical History* are the Northumbrian kings, Edwin of Deira, and Oswald of Bernicia, through whose efforts the whole Northumbrian people was brought to Christ. Both were killed in battle, Edwin in 632 and Oswald in 640, in each case against a coalition of

Celt and Saxon, ed. N. K. Chadwick, Cambridge 1964, 3. The inhabitants of the region were called *Elmetsætna*, 'people of Elmet', in the mid seventh century *Tribal Hidage* (Nicholas Brooks, 'The formation of the Mercian kingdom', in *Origins of Anglo-Saxon Kingdoms*, ed. Bassett, 159–60), and the name survives to this day in the place-names Sherburn-in-Elmet and Barwick-in-Elmet.

[27] Jackson, 'On the northern British section in Nennius', 21–2, 41–2; Kirby, *Earliest English Kings,* 90; Charles Pythian Adams, *Land of the Cumbrians: a Study in British Provincial Origins, AD 400–1120,* Aldershot 1996, 56–62. The marriage was contracted before Oswiu became king in Northumbria, and one of his first actions after succeeding his brother Oswald in 642 was to take an English wife, but his son by Riemmellt later became a sub-king in Deira (southern Northumbria). Other such dynastic marriages are known among the Northumbrians: Oswiu's elder half-brother Eanfrith had, while in exile, married into the Pictish royal family, and his son Talorcan became king of the Picts in the mid seventh century. The mother of another Pictish king, Bridei, was perhaps a daughter of Edwin, king of Northumbria; see James E. Fraser, *The Battle of Dunnichen, 685,* Stroud 2002, 22–3.

[28] For the British church in the west and its influence on the conversion of the English, see Patrick Sims-Williams, *Religion and Literature in Western England, 600–800,* Cambridge 1990, 54–86, especially 79–84.

[29] See the arguments of Bryan Ward-Perkins, 'Why did the Anglo-Saxons not become more British?', *EHR* 115, 2000, 513–33, especially 527–9.

[30] Bede's picture of British indifference and inaction may not in fact be accurate; see note 28, above.

British and English forces which saw Christian British kings in alliance with the pagan king of Northumbria's chief English rival, Penda of Mercia. Here is Bede on Cadwallon, the British king of Gwynedd (North Wales), who joined with Penda to defeat and kill Edwin of Northumbria at Hatfield Chase, in 633:

> At this point there was a great slaughter both of the Church and of the peo-
> ple of Northumbria, one of the perpetrators being a heathen and the other
> a barbarian who was even more cruel than the heathen. Now Penda and the
> whole Mercian race were idolators and ignorant of the name of Christ; but
> Cadwallon, although a Christian by name and profession, was nevertheless
> a barbarian in heart and disposition ... With bestial cruelty he put all to death
> ... meaning to wipe out the whole English nation from the island of Britain.
> Nor did he pay any respect to the Christian religion which had sprung up
> amongst [the Northumbrians]. Indeed to this very day it is the habit of the
> Britons to despise the faith and religion of the English and not to co-oper-
> ate with them in anything, any more than with the heathen.[31]

Cadwallon and the Welsh had, presumably, a different opinion on the matter, and doubtless saw the campaign as an attempt to throw off Northumbrian domination of their lands.[32] But it is perhaps this alliance, which saw the downfall of his hero Edwin, that accounts for Bede's extreme hostility to the British Church, and to the Britons in general; and the widespread dissemination of his *Ecclesiastical History* during the eighth century and beyond helps in turn to account for the spread of that hostility among the English.

It was Bede who popularized the idea of the united English people, politi-cally divided, but joined together by their common faith into a single English Church. How far this idea had spread before the late ninth century is a moot point. The rulers of Wessex bore the title 'king of the Saxons' until Alfred's day, and the eighth-century kings of Mercia were 'kings of the Angles'. But they spoke a com-mon language, known (even to 'Saxons') as 'English'.[33] One striking characteristic of the English language is the minuscule impact upon it of any British influence; only about thirty English words have British roots.[34] This monolingualism is one of the chief arguments for the extermination of the British inhabitants in areas

---

[31] *HE* ii, 20.
[32] It was Edwin, despite being harboured in exile by Cadwallon's father, King Cadfan, who had seized the island of Mona (Anglesey) from the kings of Gwynedd (*HE* ii, 9).
[33] The law-code of the West Saxon king Ine, describes his people as 'English' (Ine, 24, 46§1, 54§2, 74; see *The Laws of the Earliest English Kings,* ed. F. L. Attenborough, Cam-bridge 1922); Ine's code, however, survives only as an appendix to that of Alfred, who was acknowledged as king by the 'Anglian' Mercians as well as the West Saxons. It remains true that the four divisions of early Old English, Kentish, Mercian, West Saxon, and Northumbrian, are dialectical variations of a single language.
[34] Ward-Perkins, 'Why did the Anglo-Saxons not become more British?', 514; see also note 42 below.

under English control, but it is less telling than it may at first appear. The linguistic impact of the British language is not confined to English vocabulary. Though most towns and villages in England bear names of English origin, some have British (and even Latin) roots, and British influence is even more evident in names for rivers and other natural features.[35] The survival of Romano-British place-names in all the areas under English rule is a reminder that some of the inhabitants of such areas must have been Britons, who, whether willingly or under compulsion, adopted the manners and customs, even the language, of their English rulers.[36]

The law-code of King Ine reveals the existence of such a British population in eighth-century Wessex. They are categorized as *wealas* (singular *wealh*), the English variant of a word commonly used in several Germanic languages to mean a Latin-speaker, and specifically a Latin-speaker of Celtic origin.[37] Its primary meaning in the Old English period was much the same; it was used of the British communities in southern and western Britain, especially Wales and Cornwall ('West Wales').[38] When found in the personal names of individual Englishmen, the element *walh* or *wealh* must mean 'Welshman, Briton'; a seventh-century ruler in what is now Herefordshire, on the borders of Wales, was called Merewalh, 'famous Welshman'. But the word *walh* could have other meanings. Sometimes it denotes any foreigner; the *welisce menn* who built a castle in Hereforshire in 1051 were not 'Welshmen' but Frenchmen and Normans in the following of King Edward the Confessor.[39] The same usage is found in the OE word *wealhstod,* 'interpreter', whose literal meaning is 'someone who could understand Welsh'.[40] The word *walh* could also mean 'slave', presumably because in the English kingdoms many people of British descent were slaves, or serfs, or people of humble status.[41] A subgroup of possibly British words used until recently in some English dialects for counting sheep may reflect the status of such people.[42] It is unlikely, however, that all *wealas* of Ine's code were slaves, or even serfs, and some were of comparatively high status, like the *wealh* with five hides of land, an estate which distinguished

[35] Margaret Gelling, *Signposts to the Past,* 3rd edn, Chichester 1997, 30–105.
[36] See the map in Gelling, *Sign-Posts to the Past*, 61 (figure 1).
[37] J. R. R. Tolkien, 'English and Welsh', in *idem, Angles and Britons*, Cardiff 1963, 23–8; Gelling, *Sign-posts to the Past*, 92–6. The word *walh*, *wealh* derives originally from Latin *Volcae*, the name of a Celtic tribe; it is, of course, the ancestor of ModE 'Welsh', 'Wales'.
[38] By contrast, the native inhabitants of north Britain (Cumbria and Strathclyde) are usually *bryttisc* in OE sources.
[39] *ASC, s.a.* 1051.
[40] The word *wealhstod* was borrowed into medieval Welsh as *gwalstawt*, with the same meaning (Tolkien, 'English and Welsh', 23–4).
[41] Gelling, *Signposts to the Past*, 93–4.
[42] Ward-Perkins, 'Why did the Anglo-Saxons not become more British?', 514; Tim Gay, 'Rural dialects and surviving Britons', *British Archaeology* no. 46, July, 1999, available at www.britarch.ac.uk/ba/ba46/.

an aristocrat from an ordinary free man.[43] In general, however, it is clear that the West Saxon *wealas* were less highly-placed than their English equivalents. If an Englishman of free status was killed, his blood-price (or wergeld) was reckoned at 200 shillings, but that of a *wealh* of similar status was only 120 shillings.[44]

Wessex in Ine's time was an expanding kingdom, whose rulers were extending their power into the British-held kingdom of Dumnonia (later Devon and Cornwall) to the west; the *wealas* of Ine's code may be primarily dwellers in the recently-conquered territories. It is unlikely, however, that Wessex was the only English kingdom to have British inhabitants; a group similar to the *wealas* of Ine's code are found in the laws of King Æthelberht of Kent (d. 616 × 618), though they do not figure in the later Kentish codes, one of which was contemporary with that of Ine.[45] The presence of British communities in other English regions is signalled in place-names. Names like Walton and Walcot, whose first element is the OE word *walh* or *wealh* can be difficult to interpret, since it is hard to know whether the meaning 'serf' or 'Welshman' is intended. If the latter, the place-names Walton and Walcot might be interpreted, respectively, as 'village' and 'dwelling' of the Welsh, but if the former meaning is intended, they could mean 'village' and 'dwelling' of the serfs; a form analogous to the very common and widespread name Charlton, 'village of the free peasants'.[46] There is no ambiguity, however, in place-names containing the element *Cumbre*, derived from the British word *cumbrogi* (Mod Welsh *Cymro*), meaning 'Briton, Welshman'.[47] Such names are particularly thick on the ground in western and north-western England, the latest regions to fall under English control, where English settlement was probably sparse, and British communities are likeliest to have survived.[48]

The law-code of Alfred, king of Wessex from 870 to 899, does not distinguish any 'British' inhabitants among his subjects. This does not mean that the *wealas* of Wessex had disappeared, merely that they had come to be regarded, by themselves and their neighbours, as 'West Saxons' and hence 'English'.[49] which brings us to the

---

[43]   Ine 24§2, *EHD* i, no. 32, p. 367.

[44]   Ine 32, 34§1; *EHD* i, no. 32, p. 368. Only if the Welshman was in the king's service was his wergeld equivalent to that of an Englishman (Ine, 33).

[45]   Æthelberht 26; *EHD* i, no. 26, p. 358. For the codes of Hlothhere and Eadric (673–85) and Wihtred (695), see *EHD* i, nos 30–31, pp. 360–4.

[46]   There is an additional complication in that 'Walh' and 'Welisc' are also recorded as personal names, so that Walsall (Staffs), for instance, could be interpreted as 'hollow belonging to Walh' (Gelling, *Sign-posts to the Past*, 95). 'Wealhstod' is also recorded as a personal name; it was born by the earliest-recorded bishop of Hereford in the late seventh century.

[47]   It is found today in Cumberland, 'land of the Welsh/British', the remnant of medieval Cumbria, the southern region of the British kingdom of Strathclyde. Like 'Walh', 'Cumbra' is also found as a personal name among the English.

[48]   Gelling, *Signposts to the the Past*, 92–6.

[49]   Cornishmen (the 'West Welsh') were still speaking their native British language down

irony which underlies the notion of 'Englishness'. Whatever view one takes of the original numbers of Germanic settlers, they cannot have been sufficient to displace all the indigenous inhabitants of those parts of Britain which became 'England'. For the Britons who did not or could not fly from the invaders, the choice was simple; they had to adapt to the customs of their new rulers, and thus (eventually) gain their acceptance and become part of a single whole. In the middle ages, ethnicity as it is understood today played little part in the development of group solidarity.[50] Though 'descent' (*genus*) was one of the defining terms of 'nationhood', it was based on contemporary loyalties rather than biological realities; descent from a mythical or semi-mythical ancestor was invented retrospectively to confirm the *status quo,* and 'the myth of kinship grew with the subsequent construction of English history'.[51] Thus the idea of 'Englishness' could be embraced, not just by people of English descent, but by those of British origin as well.

A late illustration of such accomodation by a subject people to the customs of their rulers is illustrated by a legal text, the *Ordinance concerning the Dunsæte*, which emanates from the 930s, the same period which saw the composition of *Armes Prydein* and the *Brunanburh* poem.[52] The *Dunsæte* seem in origin to have been a British people living on either side of a river, possibly the Wye. At some point, perhaps in the late eighth century, their lands to the east of the river fell under English control, though what precise arrangements were made at that time are unknown.[53] In the early tenth century, however, a conference between Æthelstan, king of the English (the first to bear that title), and the Welsh kings formally recognized the River Wye as the border between the territiories of the Welsh and those of the English. The *Ordinance concerning the Dunsæte* is one result of this formal agreement, and its purpose is to regulate comings and goings across the river. The text, which is in English, opens with the words: 'this is the agreement which the wise men (*witan*) of the English and the councillors (*rædboran*) of the Welsh people have established among the *Dunsæte*'.[54] One clause is particularly relevant to our present concern:

---

to the eighteenth century.

[50] Robert Bartlett, *The Making of Europe,* London 1993, 197–204.

[51] Martin Evison, 'Lo, the conquering hero comes (or not)', *British Archaeology* no 23, April 1997, at www.britarch.ac.uk/ba/ba23/ba23feat.html.

[52] Patrick Wormald, *The Making of English Law: King Alfred to the Twelfth Century,* Oxford 1999, 381–2; see also Margaret Gelling, *The West Midlands in the Early Middle Ages,* Leicester 1992, 113–19; Sims-Williams, *Religion and Literature in Western England, 600–800,* 9, 45.

[53] Margaret Gelling (*West Midlands,* 114–18), plausibly identifies the *Dunsæte* with the men of Archenfield, that part of the Welsh kingdom of Ergyng which was attached to Herefordshire by the eleventh century.

[54] *Ðis is se gerædnes ðe Angelcynnes witan and wealhðeode rædboran betweox Dunsæte gesetton.* The text is printed, with facing translation, in Frank Noble, *Offa's Dyke Reviewed,* ed. M. Gelling, BAR British series 114 (1983), 104–9.

neither is a Welshman to cross over into English land, nor an Englishman into Welsh land, without the appointed man from that land who shall meet him at the bank and bring him back there again without any offence.[55]

It seems from this that the establishment of the Wye as the boundary between English and Welsh split the *Dunsæte*, originally a single British people, into two separate communities, one now defined as 'Welsh', and living under Welsh custom, the other as 'English' and living under English law.

Such examples are a reminder that the sharp contrast in nationality, felt on both sides of the Anglo-Welsh divide, is as much a construct as most such 'racial' animosities. Though the Welsh may be correct in feeling themselves to be the 'original' Britons, the English too have a claim to a share in the Romano-British inheritance. Since 'nationality' is itself a construct, both 'Welshness' and 'Englishness' are a matter of choice as much as a matter of biological descent. I began this paper by quoting from Freeman's *History of the Norman Conquest*, and in support of the concept of 'elective' nationality, I should like to conclude with a quotation from one of Freeman's contemporaries, W. S. Gilbert. In *HMS Pinafore*, one of the operettas which Gilbert produced with his partner, Arthur Sullivan, one of the characters is described as follows:

> He is an Englishman;
>> for he himself has said it;
>> and it's greatly to his credit
>> that he is an Englishman.
> For he could have been a Russian;
>> or French or Turk or Prussian,
>> or perhaps Italian;
> but in spite of all temptations
>> to belong to other nations,
>> he remains an Englishman;
>> a true-born Englishman.

Since I am myself, on my father's side, one of the *Cymry*, but in right of my mother, my birthplace, and my upbringing, no less English for that, this seems an appropriate coda for a paper on the origins of English, and Welsh, nationality.

---

[55] *Nah naðer tofarenne ne wilisc man on ænglisc land ne ænglisc on wylisc ðema butan gesettan landmen se hine sceal æt stæðe underfon et eft ðær butan sacne gebringan.*

The Danes and the Making of the Kingdom of the English[1]

DAVID ROFFE

'The English, the English, the English are best. I wouldn't give tuppence for all of the rest'. So sang Flanders and Swann with, I must add, tongue in cheek in the 1960s.[2] That truly was a time of warm beer, old maids cycling to communion on a Sunday morning, and fish and chips.[3] What do we have now? Well, for a start you might get into big trouble for saying English when you might mean British; warm beer has given way to cold lager and alcopops; the old maid is as likely as not to be no such thing and to be off to yoga on a Sunday morning; and England's national dish is the Indian takeaway.

England, Britain, has changed. One of the most important agents of change has been the arrival of peoples from other parts of the world. It started in the late 1940s with emigration from the West Indies and Hong Kong and gathered pace with the exodus from the Indian subcontinent from the late 50s onwards. Our last census in 2001 showed that the numbers from ethnic minorities are still relatively small: no more than 7.9% of our total population.[4] And yet the impact on our culture has been profound. The 1950s were an age of grey uniformity. We now have a vigorous multicultural society, admittedly not always at peace with itself, in which ethnic communities not only contribute to the commonweal but often provide its driving energy.

This, of course, is not an entirely new experience. England has seen successive waves of immigration throughout its history and they have often, perhaps usually, served to invigorate its society. The late nineteenth and early twentieth centuries saw Jewish immigration from the shtetls of Eastern Europe. Their

---

[1] This paper was read at the Nations of Britain Symposium at Tohoku University, Sendai, Japan, in November 2006, and remains much as it was delivered to the audience of Japanese scholars and students. I am grateful to Professor Hirokazu Tsurushima for organizing the event and for being an untiringly perfect host.

[2] For the whole song, see http://www.englandsportal.com/englishinsong.html. The song concludes 'It's not that they're wicked or naturally bad/ It's just being foreign that makes them so mad'.

[3] The notion comes from John Major's misquoting of George Orwell. It nevertheless captures an atmosphere.

[4] http://www.statistics.gov.uk/cci/nugget.asp?id=273.

progress from Whitechapel to Golders Green within two generations charts the rise of a new professional class. Before that there was the influx of Irish who provided the labour for the construction of the canals and railways which fuelled the Industrial Revolution. The seventeenth century saw the settlement of Huguenots who contributed so much to the Protestant ethic which created capitalism in the first place. Most famously of all there was the Norman colonization of England in the eleventh and twelfth centuries.

Notions of ethnicity have changed in the last twenty year or so. It is now realized that the character of societies can radically change without massive folk migration. This is no more so than in the settlement of England by the Danes. They too, I shall argue, were few in overall numbers. But they too had a hand in creating what we think of as quintessential Englishness. The Danes, or Vikings as we know them, are first recorded as raiders.[5] However, they also came as merchants and traders: one of the possible origins of the name 'viking' is people of the *wics,* that is trading places.[6] Their arrival in England was part of a wider European phenomenon. From their homelands in and around Denmark they sailed widely. To the east, they penetrated the Baltic through into Muscovy and down the Don, founding the kingdom of Kiev. From there they traded as far south as Constantinople. To the west, they followed the coast down into the Low Countries, France, Spain, and into the Mediterranean. To the north they went from Norway to the Northern and Western Isles, and then Man and Ireland. Iceland was colonized, and then Greenland, even with some penetration into North America.

Their first recorded raid in England was in 793 with an attack on the community of St Cuthbert on Lindisfarne in Northumbria.[7] The events of the next half century or so are largely unrecorded, but from 865 it would seem that the nature of the Viking assault changed. In that year there arrived what the chronicler called 'The Great Army' under the command of Ivarr the boneless (*inn beinlausi* – I cannot help feeling that this should be translated as Ivarr the legless); their intention was apparently to settle. The army spent the winter in East Anglia and in the following year crossed the Humber, and, taking advantage of an internal dispute, established itself at York. Raids into Mercia followed in 868, into East Anglia in 870, and then Wessex in 871. A second host, 'the Great Summer Army', arrived, and the combined force over-wintered in London in 872–3 and, after the Mercian king Bur-

5   For general introductions to the Viking world, see *Cultural Atlas of the Viking World,* ed. J. Graham-Campbell, C. Batey, H. Clarke, R. I. Page, and N. S. Price, London 1994; *The Oxford Illustrated History of the Vikings,* ed. P. H. Sawyer, Oxford 1997; A. Forte, R. Oram, F. Pedersen, *Viking Empires* Cambridge 2005.

6   *The Oxford English Dictionary, sv* Viking, gives a derivation from OE *wic,*, there translated as 'camp'. For a discussion, see L. Lönnroth, 'The Vikings in history and legend', in *The Oxford Illustrated History of the Vikings,* ed. Sawyer, 229–30.

7   *The Anglo-Saxon Chronicle, a Revised Translation,* ed. D. Whitelock, D. C. Douglas, and S. I. Tucker, 2nd edn London 1963 (hereafter *ASC*), 36.

gred had fled, in Repton in 873-4. In the following year the armies split and the northern contingent, now under the command of Halfdan, returned to York. In 876 Halfdan 'shared out the land of the Northumbrians' among his men and 'they began to plough and support themselves'. The summer army under Guthrum, by contrast, launched an outright assault on Wessex, but after a rearguard defence by King Alfred, the army was defeated at Edington in 878. Guthrum retreated to East Anglia in 879 where he and his men 'shared out the land'.[8] Sometime between the battle of Edington and the treaty of Wedmore in 886 a boundary between the English and the Danes was drawn up running diagonally from London north-westwards to Derbyshire and Cheshire along the line of Watling Street.[9] The area to the north was to become known as the Danelaw.[10]

Danish settlement saw a profound change in the economy and society of the region.[11] Contacts with a wider Scandinavian world fostered a booming mercantile economy based upon renewed urban life.[12] Although earlier an important trading centre, by the mid ninth century York was perhaps a city only in name. The king of Northumbria maintained a household there, as did the archbishop, but there was probably not much that was urban about it. Long-distance trade was limited, one suspects largely confined to the supply of the aristocrats settled there. Within its Roman walls to east and west of the Ouse, much of the city was not intensely developed. York would seem to have been little more than an administrative centre with a command economy. In 950, by contrast, it was a burgeoning international trading centre. Areas of the city had been re-planned and there was widespread development outside the walls where extensive industries of metal, wood, bone, antler, amber, jet, textiles and glass were established. Archaeological finds from throughout the City reveal wide-flung trading links with the Baltic and beyond.[13]

[8]   ASC, 48–50.
[9]   The Laws of the Earliest English Kings, ed. F. L. Attenborough, Cambridge 1922, 96–101, 201.
[10]   R. H. C. Davis, 'Alfred and Guthrum's frontier', EHR 97, 1982, 803–10; D. Dumville, Wessex and England from Alfred to Edgar, Woodbridge 1992, 1–27. The Danes quickly breached the boundary, moving into Bedfordshire, Buckinghamshire and Hertfordshire. The formation of the Danelaw as a legal concept was more complex and protracted. For discussions, see Dawn M. Hadley, The Northern Danelaw: its Social Structure, c.800–1100, London 2000, 3–5; C. R. Hart, The Danelaw, London 1992, 3–6. 'Danelaw' is first noted in a law code of 1008; K. Holman, 'Defining the Danelaw', in Vikings and the Danelaw, ed. J. Graham-Campbell, R. Hall, J. Jesch, and D. Parsons, Oxford 2001, 1–12.
[11]   For a discussion of the economic and social impact of the Danes, see Dawn M. Hadley, The Vikings in England: Settlement, Society, and Culture, Manchester 2006.
[12]   Pauline Stafford, The East Midlands in the Early Middle Ages, Leicester 1985, 40–62.
[13]   Hadley, The Vikings in England, 247–54.

Lincoln experienced a similar explosion in its economy with the settlement of the Danes. Like York, the Upper City seems to have been given over to purely administrative functions up to 850 or so, while the Lower City, running down the hill towards the River Witham, may have been largely deserted. By 950, however, the banks of the Witham were newly developed with the Lower City being resettled and the suburb of Wigford quickly emerging as a major trading centre. Again, archaeological finds indicate widespread manufacturing and trade.[14]

York and Lincoln were pre-eminent, but other market centres were also developing. Stamford, for example, was transformed from a Middle Saxon estate centre into a major Danish borough. It produced pottery, initially made by potters imported from Beauvais in France, of a quality otherwise unprecedented since Roman times, and there is evidence of extensive metal working. In the early tenth century defences were laid out to define a new town on the north of the Welland.[15] Derby, formerly known as *Northworthig* in English, seems to have developed at the same time at a crossing of the River Derwent away from the Roman defences of Little Chester.[16]

A similar picture was to be found in East Anglia. Norwich was stirring as a major mercantile centre and Ipswich, a Middle Saxon *wic*, was revitalized. The rural economy itself was booming with a lively land market.[17] This was all by way of contrast with the south and west of England. There were no trading centres that could compare with those of the east except London and Winchester. The richness of the Danelaw was prodigious. The tenth century has been characterized as a period of *reconquest* of the area.[18] But for Wessex, and to a great extent Mercia, it was a conquest. The wealth of the Danelaw was a great prize. The winning of it was to create England and then shape its distinctive institutions.

In 886 this was all in the future. The Danes had looked like overrunning the whole of England. Edington was to prove a turning point. Alfred's restructuring of English society was the key to a counter offensive against the Danes. Up to the ninth century military service had been an essentially personal affair, it depended on the bond between lord and man.[19] It proved an inadequate means of defence against the hit-and-run tactics of the Danes, since local lords often preferred to come to term than stand and fight. Alfred introduced what was effectively a stand-

---

[14] Hadley, *The Vikings in England*, 157–8, 162–74.

[15] C. M. Mahany and D. R. Roffe, 'Stamford: the development of an Anglo-Scandinavian borough', *ANS* 5, 1983, 199–219; Hadley, *The Vikings in England*, 158–74.

[16] Hadley, *The Vikings in England*, 155–7, 162–3, 166–9, 172–3.

[17] For a nuanced reinterpretation of the evidence, see D. M. Metcalf, 'Monetary circulation in the Danelaw, 973–1083', in *Anglo-Saxons: Studies Presented to Cyril Roy Hart*, ed. Simon Keynes and A. P. Smyth, Dublin 2006, 159–85.

[18] W. M. Aird, 'Northumbria and the making of the kingdom of the English', below.

[19] R. P. Abels, *Lordship and Military Obligation in Anglo-Saxon England*, London 1988, 58–78.

ing army by imposing military service on all land regardless of lordship. Drawing on continental models, he built a network of boroughs. To each was assigned a certain number of hides and the men who held them were responsible for the upkeep of the defences of the central borough and its garrisoning in times of need. The system provided bases for a standing army that could take to the field both defensibly and offensively.[20]

By the death of Alfred in 899 Wessex had been secured against further Danish expansion. The stage for conquest was set. The first major set-back for the Danes in its own backyard occurred in 910 when the army of the North was routed at Tettenhall in Staffordshire.[21] With much of its leadership killed, the Danes at York were paralyzed and the Danes of the East Midlands were forced to look to their own defence. It was from this time that boroughs were fortified at Stamford, Leicester, and possibly Derby. Meanwhile, the Danish boroughs to the south – Huntingdon, Cambridge, Hertford, Northampton – were made ready.[22] One by one Alfred's son Edward the Elder picked them off between 912 and 918, building new boroughs where they were required. At the same time, Edward's sister, Æthelflæd, Lady of the Mercians, attacked from the west, again founding boroughs to secure the northern boundary of Mercia and penetrate further east. On her death in 918, Edward succeeded to Mercia and by 920 was the undisputed king of England south of the Humber.[23]

East Anglia was never again to be independent. The East Midlands were briefly and reluctantly to succumb to the Norse kingdom of Dublin and York between 939 and 942, but thereafter remained an integral part of the kingdom. With the fall of York and Northumbria to Wessex rule in 954, the England of Domesday Book had come into existence.[24] By and large it was to remain united thereafter. It was to be conquered by the Danish kings Swein and Cnut in 1016 after renewed Danish raids in the late tenth century. This, however, was far from the revenge of the Danelaw. By then it had long been 'English'.

The process of conquest was long interpreted by English historians in ethnic terms: it was assumed that it was the conquest of one race by another. The differ-

[20] *The Defence of Wessex: the Burghal Hidage and Anglo-Saxon Fortifications*, ed. D. Hill and A. R. Rumble, Manchester 1996.

[21] *ASC*, 61–2.

[22] Archaeological evidence suggests extensive urban replanning at the same time. See A.P. Smyth, *Scandinavian York and Dublin,* Dublin 1987, 75, 102; R. A. Hall, 'The Five Boroughs of the Danelaw: a review of present knowledge', *ASE* 18, 1989, 149–206; D. R. Roffe, 'Nottinghamshire and the North: a Domesday Study', PhD thesis, Leicester, 1987, chapter 10, at http://www.roffe.co.uk/phdframe.htm.

[23] *ASC*, 61–8.

[24] S. Keynes, 'The Vikings in England', in *The Oxford Illustrated History of the Vikings,* ed. Sawyer, 48–82. For an eminently accessible account, see P. Wormald, 'The Making of England', *History Today* 45:2, 1995, 26–32.

ences between the Danelaw and the rest of England are indeed pronounced. This is no more so than in its organization of land. The most cursory of glances at the Domesday account of the region shows just how far the Danelaw manor differed from what we conceive of as the norm.[25] We think of a compact area, perhaps a village, over which the lord has more or less full rights. In the Danelaw generally none of this applies. Villages are divided and manors, more usually called 'sokes', have lands scattered all over the place. Above all the peasants, known as sokemen, owned their own lands and had a high degree of freedom. Lordship was relatively weak: the Danelaw was predominantly a region of free communities of sokemen.[26]

It was also a region with its own distinctive place-names.[27] In some parts of Lincolnshire and Yorkshire as many as two third are Danish. Typically, they are formed from a Danish personal name compounded with Danish *by*, 'village' or *torp*, 'hamlet'. Hence, Whitby, perhaps 'Hviti's village' and Scunthorpe, 'Skuma's hamlet'.[28] Land, moreover, was often measured in ploughlands, that is in terms of arable. Elsewhere in England the hide was more usual. It was, theoretically at least, a measure of the total land in arable, pasture, meadow and woodland, needed to support a family. All of this fostered the notion that the Danelaw was a more or less homogeneous area of Danish settlement and sensibilities. In the eleventh- and twelfth-century law codes the Danelaw is said to have had its own distinctive laws. To many historians the conclusion seemed clear: the pronounced freedom of the Danelaw was a direct result of colonization by the rank and file of the free Viking armies.[29]

[25] *Domesday Book*, ed. R. W. H. Erskine, A. Williams, and G. H. Martin, London 1986–2000. For the 'Danelaw' Counties, see Yorkshire, Lincolnshire, Nottinghamshire, Derbyshire, Huntingdonshire, Cambridgeshire, Hertfordshire, Bedfordshire, and Buckinghamshire in volume i, Great Domesday Book (*GDB*), and Norfolk and Suffolk in volume ii, Little Domesday Book (*LDB*). Many of the distinctive forms are Domesday artefacts. See D. R. Roffe, *Domesday: the Inquest and the Book*, Oxford 2000, 186–223; D. R. Roffe, *Decoding Domesday*, Woodbridge 2007, 29–61.

[26] For the basic analyses of the societies of the region, see F. M Stenton, *Types of Manorial Structure in the Northern Danelaw*, Oxford 1910; D. C Douglas, *The Social Structure of Medieval East Anglia*, Oxford 1927. For a revisionist review, see Hadley, *The Northern Danelaw: its Social Structure, c.800–1100*.

[27] See the English Place-Name Society volumes for the Danelaw counties and G. Fellows Jensen, *Scandinavian Settlement Names in the East Midlands*, Copenhagen 1978, for identification and analysis of the raw data.

[28] A. D. Mills, *A Dictionary of English Place-Names*, Oxford 1998, 288, 356. For a recent discussion of the place-name evidence, see M. Townend, 'Viking age England as a bilingual society', in *Cultures in Contact: Scandinavian Settlement in England in the Ninth and Tenth Centuries t*, ed. D. M. Hadley and J. Richards, Turnhout 2000, 89–105.

[29] See, for example, F. M. Stenton, 'The Danes in England', *Proceedings of the British Academy* 13, 1927, 203–46; H. R. Loyn, *The Vikings in England*, London 1977; K. Cameron, 'Scandinavian settlement in the territory of the Five Boroughs: the place-name evidence', in *Place-Name Evidence for the Anglo-Saxon Invasion and Scandi-*

The reality is at once more complex and interesting. The Danelaw undoubtedly had a Danish cultural identity. Danish was evidently spoken by many and the English of the area became Scandinavianized.[30] Coins, personal jewellery, and monumental sculpture all exhibit distinctive Danish influences. They are some of the glories of pre-Conquest art in England.[31] This, however, was but a veneer on a society that was still essentially English. Far from being specifically Danish, the hallmark tenurial forms and freedoms of the Danelaw were characteristic of pre-Viking English society in general.[32] What are now called 'multiple estates' were a common feature of pre-Viking England. Villages were grouped together, usually in twelves, to provide food for the king. One village might supply ale, another barley, and so on. The peasants who made the renders might also be obliged to provide sundry other minor services, but were otherwise free and had full rights over their lands just like sokemen. Remnants of this tributary society survived into the post-Conquest period in non-Danish areas – notably in Northumbria and Cumbria in the far north – and are almost identical in form to the sokes of the Danelaw.[33]

In this context the Danish place-names begin to look less like evidence of a mass migration from Scandinavia.[34] The Danish leaders, jarls, clearly took over the great sokes. Most of these have English names and had long been major centres of tribute.[35] The Danish place-names within the sokes, the *by* and the *torp* names, indicate that the dues from some of the villages attached to them were granted to their men: the compounded personal names are a record of their identities. It was a small Danish aristocracy that took control in the Danelaw. In some areas of Lincolnshire and Yorkshire there may have been a degree of secondary immigration from Denmark after the initial settlement.[36] But otherwise it was business as usual.

---

navian Settlements: Eight Studies, ed. K. Cameron, English Place-Name Society Occasional Publications, Nottingham 1975, 115–71.

[30] Townend, 'Viking age England as a bilingual society'.

[31] Hadley, *The Vikings in England*, 120–8.

[32] G. R. J. Jones, 'Multiple estate and early settlement', in *Medieval Settlement*, ed. P. H. Sawyer, London 1976, 15–40; Stafford, *The East Midlands in the Early Middle Ages*, 30–2; *The Kalendar of Abbot Samson of Bury St Edmund's and Related Documents*, ed. R. H. C. Davis, Camden Society 3rd series 84, 1954, xliv–xlvii.

[33] See, for example, Leominster in Herefordshire (*GDB*, ff. 180–1). This is not to say, however, that all Domesday estates of this kind, either in the Danelaw or beyond, were necessarily ancient: sokes could and did change structure throughout their history (Roffe, *Decoding Domesday*, 150–162).

[34] G. R. J. Jones, 'Early territorial organization in Northern England and its bearing on the Scandinavian settlement', in *The Fourth Viking Congress*, ed. A. Small, 1965, 67–84.

[35] Many are associated with large, 'regional', pagan Saxon cemeteries that seem to have served a region. See, for example, Sleaford in Lincolnshire: *Sleaford*, ed. C. M. Mahany and D. R. Roffe, South Lincolnshire Archaeology 3, Stamford 1979.

[36] In some areas Danish field names are thick on the ground, perhaps suggesting a greater concentration of Danish-speaking farmers.

English sokemen continued to render the same sorts of dues as they always had done.

With power goes sensibilities. Danish culture, language, and values inevitably became widespread. However, acculturation is never a one-sided affair.[37] The Danish aristocracy soon began to put down local roots. The Danelaw had never been a social or political unity. In large measure the divisions of the original settlement in the late ninth century were to persist. Historians have traditionally made the distinction between the Northern and Southern Danelaw.[38] The River Welland which divides the two areas was already an important boundary in the ninth century. The Midlands and East Anglia to the south were to continue through the tenth and eleventh centuries with their own political and social networks. The Northern Danelaw was divided by the Humber. Again, the boundary between the two areas was of long standing: it marked the divide between Northumbria on the one side and Lindsey and Mercia on the other. Yet again, each had its own networks of power. Even as late as 1066 these regions remained quite distinct. With the exception of a handful of figures of national standing, very few family interests crossed the Humber and Welland boundaries.

From the very beginning of the Danish settlement local identities were forged within these areas. In the late ninth century links were made with local English families. In 865 the Danes probably allied themselves with a local faction in York.[39] In the mid 870s such an alliance with locals is all-but explicit. After the flight of Burgred of Mercia from Repton in 873, the Danes, according to the Anglo-Saxon Chronicle, installed Ceolwulf, 'a foolish king's thegn', as king. The reality seems to be that Ceolwulf had executed a coup with the aid of the Danes, for he was a member of a rival Mercian dynasty.[40] How common were these marriages of convenience in the early stages of the settlement is impossible to gauge, but one suspects that they must have been a significant factor in the settlement. In the 940s and 950s Archbishop Wulfstan and the men of York allied themselves with successive kings of York and Dublin in the cause of Northumbrian independence from Wessex.

[37] For a succinct account of the processes of acculturation and its mutual nature, see Dawn M. Hadley, 'Viking and native: re-thinking identity in the Danelaw', *Early Medieval Europe* 11, 2002, 45–70.

[38] D. R. Roffe, 'The historical context', *Anglo-Saxon Settlement on the Siltland of Eastern England*, Lincolnshire Archaeology and Heritage Reports Series 7, 2005, 264–88; D. Stocker, 'Monuments and merchants: irregularities in the distribution of stone sculpture in Lincolnshire and Yorkshire in the tenth century', in *Cultures in Contact*, ed. Hadley and Richards, 179–212; D. Stocker and P. Everson, 'Five town funerals: decoding diversity in Danelaw stone sculpture,' *Vikings and the Danelaw*, ed. Graham-Campbell *et al.*, 223–43.

[39] *ASC*, 46–7.

[40] A. Williams, A. P. Smyth, and D. P. Kirby, *A Biographical Dictionary of Dark Age Britain: England, Scotland and Wales, c.500–c.1050*, London 1991, 78. Intermarriage was probably also a significant force towards integration.

Similar alliances were forged in the course of the second Danish conquest in the eleventh century.[41]

The early tenth century saw further localization of loyalties in the newly-fortified boroughs. After the defeat of the army of the North at Tettenhall in 910 the Anglo-Saxon Chronicle repeatedly refers to Danes of named boroughs. So, we hear of 'all those who belong to Northampton', 'the men of Huntingdon' and so on. Sometimes these armies or boroughs might act together against the English. In 916 the 'army of Northampton and Leicester' broke out and raided into Oxfordshire and then besieged Luton. However, although boroughs might cooperate with each other against the advancing English, there were no formal alliances.[42] The borough had become the focus of loyalty and communal action.

Indeed, throughout the century loyalties to place seem to have been stronger than race. In 939 the men of the five boroughs of Lincoln, Stamford, Nottingham, Leicester, and Derby may have welcomed the annexation of the East Midlands by Olaf Guthrithson, the king of York, but they soon repented of their decision when Olaf's Norse army threatened their interests. They supported King Edmund in the 'redemption of the five boroughs'.[43] Later in the century the men of Lindsey were accused of not fighting King Swein of Denmark - again, it might be added, in West Saxon sources - because they were fellow Danes. It seems more likely, however, that they acted to minimize the wasting of their lands.[44] They were similarly pragmatic in 1013 when faced with a similar threat.[45] From early on, it would seem, the men of the Danelaw thought of themselves less as Danes than men of York, men of Lincoln, men of Nottingham, and so on.

These were identities that were no more nor less easy to incorporate into the kingdom of England than any other. In the event successive kings of Wessex had as many problems with English Mercia as the Danelaw.[46] Most immediately in the aftermath of conquest, forfeited lands were probably granted to outsiders to bolster the crown's influence in the Danelaw. The expedient was used in the northern Danelaw after 942.[47] But wholesale confiscation was never an option. The region was integrated into the kingdom by reorganizing existing communities in a new system of local government, that of the shire.

[41] For a succinct account, see Hadley, *The Vikings in England*, 28–80.
[42] *ASC*, 61–8. The Five Boroughs was apparently a late tenth-century, English, innovation (D. R. Roffe, 'Hundreds and wapentakes,' *The Lincolnshire Domesday*, eds A. Williams and G. H. Martin, London 1992, 33–9).
[43] *ASC*, 71.
[44] *John of Worcester* ii, 443; *ASC*, 83.
[45] *ASC*, 92–3.
[46] Regional identities remained into the eleventh century and beyond.
[47] Hart, *The Danelaw*, 134–5. For something of the process of forfeiture and grant in Huntingdonshire and Cambridgeshire, see *Liber Eliensis*, ed. E. O. Blake, Camden Society 3rd ser. 92, 1962, 98–9.

The system seems to have been introduced into the Southern Danelaw at much the same time as it was into east and central Mercia.[48] Like Alfred's burghal system, it was based upon boroughs. From the Thames to the Welland there was a reassessment of land in hides, here less a measure of land than of obligation to the king in payment of taxes, maintenance of the peace, and military service. From the start it was an assessment on communities rather than individuals. Five or ten hides were assessed on each village and the inhabitants acquitted the duties incumbent on them in common.[49] A hundred hides, notionally ten or twenty villages, made up a hundred. Each hundred had its own court to which the free men of the hundred owed suit. It was the forum in which disputes between them might be settled. Again, it was the community at large that took responsibility for the business of maintaining the peace and organized military service. In their turn hundreds in groups of twelve, eighteen, twenty-four, or thirty-two, were assigned to central boroughs. The chief men of each hundred paid suit to its court. It too was a communal court: it was the men of the shire who decided the matters that came before it. However, it was the king's representative, the shire reeve or sheriff, who presided, although the earl and bishop sat with him.

In contrast to Wessex and East Anglia, each shire was named after its central borough. Hence, Cambridgeshire after Cambridge, Huntingdonshire after Huntingdon and so on. The system seems to have been in place c.950 when it is first described in the Hundred Ordinance.[50] It may have been introduced in the early years of the century by Edward the Elder or his son Athelstan,[51] but on balance a later date might be preferred. North of the Welland the process was more protracted. After the conquest of the area, a rudimentary burghal system seems to have been introduced in the area of the five boroughs. Mints were established in the reign of Athelstan, and the tolls boundaries of Nottingham and Derby suggest that defined territories were assigned to these boroughs.[52] These, however, were

[48] H. R. Loyn, *The Governance of Anglo-Saxon England, 500–1087*, London 1984, 131–54. For detailed examinations of each county, see F. R. Thorn, 'Hundreds and wapentakes', in the various volumes of *Great Domesday Book: County Edition*, ed. Ann Williams, R. W. H. Erskine and G. H. Martin, 30 vols, London 1986–92.

[49] Recent statistical analyses of Domesday data have argued for a bottom-up assessment based on something like measured survey (J. McDonald and G. D. Snooks, 'Were the tax assessments of Domesday England artificial? The case of Essex', *EHR* 38, 1985, 353–73). But the evidence for a top-down assessment is overwhelming (R. A. Leaver, 'Five hides in ten counties: a contribution to the Domesday Regression debate,' *Economic History Review* 41, 1988, 525–42). For a critique, see Roffe, *Decoding Domesday*, 191–7).

[50] *The Laws of the Kings of England from Edmund to Henry I*, ed. A. J. Robertson, Cambridge 1925, Hundred Ordinance.

[51] D. Hill, 'The shiring of Mercia – again', in *Edward the Elder, 899–924*, ed. N. J. Higham and D. H. Hill, London 2001, 144–59.

[52] D. R. Roffe, 'The origins of Derbyshire,' *The Derbyshire Archaeological Journal* 106,

very different from the later shires of Nottingham and Derby. Moreover, there appears to have been no reassessment at this time. Shiring on the Southern Danelaw model was a later tenth or early eleventh century phenomenon.

In outline it followed the principles apparent south of the Welland, but it took integration of local communities to a higher level.[53] Here the basic unit of assessment was the carucate, that is the ploughland. Carucates were grouped in twelves, known locally and confusingly as hundreds, to form tithings, that is villages or groups of villages that were responsible for policing. The twelve-carucate hundreds were in their turn grouped into wapentakes and then groups of wapentakes were assigned to boroughs. The wapentake and boroughs had their own courts like the hundreds of hidated England, but the ultimate authority in the area was the meeting of the Five Boroughs.[54] It probably met in Nottingham.

The regional assembly, apparently paralleled in Mercia,[55] was short-lived. It is not evidenced after 1016 and the Five Boroughs were re-organized into the four shires of Lincoln, Leicester, Nottingham and Derby that subsequently functioned in very much the same way as the shires south of the Welland. East Anglia seems to have been shired at much the same time, although its assessment in carucates and division into hundreds may be earlier.[56]

This elaborate structure of local administration has usually seen as a species of military government. It was the means, it is argued, by which kings of Wessex imposed their will on a conquered people. The notion has had credence not the least because the system undoubtedly had military functions.[57] The local militia, the *fyrd*, was mustered through the hundred and, more widely, groups of shires can be seen to have had wider strategic roles. As we have seen, the Welland marks a pronounced cultural boundary between the Northern and Southern Danelaw. To the north there was a higher concentration of Danish settlement and the area to the south may well have been organized as some sort of march in the first half of the tenth century. Certainly, the Five Boroughs acted as such in the second half

1986, 102–22.

[53] D. R. Roffe, 'The Lincolnshire hundred,' *Landscape History* 3, 1981, 27–36; Roffe, 'Hundreds and wapentakes,' *The Lincolnshire Domesday*, ed. Williams and Martin, 33–9.

[54] The institution of the Five Boroughs is first noticed in Æthelred II's Wantage Code of c.997. The integration of tithing (policing functions), carucate, hundred, and wapentake suggests that the system cannot have been any earlier than the second half of the tenth century. Before that date, warranty seems to have been largely a matter for the kin and peace guilds.

[55] A. Williams, '*princeps Merciorum gentis*: the family, career and connections of Ælfhere, ealdorman of Mercia 956–83', *ASE* 10, 1982, 161–6

[56] L. Marten, 'The shiring of East Anglia: an alternative hypothesis', *Historical Research* 81, 2008, available online at http://www.blackwell-synergy.com/toc/hisr/0/0.

[57] Roffe, 'Hundreds and wapentakes', *The Lincolnshire Domesday*, ed. Williams and Martin, 31–9.

as a buffer against the still unstable Northumbria.

The shire system, however, was much more than just a muster list. It was no doubt efficient in defending the locality in times of war, but its primary role was the maintenance of the peace. At every level, from village to borough, it enlisted the support of the free communities of the shire to that end. Title to land, law-worthiness, and free status all depended on cooperation: if a free man failed in his obligations he was in danger of losing everything. In an age of rampant neo-conservatism it is often forgotten that taxation is our subscription to a civil and civilized society. No less did the shire give as much as it took. Courts of hundred and shire preserved freedom and in so doing consolidated social cohesion.[58] Patronage was, of course, part of the equation. The prospect of preferment in the shire court oiled the wheels. But, once instituted, the shire had its own dynamic.

The outcome was a system of local government that was all-but unique in the Middle Ages. King and subject made common cause against disruptive forces, be they invaders, felons, or over-mighty lords. By tapping into local communities in this way, both in the Danelaw and beyond, successive kings prevented the privatization and localization of power that was so characteristic of Western Europe after 1000. Thus it was that lordship was relatively weak and ancient forms of social organization more prevalent north of the Thames. 'Feudalism' never took a hold.

Perfected in the Northern Danelaw, the shire became the model for the rest of England. It was introduced into Yorkshire, probably in the reign of Cnut in the early eleventh century. Elements were transplanted to the far North later in the same century and the next. It subsequently made its way with the Normans to Wales and Ireland.[59] Less obviously, the model also influenced the organization of society in the heartlands of Wessex itself. The burghal system introduced by King Alfred is usually seen as the prototype of the shire. Clearly its military organization was an influence. However, it was little more than that. The network of boroughs in the south and west organized Wessex for war and not much else. The system became largely redundant in the tenth century. Many boroughs lost their status, some even slipped out of sight and are now lost.[60] But militarization of the kingdom had inevitably led to strong lordship and local government devolved upon great estates, both royal and non-royal. The hundreds that are later found in Wessex, and western Mercia which came under the influence of Wessex at any early period, look very much as if they have been imposed upon these estates in an

---

[58]   Roffe, *Decoding Domesday*, 183–209.
[59]   Tithings and then frankpledge, for example, do not seem to have been transferred. Maintenance of law and order was generally vested in sergeants of the peace (R. Stewart-Brown, *The Serjeants of the Peace in Medieval England and Wales,* Manchester 1936).
[60]   South of the Thames shires perpetuate the names of earlier kingdoms where, to the north, they are all named after central boroughs.

attempt to bring them into line with the Danelaw and Mercia.[61] Wholesale reform was never to be attempted. The Anglo-Saxon kingdoms and their subdivisions remained the units of administration at the shire level. But after the Norman Conquest changes in organization and procedure continued to be influenced by the structure of the shire north of the Thames.[62]

What, then, of the Danes in the making of the kingdom of the English? England was not yet a nation in any modern sense in the pre-Conquest period. It was a collection of local communities with their own interests and identities. The communities of the Danelaw fitted neatly into this habitat. Danish settlers were never great in numbers and they had rapidly integrated themselves into English society. As with communities elsewhere in their expanding realm, the kings of Wessex incorporated them into an England by recognizing and reinforcing their local interests and identities. The process saw the emergence of what was to be the predominant character of the kingdom of the English throughout the medieval period. It is paradoxical that in becoming so English the Danes were instrumental in creating Englishness. Had Flanders and Swann been living in the Danelaw in the early eleventh century, they would still have been singing 'The English, the English, the English are best'.

[61] The *manerium cum hundredo*, that is the hundred as an off-shoot of a royal estate, has been held to be the archetype of the hundredal system throughout the country (H. M. Cam, '*Manerium cum hundredo*: the hundred and the hundred manor', *EHR* 47, 1932, 355–76). However, north of the Thames the equation has little reality – the hundred is essentially independent of tenure. Its occurrence in Wessex, then, is more likely to reflect the, perhaps later, grant or assumption of an intrinsic hundred, that is, a private hundred. For a full discussion, see Roffe, *Decoding Domesday*, 283–4. For the reorganization of hundreds in Wessex, see D. R. Roffe, 'The hide and local government in Anglo-Saxon England', National Museum of Japanese History, forthcoming.

[62] For example, south of the Thames shires met in traditional meeting places peripheral to the burghal hidage boroughs; only after the Conquest were they brought within their confines. North of the Thames, by contrast, shires had probably always met in the central boroughs.

Northumbria and the Making of the Kingdom of the English

WILLIAM M. AIRD

In the first chapter of the first book of his *Historia gentis Anglorum ecclesiastica*, 'The Ecclesiastical History of the English people', completed by 731, the monk, Bede, who has a strong claim to be the father of English historical writing, noted that

> At the present time there are five languages in Britain, just as the divine law is written in five books, all devoted to seeking out and setting forth one and the same kind of wisdom, namely the knowledge of sublime truth and of true sublimity. These are the English, British, Irish, Pictish, as well as the Latin languages; through the study of the scriptures, Latin is in general use among them all.[1]

Bede was a monk at the Northumbrian monastic complex of Jarrow-Monkwearmouth, one of the most sophisticated centres of learning in early medieval Britain. Although Bede was making a point about the correspondence between the number of languages in Britain and the five books of Old Testament Biblical Law in the Pentateuch, his statement about the five languages of Britain was probably based on personal experience, for Northumbria throughout the Middle Ages was a cultural melting-pot, where different ethnic groups co-existed side-by-side and interacted with one another.

Bede was writing at a time when what we now call England was divided into a number of independent kingdoms. As well as Northumbria, the 'English', Germanic settlers who had crossed the Channel in the century or so after the end of the Roman occupation of Britain, had established Wessex, Kent, East Anglia and Mercia as well as other, smaller kingdoms, driving out, or establishing their lordship over the native British inhabitants. Northumbria itself, in the centuries before the Scandinavian invasions of the ninth and tenth centuries, was made up of two separate kingdoms, Deira, between the Rivers Humber and the Tees, and Berni-

---

[1] *Haec in presenti iuxta numerum librorum quibus lex diuina scripta est, quinque gentium linguis unam eandemque summae ueritatis et uerae sublimitatis scientiam scrutatur et confitetur, Anglorum, videlicet Brettonum Scottorum Pictorum et Latinorum, quae meditatione scripturarum ceteris omnibus est facta communis. HE, i.1,16–17.*

cia, which comprised the lands between the River Tees and the Firth of Forth.

This paper, therefore, examines the place that the ancient kingdom of Northumbria had in the making of a unified kingdom of the English. Given the constraints of time, the paper focuses on the two centuries from around 950 to 1156, and deals predominantly with the area between the Rivers Tees and Forth, that is the Northumbrian kingdom of Bernicia. The paper argues that the West Saxon kings of the tenth century and their Danish and Norman successors in the eleventh and twelfth centuries had to compete for influence in the region with another emerging kingdom, namely that of the Scots, whose own territorial ambitions extended over the whole of the former kingdom of Bernicia.

Until fairly recently the historiography dealing with Northumbria in this period has been dominated by the theme of the political unification, or 'making' of the kingdom of England. The idea behind this is that England's pre-existing 'national' unity was already in place, waiting to be rediscovered, and was given political expression by Alfred the Great and his immediate successors in the tenth century: Alfred's West Saxon dynasty '*re*-conquered' or unified England and, in so doing, gave the English a political unity through which to express their enduring ethnic and national identity.[2]

The idea of reuniting the disparate branches of a single ethnic group through a war of liberation is a common theme in the historiographies of nation-states. The idea of *re*-conquest, rather than conquest allows aggression to be justified and legitimized in a national myth. The West Saxon conquest of 'England' has thus been portrayed as a *re*-conquest, a war of liberation, bringing under the political rule of one dynasty an ethnically coherent people. In historical accounts of the process, 'West Saxon' political ambition subtly and imperceptibly grows into 'English' political identity. As the natural leaders of their ethnic group, the West Saxon kings thus restored, rather than created, the kingdom of the English, and established it as the only legitimate political expression of the ethnic unity of the English.[3]

This interpretation of England's history has tended to obscure the importance of other elements in the historical development of the nation state. Regional narratives give place to an overarching national story. Recently, however, there has been renewed interest in the older socio-political and cultural regions of Britain.[4] In the specific case of Northumbria, the 'national narrative' has also influenced the characterisation of the role of key agents in the formation of the region's early

[2] A useful review of the literature is Sarah Foot, 'The historiography of the Anglo-Saxon "nation-state"', in *Power and the Nation in European History*, ed. L. Scales and O. Zimmer, Cambridge 2005, 125–42.

[3] Stenton, *Anglo-Saxon England*; cf. Eric John, 'The West Saxon conquest of England', in *idem, Reassessing Anglo-Saxon England*, Manchester 1996, 83–98; Pauline Stafford, 'Kings, kingship and kingdoms', in *From the Vikings to the Normans*, ed. Wendy Davies, Oxford 2003, 11–39.

medieval history. For example, the contribution of Scandinavian settlers in the region has generally been viewed negatively in this 'liberation narrative' of West Saxon triumph. Similarly, and especially with reference to the most northerly parts of Northumbria, the influence of another emerging kingdom has also been underplayed.

The Kingdom of the Scots began to coalesce in the tenth and eleventh centuries, and its territorial ambitions extended south into Bernician Northumbria.[5] In examining the history of Northumbria in this period, we might move away from the West Saxon 'master-narrative' and question the assumption that the region was predestined to be included in the kingdom of England. Here, the Scots and Scandinavians are seen as key contributors to the history of Northumbria, agents of formative change and not merely obstacles to its inevitable incorporation into the kingdom of England. Finally, the terms historians have employed in describing the North of England conceal significant divisions with the region itself.[6]

Fortunately, there are sources, produced in Northumbria, upon which to base this interpretation. To an extent these northern sources represent an alternative to the West Saxon kings' 'house history', the *Anglo-Saxon Chronicle*, which was originally designed to promote the image and political aspirations of Alfred and his successors.[7] The sources emanating from the archiepiscopal see of York and, particularly for the purposes of this paper, the ecclesiastical community serving the shrine of St Cuthbert, provide a distinctively 'Northumbrian' perspective on the developments of this period.[8]

Historians are no longer confident about the conclusions to be drawn from the evidence of the Scandinavian presence in Northumbria. For example, placename evidence, once seen as a guide to the extent of Scandinavian settlement, has

---

[4]   See, for example, William Aird, *St Cuthbert and the Normans; the Church of Durham, 1071–1153*, Woodbridge 1998; Dawn Hadley, *The Northern Danelaw: its Social Structure c.800–1100*, London 2000.

[5]   A. A. M. Duncan, *The Kingship of the Scots, 842–129; Succession and Independence*, Edinburgh 2002.

[6]   For convenient maps of these areas, see David Hill, *An Atlas of Anglo-Saxon England*, Oxford 1981.

[7]   R. H. C. Davis, 'Alfred the Great: Propaganda and Truth', *History* 55, 1971, 169–82, reprinted in *idem, From Alfred the Great to Stephen*, London 1991, 33–46. There is a revealing map in Hill, *Atlas*, 20, which graphically illustrates the 'Southumbrian' geographical bias of the *Anglo-Saxon Chronicle*.

[8]   There is a convenient collection of materials for the Church of York in *Sources for York History to AD 1100*, ed. D. W. Rollason, D. Gore and G. Fellows-Jensen, York 1998. For the historical tradition in the Church of St Cuthbert, see Antonia Gransden, *Historical Writing in England c.550–1307*, London 1974, 114–23 and Symeon, *Libellus*, lxviii–xc. In addition, see C. R. Hart, *The Early Charters of Northern England and the North Midlands*, Leicester 1975.

been questioned.[9] As a consequence, the extent and nature of the Scandinavian settlement has been re-examined and, for some, the presence of Viking kings at York in the later ninth and tenth century no longer marks a definitive crisis point for the survival of native Northumbrian institutions. Indeed, it is suggested that the Viking settlement enhanced, rather than diminished, the power and prestige of these institutions. For example, drawing analogies with similar configurations in the German empire of the same era, a persuasive case has been made for characterising the archbishops of York, or the bishops of the Church of St Cuthbert, as 'prince-bishops' wielding a great degree of political as well as ecclesiastical power.[10]

The mere fact of the existence of archbishops and their clerical communities at York and Chester-le-Street/Durham during the Scandinavian period, suggests at least a pragmatic tolerance of Christianity by the Vikings.[11] In fact, these churches prospered in this period. In addition, Archbishop Wulfstan I of York (931–56) demonstrated a decidedly ambivalent attitude to the West Saxons kings.[12] He was ready to make use of the Scandinavians in his see and even fought alongside Olaf Guthfrithsson in 939 against Edmund and Eadred of Wessex.[13] It was not in the interests of the Scandinavians to disrupt the commercial activities of the city of York, and perhaps the success of the viking-age city should be seen as the result of a flourishing partnership between the immigrants and the natives. The Scandinavian kings of York were, in effect, employed by these archbishops as mercenaries, defenders of the region against the encroachments of other external enemies, including the West Saxon kings.[14] Here, regional interests took precedence over

---

[9]   See, for example, Dawn Hadley, 'In search of the Vikings: the problems and possibilities of interdisciplinary approaches', in *Vikings and the Danelaw: Select Papers from the Proceedings of the Thirteenth Viking Congress*, ed. James Graham-Campbell *et al.*, Oxford 2001, 13–30, and *eadem*, 'Viking and native: re-thinking identity in the Danelaw', *Early Medieval Europe* 11, 2002, 45–70.

[10]   D. W. Rollason, *Northumbria 500–1100: Creation and Destruction of a Kingdom* , Cambridge 2003, 229.

[11]   Lesley Abrams, 'The conversion of the Danelaw', in *Vikings and the Danelaw,* ed. Graham-Campbell, 31–44.

[12]   Dorothy Whitelock, 'The dealings of the kings of England with Northumbria in the tenth and eleventh centuries', in *The Anglo-Saxons: Studies in some Aspects of the History Presented to Bruce Dickens,* ed. P. Clemoes, London 1959, 70–88; reprinted in *eadem, History, Law and Literature in Tenth- to Eleventh-century England*, London 1981.

[13]   C. R. Hart, 'Wulfstan (d. 955/6)', in *ODNB*; cf. Simon Keynes, 'Wulfstan I, archbishop of York (951–56)', in *The Blackwell Encyclopedia of Anglo-Saxon England*, ed. M. Lapidge, J. Blair, S. Keynes and D. Scragg, Oxford 1999, 492–93.

[14]   The utilisation of the Vikings in this way by Carolingian rulers has been explored by S. Coupland, 'From poachers to gamekeepers: Scandianavian warlords and Carolingian kings', *Early Medieval Europe* 7, 1998, 85–114.

any idea that York and its hinterland properly 'belonged' to an overarching kingdom of the English.[15]

Similarly, the Community of St Cuthbert benefited in the long term from its dealings with the Scandinavian settlers.[16] The Community was originally based on Holy Island (Lindisfarne), near the Bernician royal centres of Yeavering and Bamburgh. According to an eleventh-century text, the *Historia de Sancto Cuthberto* ('The History about St Cuthbert'), in 875, the Community began a period of seven years wandering about Northumbria, before settling at Chester-le-Street (County Durham).[17] The *Historia* presents a dramatic view of the effects of the Viking incursions in the region. The coffin containing the undecayed body of Cuthbert was wheeled around Northumbria by a band of refugees led by seven companions, chased by the pagans, who had driven them from Lindisfarne. This 'foundation myth' account obscured the reality of the situation, which was that the Community of St Cuthbert visited ecclesiastical sites over which it later asserted proprietary claims.[18]

The Community of St Cuthbert established close political relationships with Scandinavian leaders and the *Historia de Sancto Cuthberto* describes the inauguration of a Scandinavian king by the saint and his community. In gratitude, this king, Guthred, then granted all the land between the rivers Tyne and Wear, which became the core of 'liberty of St Cuthbert'.[19] The inhabitants of the estates of St Cuthbert became known as the *Haliwerfolc*, or 'the people of the holy man'. The name was eventually extended to the land itself, and this identity, associated with an ecclesiastical institution, transcended other ethnically-derived identities. By the time that the *Historia* was compiled, the West Saxon kings were also given key roles in the protection of the Church of St Cuthbert, reflecting the Community's desire to be associated with the successful dynasty, but not to the exclusion of other possible benefactors.[20]

The Community of St Cuthbert retained its landed interests north of the River Tyne in the region dominated by the House of Bamburgh. Scandinavian settlement was concentrated south of the Tees, so the contact that the earls of Bamburgh had with the Scandinavians was confined to dealing with military incursions. In order to counteract these attacks, the earls of Bamburgh allied with the Scots. For exam-

[15]   Rollason, *Northumbria*, 265.
[16]   Aird, *St Cuthbert*, 34–44.
[17]   *Historia de Sancto Cuthberto*, §20, pp. 58–9.
[18]   David Rollason, 'The wanderings of St Cuthbert', in *Cuthbert, Saint and Patron*, ed. D. W. Rollason, Durham 1987, 45–61.
[19]   *Historia de Sancto Cuthberto*, §13, pp. 52–3.
[20]   Luisella Simpson, 'The Alfred/St Cuthbert episode in the Historia de Sancto Cuthberto: its significance for mid-tenth century history', in *Saint Cuthbert, his Cult and Community to AD 1200*, ed. G. Bonner, D. W. Rollason and Clare Stancliffe, Woodbridge 1989, 397–412.

ple, Ealdred of Bamburgh was driven into Scotland by the Viking leader Rægnald in 914, where he enlisted the aid of Causantin (Constantine) II (900–44). It is possible that Ealdred and Causantin were also assisted by a certain Elfred, one of the men of St Cuthbert. These allies were defeated by Rægnald at Corbridge in 914 and the Scandinavian attempted to settle his own men on the lands of St Cuthbert.[21] Despite this, the Community of St Cuthbert managed to acquire a great number of landed estates during the course of the tenth century. Many of these were the possessions of other ecclesiastical institutions, which had fared less well against the Scandinavians. For example, the lands of the church of Hexham were almost certainly absorbed in this way. By the end of the tenth century, the Church of St Cuthbert was laying claim to estates in a region extending from Lothian in the north to the Yorkshire in the south, and from Carlisle in the west to Durham in the east.[22]

Alfred's West Saxon successors began to encroach on Viking areas of influence in the tenth century. It was understandable that the West Saxon monarchy should attempt to neutralise the potential threat represented by the Northumbrians. In 909, Edward the Elder 'ravaged' the region over a period of five weeks.[23] In 927 Æthelstan (924–39) captured York and seven years later made a grant of Amounderness, a sizable area of the North-West, to York's Church of St Peter.[24] Similar grants were made to the Church of St Cuthbert. The *Historia de Sancto Cuthberto* preserves the text of a charter by Æthelstan, recording his grant of several liturgical manuscripts, ecclesiastical vestments, vessels, bells, gold and silver drinking horns, banners, a lance and golden armlets. The estate of Bishop Wearmouth with its dependent settlements was also confirmed to St Cuthbert. Whether the king had any effective power over these estates, or whether he was simply confirming possession or recognising claims, is another matter, but what Æthelstan and the clerics serving St Cuthbert were probably doing was mutually reinforcing each other's claims to authority.[25] Æthelstan was also credited with confirming the right of sanctuary to the Church of St Cuthbert.[26]

Æthelstan's example was followed by his brother Edmund (939–46) who, during a campaign against the Scots, 'made a diversion to the Church of St Cuthbert, knelt before his tomb, poured out prayers and commended himself and his men to God and the holy confessor.'[27] In the early eleventh century, the *Historia*

[21] Rollason, *Northumbria*, 274.
[22] Aird, *St Cuthbert*, 9–59.
[23] It has been argued, however, that Edward's success in the North was exaggerated by medieval and modern writers alike; cf. Lesley Abrams, 'Edward the Elder's Danelaw', in *Edward the Elder, 899–924*, ed. N. J. Higham and D. H. Hill, London 2001, 128–43.
[24] Hart, *Early Charters of Northern England*, no. 119, pp. 117–18.
[25] *Historia de Sancto Cuthberto*, §§26–27, pp. 64–67 and 108–110.
[26] Rollason, *Northumbria*, 272–73; D. Hall, 'The sanctuary of St Cuthbert', in *St Cuthbert: his Cult and Community*, ed. Bonner *et al.*, 425–36.
[27] *Historia de Sancto Cuthberto*, §28, pp. 66–7 and 110–11.

de Sancto Cuthberto added the story of St Cuthbert's help for Alfred in the middle of his struggles with the Danes. Clearly, in the historical traditions of the Church of St Cuthbert, it became necessary to suggest a close association between their patron and the royal house of Wessex. How early this relationship was established and whether it was of any lasting help to the clerics at Chester-le-Street is another matter, given that the centre of West Saxon power lay so far to the south. For the inhabitants of Bernicia, a more immediate problem was presented by the growth of the power of the kings of Scotland.

At the beginning of the tenth century, the kings of 'Alba' claimed to rule a diverse collection of peoples. Although the heartland of these kings lay north of the line of the Rivers Forth and Clyde, they had ambitions further south in Cumbria and Northumbria. The extension of political control over these disparate ethnic communities helped to create the idea of a Scottish political identity. The diverse ethnic character of the kingdom of Scots meant that the Anglian roots of Bernicia, or the British origins of Strathclyde-Cumbria, were no obstacle to their incorporation. Only if 'Englishness' is seen in rigidly irredentist terms, does the prospect of the incorporation of Northumbria into an enlarged Scottish kingdom seem implausible.[28]

During the tenth century, the Kings of Alba intervened more often in Northumbria, especially as Bernicia was under the relatively fragile lordship of the earls of Bamburgh. Taking advantage of the problems caused by the Scandinavian kings of York and the remoteness of the West Saxon kings, the Scots made substantial inroads. For example, in around 950, Maelcoluim (Malcolm) I plundered as far as the Tees, seizing many people and cattle.[29] This method of waging war, the slaving and plunder raid was to characterise Scots incursions into Northumbria well into the twelfth century.

When the sources mention the Scots kings in connection with their West Saxon counterparts in the tenth century, they are usually one of several parties agreeing to recognise the overlordship of the southern ruler. For example, in 923, according to the *Anglo-Saxon Chronicle*, 'the king of the Scots and all the nation of the Scots chose him [Edward the Elder] as father and lord; and [so also did] Rægnald and Eadwulf's sons and all those who live in Northumbria, both English and Danish and Norwegians and others; and also the king of the Strathclyde Britons and all the Strathclyde Britons.'[30] It must be borne in mind that this is a southern source and necessarily emphasises, and probably exaggerates, the power of the West Saxons, but the entry does demonstrate the diversity of contending powers in the region. Similarly, the entry for 934 claimed that Æthelstan attacked and subdued Scotland and when the Scots and their Norse allies retali-

28 Duncan, *Kingship of the Scots*, 5.
29 Duncan, *Kingship of the Scots*, 24.
30 *Scottish Annals*, 65.

ated, they were defeated at *Brunanburh*. Æthelstan's successor, Edmund, 'brought all Northumbria into his domain', driving out the Scandinavians in 944, and the following year he 'raided across all the land of Cumbria and ceded it to Malcolm, king of Scots, on the condition that he would be his co-operator both on sea and on land.'[31]

During Eadred's reign, Maelcoluim raided as far as the Tees, probably taking advantage of the readmission of the Scandinavian Olaf to York in 949–50. The steady southerly progress of Scots lordship in Bernician Northumbria was recognised in the mid-970s. After an imperial coronation ceremony at Bath in 973, Edgar of Wessex demonstrated his overlordship in an elaborate ritual conducted at Chester. There eight 'under-kings', who included Cinead (Kenneth) II king of Scots, Malcolm king of the Cumbrians and Maccus king 'of many islands', took the oars of a boat steered by Edgar himself and rowed their lord along the River Dee.[32] A Durham source, the *Historia Regum Anglorum* ('History of the Kings of the English'), compiled in the twelfth century, describes Edgar as dividing the Northumbrian ealdormanry into a southern part and a northern one extending from the Tees to *Myreforth*, which might indicate the mud-flats between the mouth of the River Esk and the Solway Firth.[33] The *Historia Regum* also states that Edgar gave Lothian to Cinaed and sent him home with great honour. If accurate, this also suggests that the Scots may have already been in possession of northern Bernicia and Edgar was thus recognising a *fait accompli*.[34]

For information on the earls of Northumbria in the early eleventh century, historians are able to make use of another tract produced by the Community of St Cuthbert. The *De Obsessione Dunelmi et de probitate Uchtredi comitis, et de comitibus qui ei successerunt* ('Concerning the Siege of Durham and the Probity of Earl Uhtred and the earls who succeeded him') is an anonymous work probably written by a member of the Church of St Cuthbert between 1070 and 1100.[35] It

[31] *ASC*, Swanton, *s.a.* 'A' 944, 945, p. 110.

[32] *Worcester Chronicle*, s.a. 973 in *Scottish Annals*, 76–77.

[33] Duncan, *Kingship*, 24.

[34] Duncan, *Kingship*, 25 and note 58. Roger of Wendover added the detail that Cinaed's service for this concession was to attend the king's annual crown-wearing feasts, for which purpose he was granted residences along his route south. There has been some debate over the date of the acquisition of Lothian by the Scots. In particular, the failure of the *Anglo-Saxon Chronicle* to mention it, together with the assertion by northern sources that Lothian was given in 1018, has raised doubts; for discussion of these points, see Duncan, *Kingship*, 25. Whatever arrangements Cinead had made with Edgar, there is evidence that suggests that the Scots continued to view Northumbria as a legitimate target. For example, in 980 a northern 'ship-army' raided as far south as Chester; *ASC*, Swanton, *s.a.* 'C' 980, p. 124.

[35] C. J. Morris, *Marriage and Murder in Eleventh-century Northumbria: a Study of 'De Obsessione Dunelmi'*, University of York Borthwick Paper no. 82, York 1992.

deals with the descent of certain landed estates belonging to that Church, but also includes information on the rulers of Northumbria in the eleventh century.[36]

The *De Obsessione* describes a siege of Durham by the Scots probably in 1006. The text also outlines the relationship between Earl Uhtred and the West Saxon king Æthelred II, as well as his association with the Church of St Cuthbert. It was with Uhtred's assistance that the Community relocated to Durham from Chester-le-Street in 995. Durham's naturally defensive site made it a more secure location for the Community and, according to Durham tradition, Uhtred recruited men from the area between the Rivers Coquet and Tees to clear the peninsula surrounded by the River Wear.[37]

During the siege, Uhtred organized the defence of Durham as his father, the elderly Earl Waltheof, had refused to leave the stronghold at Bamburgh. As a reward for his efforts Æthelred II granted him Waltheof's title in addition to the earldom of York. Despite the evidence presented by the *De Obsessione*, it is unlikely that the West Saxon kings were able regularly to impose their will on Northumbria in the period leading up to the succession of Cnut. Æthelred's reign ended with the invasion of Swegn and his son Cnut of Denmark in 1016.[38] Briefly, Northumbria had provided Æthelred's son, Edmund Ironside, with the resources to resist the Danes, but after his death on 30 November 1016, Cnut was secure in England. Cnut (1016–1035) followed the example of his tenth-century West-Saxon predecessors by visiting Northumbria in order to establish his lordship.

There was also the continuing threat of the Scots kings. As well as the siege of Durham, the Scots under Maelcoluim II and in alliance with Owen, king of Strathclyde, had defeated the Northumbrians at Carham-on-Tweed in 1018.[39] This battle was also associated with the concession of Lothian to the king of Scots, by Earl Uhtred's successor, Eadulf. This is probably to be interpreted as a formal recognition of the Scots possession of Lothian since the 970s, although it is possible that Earl Uhtred had been making successful inroads there before his death.[40]

In order to deter further incursions, and to make clear his claims to rule all of England, Cnut invaded Scotland in 1027 forcing Maelcoluim II and two other kings Mælbætha and Iehmarc to submit to him.[41] Cnut also appointed Eric of Hlathir (1016–23 × 1033), one of his own military commanders, earl of Northumbria, although his jurisdiction probably excluded the liberty of St Cuthbert and the

---

[36] Rollason, *Sources*, 24–5; Morris, *Marriage and Murder*; B. Meehan, 'The siege of Durham, the battle of Carham, and the cession of Lothian', *SHR* 55, 1976, 1–19.

[37] Aird, *St Cuthbert*, 46–7.

[38] M. K. Lawson, 'Cnut (d. 1035)', *ODNB*.

[39] *Historia Regum*, sa. 1018; see Duncan, *Kingship of the Scots*, 28 and n.3. On Owen of Strathclyde, see Duncan, *op. cit.*, 29 and note 6.

[40] Meehan, 'The Siege of Durham', 1–19.

[41] B. T. Hudson, 'Cnut and the Scottish Kings', *EHR* 107, 1992, 350–60. For the date, see Duncan, *Kingship of the Scots*, 29–30.

lands of the earls of Bamburgh. Eric was followed by the Scandinavian, Siward (1023 × 1033–55), who extended control over the district north of the Tyne by marrying into the House of Bamburgh and establishing relationships with the two most important ecclesiastical institutions in Northumbria.[42] The *Historia de Sancto Cuthberto*, tells us that Cnut granted St Cuthbert an estate at Staindrop (County Durham) and its dependencies, as well as Brompton in Yorkshire. These grants should probably be associated with a barefoot pilgrimage that Cnut is said to have made to Cuthbert's shrine from Garmondsway, a distance of about five miles from Durham.[43] The pious nature of the visit recalls those of Cnut's West Saxon predecessors and is in keeping with his desire to present himself as a thoroughly Christian king. Given the recent paganism of elements of the Danish army, Cnut's extravagant piety was as much a political statement as a religious one.[44]

Despite these attempts to forge stronger links with the kings of the English, Northumbria, especially north of the Tees, was still largely beyond the reach of royal government. Judging by the evidence presented by the *Domesday Book*, the West Saxon and Danish kings still held relatively little land in the North East of England. These rulers managed to bring Yorkshire and a small part of Cumbria into the royal taxation system of the geld, and, at some point, the administrative divisions familiar south of the Humber were introduced into Yorkshire.[45] The Scandinavian origins of the terms *wapentake* and *riding* suggest that the Danes retained some influence in the region, although it is difficult to demonstrate that this is a legacy of the tenth century, rather than of the eleventh. Despite these innovations, it is still possible to identify earlier administrative divisions, the small 'northern shires'.[46]

After the brief reigns of Harold Harefoot (d. 1040) and Harthacnut (d. 1042), the West Saxon royal dynasty was restored to England in the person of Edward the

[42] W. M. Aird, 'Siward, earl of Northumbria (d. 1055)', *ODNB*.
[43] Symeon, *Libellus*, 166–67.
[44] For example, in June 1023, Cnut attended the translation from London to Canterbury of the relics of St Ælfheah, the archbishop murdered by the Danes in 1012. Lawson, 'Cnut (d. 1035)'.
[45] The county was 'shired' and divided into three 'Ridings' (*trithings* = third parts). These divisions were, in their turn, made up of *wapentakes*, seen as the northern version of the southern hundred; e.g. *GDB* fo. 315 'Skyrack Wapentake'; fo. 316v, 'Staincross wapentake', etc.
[46] These are also known as 'sokes' or 'multiple estates'; see K. M. Hall, 'Pre-Conquest estates in Yorkshire', in *Yorkshire Boundaries*, ed. H.E.J. Le Patourel, Moira H. Long and May F. Pickles, Leeds 1993, 25–38. Other areas of the north, such as south Lancashire were subsumed in the Domesday accounts of Cheshire and north Lancashire, and those parts of Cumbria that remained free of Scots lordship appeared in the Yorkshire folios. There are hints that royal officials may also have been active in eleventh-century Yorkshire before the settlement of the Normans, but the evidence is far from conclusive; Rollason, *Northumbria*, 270 and note 19.

Confessor (1043–66). Although in his early years Edward attempted to impose his own will on affairs, it became clear, as the reign progressed, that the Godwine family dominated his regime.[47] One by one, members of the family acquired the major earldoms of England and, in 1055, Tosti became earl of Northumbria. Tosti based his regime in York, but attempted to extend his influence into Bernicia. His position was difficult as he had few 'natural' supporters in either region and there are suggestions that his regime had to overcome opposition in the Church of St Cuthbert.[48] According to a miracle story preserved at Durham, one of Tosti's men was struck down when he attempted to force an entry to the church in order to arrest a fugitive.[49]

Opposition to Tosti's rule coalesced in 1065 and the earl was driven out of Northumbria. In addition to attempting to levy heavy taxes and impose West Saxon law rather than the *Laws of Cnut*, which recognised northern custom, Tosti executed prominent members of the local nobility.[50] The rebels attacked the earl's residence at York and marched south, announcing that Morkar, the brother of Earl Edwin of Mercia, was their new ruler.[51] The Community of St Cuthbert may have encouraged the rebellion by exhuming the relics of King Oswine of Deira, a seventh-century martyr.[52] So, on the eve of the Norman invasion of the kingdom of England, Northumbria had asserted its independence.[53]

The invasion of England by William the Conqueror and his allies in the autumn of 1066 presented a familiar set of problems for those living north of the Humber. As with the Danish Conquest of 1016, the Northumbrians were faced with an outside power whose ambitions were to extend effective rule as far as possible. The combined forces of Bernician and Deiran Northumbria had driven out Tosti Godwineson and installed Morkar as earl. It is to be doubted whether Morkar's authority ran north of the River Tees and there is certainly evidence of the continuing importance of members of the House of Bamburgh there.[54]

[47] Frank Barlow, *Edward the Confessor*, London 1970; *idem*, *The Godwins*, London 2002; Emma Mason, *The House of Godwine: the History of a Dynasty*, London 2004.

[48] Aird, *St Cuthbert*, 54–9.

[49] 'Capitula de miraculis et translationibus sancti Cuthberti', in *Symeonis Monachi Opera Omnia,* ed. Thomas Arnold, Rolls Series, vol. i, London 1882, 243–45; cf. Symeon, *Libellus*, 176–77.

[50] Aird, *St Cuthbert*, 57.

[51] It is possible that the rebels chose an 'outsider' in order to bring the separate regions together, but Morkar's family had well-established connections with Northumbria; cf. P. H. Sawyer, *The Charters of Burton Abbey*, London 1979, xliii–xliv; cf. W. E. Kapelle, *The Norman Conquest of the North: the Region and its Transformation 1000–1135*, London 1979, 100–101.

[52] Kapelle, *Norman Conquest of the North,* 98; cf. Aird, *St Cuthbert,* 57–8.

[53] B. Wilkinson, 'Northumbrian separatism in 1065–66', *Bulletin of the John Rylands Library* 23, 1939, 504–26.

[54] According to the *Historia Regum*, Morkar 'handed over the earldom beyond the Tyne'

For the Northumbrians the crucial battles of 1066 were those fought near York, at Fulford Gate and Stamford Bridge. Earl Tosti, driven out of the kingdom by his brother Harold, returned to make a bid for power after the accession of Harold in January 1066. Beginning with raids on the south coast in April, Tosti's fleet moved north to attack Lindsey. An army, including 'Northumbrians' and led by Earls Edwin and Morkar, drove Tosti north to the mouth of the River Tyne, where he joined the fleet of Harald Hardrada, king of Norway (1015–1066), who was pursuing a claim of his own to England, based on his kinship with the Danish kings.[55] On 20 September 1066, King Harald and Tosti defeated Earls Edwin and Morkar, and, a few days later, York surrendered.[56] King Harold Godwineson, awaiting the arrival of William of Normandy, was forced to ride north to deal with the Norwegian threat. The armies met at Stamford Bridge, east of York, on 25 September 1066, where Harold defeated and killed his brother and Harald Hardrada.[57]

William the Conqueror's coronation at Westminster on Christmas Day, 1066, did not automatically bring him the submission of Northumbria. In his dealings with the region and its centres of power, the new king employed methods recognisable as those of his predecessors. In the years immediately following Hastings, William attempted to rule through native Northumbrians. In 1067, Earl Morkar of Northumbria was arrested by the Conqueror, and his earldom was granted to Copsi, who had served as Tosti's lieutenant. Copsi was appointed to the earldom north of the River Tyne, for he targeted Osulf of Bamburgh, but at the ancient comital centre of Newburn-on-Tyne, Osulf trapped and killed Copsi.[58] Later that year, Osulf himself was killed and the earldom was purchased by his kinsman, Gospatric.[59]

As Norman settlement pushed further north, royal administrators appeared at York and Durham. In 1068, Gospatric and a group of English nobles, including the West Saxon claimant to the throne, Edgar the Ætheling, fled north to Scotland. There Edgar's sister Margaret married Maelcoluim (Malcolm) III, thereby giving

to Osulf, son of Earl Eadulf. Whether Morkar actually appointed Osulf is another matter and it is, once again, more likely to be a question of the formal recognition of already existing authority; cf. 'Historia Regum', *s.a.* 1072, in *Symeonis,* II, 198.
55 C. Krag, 'Harald Hardrada (1015–1066)', *ODNB.*
56 *ASC,* Swanton, *s.a.* 'CDE' 1066.
57 J. Bradbury, *The Battle of Hastings,* Stroud 1998; M.K. Lawson, *The Battle of Hastings, 1066,* Stroud 2002.
58 W. M. Aird, 'Copsi, earl of Northumbria (d. 1067)', *ODNB.*
59 W. M. Aird, 'Osulf, earl of Bamburgh (d. 1067)', *ODNB.* Gospatric had married the daughter of Uhtred of Northumbria and his wife Ælfgifu, daughter of Æthelred II. Like Copsi, Gospatric may have been a member of Tosti's entourage, and his knowledge of the region, together with his connections with Bamburgh, may have led him to purchase the earldom from the Conqueror. 'Historia Regum', *s.a.* 1072, in *Symeonis,* II, 199.

the Scots king an excuse to claim the southern regions of Bernicia.[60] In January 1069, Robert Cumin, sent north by the Conqueror to secure the earldom after Gospatric's desertion, was murdered, along with his troops at Durham. Whether the Community of St Cuthbert was a party to the insurrection is unclear, but the earl's death heralded a general rising in Northumbria.[61]

The Conqueror's reaction to the rebellion in Northumbria was a winter campaign of such ferocity that it was singled out by medieval historians as an atrocity. William's troops plundered and destroyed to such an extent that famine was induced and with it a great mortality.[62] The so-called 'Harrying of the North' left an indelible impression on the English-born, Norman monk, Orderic Vitalis, writing some seventy-five years after the event: 'My narrative has frequently had occasion to praise William, but for this act which condemned the innocent and the guilty alike to die by slow starvation I cannot commend him.'[63]

The slaughter induced Bishop Æthelwine and the Community of St Cuthbert to abandon Durham for the comparative safety of Lindisfarne.[64] Earl Gospatric, had warned the clergy at Durham of the approach of the Normans, but, according to later tradition there, he had taken advantage of their absence to plunder the church. Despite his involvement in the attack on York, William I accepted Gospatric's surrender and allowed him to retain his earldom. It was not until 1072, when the Conqueror led an expedition into Scotland, that he was deposed. The earl fled north, where his family secured the earldom of Dunbar from Maelcoluim III. As a successor to Gospatric, William appointed Waltheof, who had close connections with the Northumbrian nobility.[65]

King William's relationship with the Church of St Cuthbert provides an interesting commentary on the difficulties the Normans experienced in extending their rule beyond Yorkshire. After Bishop Æthelwine fled his see in 1071, the king appointed a Lotharingian cleric, Walcher as bishop. On his return from an expedition to Scotland, in 1072, the Conqueror visited Durham. Two accounts of his visit survive, each presenting a different view of the king's relationship with the saint. Symeon of Durham, writing in the early twelfth century, suggested that the

---

[60] 'Historia Regum', *s.a.* 1068, in *Symeonis*, II, 186.

[61] Aird, *St Cuthbert*, 70–75.

[62] For discussion of the evidence, see D. M. Palliser, 'Domesday Book and the Harrying of the North', *Northern History* 29, 1993, 1–23.

[63] *Orderic* ii, 232–33.

[64] 'Historia Regum', *s.a.* 1069, in *Symeonis,* II, 189.

[65] Despite his involvement in the rebellions of 1068–70, Waltheof was pardoned by the king and, presumably in an attempt to secure his loyalty, married to the Conqueror's niece, Judith. Unfortunately, Waltheof stepped into the middle of a bloodfeud between the House of Bamburgh and members of the York nobility, which had persisted over several generations. The details are given in R. A. Fletcher, *Bloodfeud: Murder and Revenge in Anglo-Saxon England*, London 2002.

Conqueror threatened violence against the Community of St Cuthbert, if they could not prove that the saint's incorrupt body was present.[66] An earlier account, however, tells us that the king approached the shrine reverently, heard the story of the saint's life and, as a consequence, made gifts to the church.[67] This earlier account seems more in keeping with the policies of the Conqueror's predecessors: it was in the king's interests to win allies for the new bishop, rather than alienate the locals with threats of violence.

In 1075, after the arrest and subsequent execution of Earl Waltheof, the Conqueror abandoned his policy of ruling through members of the native nobility.[68] The earldom of Northumbria, here meaning the Bernician lands between the Tyne and the Tweed, was entrusted to Bishop Walcher. The bishop managed to rule until 1080, when he and members of his household were murdered at Gateshead on the River Tyne. The immediate context of the bishop's death was an invasion of the region by Maelcoluim III of Scotland. Walcher's regime necessarily relied on co-operation with members of the Northumbrian aristocracy and they protested at the bishop's ineffectiveness in the face of the Scots attack. Local rivalries also added to the volatility of the situation and members of a prominent native family were murdered by the bishop's kinsman. Despite protesting his innocence, Walcher and his men were murdered by members of the House of Bamburgh.[69] The incident demonstrated that it was virtually impossible to ensure the survival of a regime loyal to the Norman monarchy in the region, without there being widespread settlement of French landholders.

Walcher's successor was William of Saint-Calais, a monk and former abbot of Saint-Vincent, Le Mans. One of the key problems for Bishop William was the deep-rooted power of the families of the North-East on the estates of the Church of St Cuthbert. In 1083, he managed to sever their controlling interests when he reformed the Community of St Cuthbert, insisting that its members accept the Benedictine Rule or leave the church.[70] There has been some debate as to how far

---

[66] Symeon, *Libellus*, 196–97.

[67] 'Cronica Monasterii Dunelmensis' in H. H. E. Craster, 'The Red Book of Durham', *EHR* 40, 1925, 528.

[68] C. P. Lewis, 'Waltheof, earl of Northumbria (c.1050–1076)', *ODNB*.

[69] Aird, *St Cuthbert*, 97.

[70] The bishop was assisted in his task by the fact that, at the beginning of the 1070s, there had been something of a monastic revival in Northumbria. Symeon of Durham described how three monks, inspired by reading Bede's *Historia Ecclesastica*, set out for Northumbria to visit the shrines of the saints described by the venerable doctor. Led by Aldwin, prior of the abbey of Winchcombe in the Vale of Evesham, they made their way north to York and then on to the Tyne. With Bishop Walcher's aid, the monks established themselves at *Munecaceastre* ('Monkchester') and then at Jarrow, Bede's former home. The whole account of Aldwin and his companions, the re-establishment of Benedictine monasticism in Northumbria and the reformation of the Community of St Cuthbert in 1083, has the characteristics of the foundation narratives, which often

the reformation in 1083 was a violent one, but, given the precarious nature of Norman rule in Bernician Northumbria at this date, the violent removal of members of the Community of St Cuthbert would seem imprudent. A more subtle approach was to reform the Community. Accepting the Rule of St Benedict regularised the status of the monks and forced them to choose between their wives and families and their service at the saint's shrine. The lack of explicit accounts of violence suggests that the latter course was adopted.

The key to a more complete integration of the region into the kingdom of England was the settlement of French families in Northumbria. French lords were established on compact lordships which gave them a greater measure of military security and economic viability.[71] The process of settlement moved north during the final decades of the eleventh century, but it was not until well into the reign of Henry I (1100–1135) that French lordships were established to the north of the River Tyne.

Throughout this period of the extension of Norman power into Northumbria, the kings of Scots also advanced claims to lordship. Maelcoluim III's five attacks on Northumbria were as much about demonstrating his right to intervene in the affairs of the region, as they were plundering expeditions. The Community of St Cuthbert was careful to establish links with the kings of the Scots, as much out of self interest as self-preservation, for the Church of St Cuthbert claimed estates in Lothian as far north as the River Forth and on either bank of the River Tweed, the recognised frontier between Scots and English Northumbria. In 1093, Maelcoluim III and his English wife, Margaret, attended the foundation of Bishop William's new cathedral church at Durham and on the same occasion an agreement (*conventio*) was drawn up, by which the monks of Durham granted the Scots royal couple the privileges of confraternity, a share in the spiritual benefits of membership of the Church of St Cuthbert. Their names were entered in the *Liber Vitæ* ('The Book of Life') and their obituaries commemorated.[72]

In that it was the home of Bede, the kingdom of Northumbria, was the birthplace of the idea of English identity. Yet, as the history of the region from c.950 to 1156 demonstrates, it was here that notions of 'English' identity and the 'natural' political unity of all the English were challenged. Historical models which portray the West Saxon conquests of the tenth century as '*re*-conquest' or 'unification' are liable to undervalue the continuing distinctiveness of the lands between the Humber and the Forth. Similarly, a history of Northumbria in this period should recog-

---

accompanied the establishment of monastic communities in this period. When Bishop William introduced the Rule of St Benedict to the Community of St Cuthbert in 1083, he relied on Aldwin as his first prior; Aird, *St Cuthbert*, 131–36.

[71] Paul Dalton, *Conquest, Anarchy and Lordship: Yorkshire 1066–1154*, Cambridge 1994; Aird, *St Cuthbert*, 184–226.

[72] Aird, *St Cuthbert*, 227–67.

nise the role of the emerging kingdom of the Scots as much as that of the West
Saxon kings and their Danish and Norman successors. The kings of Scots claimed
Lothian as heirs to Bernicia and their ambition extended south of the Rivers Tyne
and Solway until Malcolm IV was forced by the Angevin king Henry II to recognise
that the northern counties of England had been reintegrated into the kingdom of
England.

The Anglo-Scottish border was, however, a permeable frontier. Lords of
French extraction settled on estates in both Scotland and England, creating political dilemmas for their descendants which persisted into the later Middle Ages.
Similarly, the Church of St Cuthbert maintained claims to estates in Lothian
throughout the medieval period. Pilgrims from Scotland made their way to
Durham and to the other shrines of the North-East of England in search of communion with the ancient Northumbrian saints, whose beneficence was not confined solely to the inhabitants of England or Scotland.[73] It should come as no
surprise, therefore, given these developments, to discover that the earliest Scottish charters were preserved in the archives of the Church of the Northumbrian
saint Cuthbert.

So, in this review of the historical development of the northernmost part of
the kingdom of England from the mid-tenth to the mid-twelfth centuries, it is
important to recognise that all of the ethnic groups recognised by Bede in the
eighth century still had a stake in the region, in addition to the descendants of the
Scandinavian and Norman settlers of the tenth to twelfth centuries. England was
and, indeed, still is a political entity composed of many ethnic groups. 'Englishness' does not refer to a single ethnicity, but, rather to a combination of ethnicities. Finally, then, it is difficult to understand the historical development of
Northumbria and its place in the making of the kingdom of England, if one starts
with the idea that the region always was, and was always going to be, 'English'.

---

[73] G. W. S. Barrow, 'Scots in the Durham Liber Vitae', in *The Durham Liber Vitae and its Context*, ed. D. Rollason, A. J. Piper, Margaret Harvey and Lynda Rollason, Woodbridge 2004, 109–116.

Normans and the Kingdom of the English

EMILY ALBU

When American schoolchildren study world history, one of the few dates that they learn to associate with a famous event is 1066.[1] At the Battle of Hastings, they read in their seventh-grade textbooks, Duke William of Normandy defeated the English king Harold "and established a line of Norman kings in England." With this conquest, the textbooks continue, William introduced feudal institutions to the island from the continent. "Supported by feudalism, strong rulers brought order to England". In fact, the schoolbooks proclaim, "by the start of the High Middle Ages, around 1000 C.E., the feudal system had brought stability to much of Europe."[2] Finally, it was England's turn to adopt the orderly ways of Europe, thanks to the Normans.

Many elements of this explanation may surprise you, but it follows the view I learned decades ago in grammar school and encountered again as an undergraduate when I first read Charles Homer Haskins' popular book, *The Normans in European History*.[3] Today much of scholarly opinion has moved to a quite different assessment of the Norman impact on England, and we might scarcely know where to begin with a critique of this textbook analysis. Let us start with a basic question, one that has itself provoked debate: who really were those Normans who attacked the English in 1066?

Normans traced their ancestry to Scandinavian raiders who plundered northern France in the early tenth century. Rollo or Rolf, probably the son of a Norwegian earl, led a fearsome band of marauders, mostly Danes, who harried the coasts of Scotland and Ireland before attacking French lands at the mouth of the river

---

[1]   This is a lightly revised and updated version of the paper first delivered at Tohoku University, Sendai in November 2006 and published in *Seiyoshi Kenkyu (Study of Occidental History)* 36, 2007, 199–210. I am grateful to Professor Hirokazu Tsurushima for organizing the symposium and for being such a gracious host; and to Professor Hideyuki Arimitsu for his expert editorial work with the journal article.

[2]   *History Alive! The Medieval World and Beyond (Student Edition)*, ed. Laura Alavosus *et al.*, Palo Alto, CA 2005, 23. In recent decades, scholars have taken a critical look at the usefulness of the term 'feudalism'; Marjorie Chibnall has reviewed and analyzed that debate in 'Feudalism and Lordship' in *A Companion to the Anglo-Norman World*, ed. Christopher Harper-Bill and Elisabeth van Houts, Woodbridge 2002, 123–34.

[3]   C. H. Haskins, *The Normans in European History*, New York 1915.

Seine.[4] According to the traditional account, the French king, Charles the Simple, made a treaty with Rollo at Saint-Clair-sur-Epte in 911. By this agreement Rollo and his men received Rouen and some lands around it, and in return they promised to defend the Seine and Paris against other invaders. Charles hoped that these Scandinavians would serve as a buffer against their brethren from the north. Rollo's men did not always prove reliable protectors. They were just as likely to threaten Paris as to protect the city. But they did settle into northern France, the former Merovingian region of Neustria, and expand the territory eventually called *Northmannia*, Land of the Northmen, Normandy. They embraced Christianity. They intermarried with the French inhabitants and adopted the French language for everyday commerce, while Latin became the language of their clerics at court and church. In many ways Normans came to look and sound very much like their French neighbors.

At some level, however, they developed and maintained a distinctive Norman identity. Small but perceptible waves of newcomers from Scandinavia, for instance, reinforced knowledge of the old language and the old ways. Rollo's grandson, Duke Richard I, was bilingual and apparently quite adept at communicating with both Scandinavian mercenaries and the French king against whom those Scandinavians had been recruited. Richard also married a pagan-born Danish woman, further fostering the old Scandinavian ties of kinship. It is likely that Scandinavians at every level of society assimilated more slowly than historians have imagined.[5]

All Norman dukes, from William I Longsword (c. 931–42) to the English king John (duke of Normandy, 1199–1204), traced their ancestry back to Rollo, Longsword's father.[6] William the Conqueror was Rollo's great-great-great grandson. Still, Normans did not think of themselves as exclusively the creation of a Scandinavian-French union. As Marjorie Chibnall and others have reminded us, ancient and medieval peoples were typically racially mixed groups, the products "not of blood, but of history."[7] And the Norman people even more self-consciously than most others celebrated their diversity. According to their myth-making his-

---

[4]   For a concise and authoritative account of the creation of Normandy, see Marjorie Chibnall, *The Normans*, Oxford 2000, 9–37.

[5]   Emily Albu, 'Scandinavians in Byzantium and Normandy,' in *Peace and War in Byzantium: Essays in Honor of George T. Dennis, S. J.*, ed. Timothy S. Miller and John Nesbitt, Washington, D.C. 1995, 114–22.

[6]   For a genealogy chart of Norman dukes, see Emily Albu, *The Normans in Their Histories: Propaganda, Myth, and Subversion*, Woodbridge 2001, xi. Only in the last years of Richard I (died 996) or perhaps as late as Richard II (996–1026) did Rollo's heirs gain the ducal title, see K. F. Werner, 'Quelques observations au sujet des débuts du 'duché' de Normandie,' in *Droit privé et institutions régionales: Études historiques offertes à Jean Yver*, Paris 1976, 691–709.

[7]   Chibnall, *The Normans*, 3.

torians, the Normans welcomed a variety of peoples into their *gens Normanno-rum*. The first historian of the Normans, Dudo of Saint-Quentin, established their mythic origins with his account of a dream vision.[8] In Dudo's now-familiar story, the pagan Rollo sailed to England by mistake, having falsely interpreted an earlier dream. In England Rollo had a second dream in which he stood on a mountain towering high over France. From that mountain top flowed a sweet-scented spring, curing him of leprosy and lust. As he slept, the freshly healed Rollo saw, far below and flying in dense flocks from the distant horizon, thousands of birds of many species and various colors, but all with red left wings. After these birds bathed in the spring, they ate together and nested together peaceably, and followed Rollo's bidding. When he awoke, Rollo asked a Christian captive to interpret the dream. From him Rollo learned that the mountain stood for the church in France. The healing spring was the holy baptism, washing away the leprosy of wickedness and sin. The countless birds represented the men of many lands destined to carry Rollo's shields and restore the walls of ruined cities in Rollo's name. The feast symbolized the body and blood of Christ, and the nests, the rebuilt city walls. Christianity would lead Rollo to worldly power, as the Christian prisoner explained: "*You* the birds of various kinds will attend; *you* the men of various realms will obey as they lie down in service to you" (*Tibi aves diversarum specierum obtemperabunt; tibi homines diversorum regnorum serviendo accubitati obedient*).[9]

Rollo was naturally pleased by this promise of a large force drawn from many peoples yet obedient to his authority. This origin myth proved surprisingly potent and durable. Or perhaps we should not be surprised, as it was apparently authorized by Dudo's patrons, Rollo's grandson Duke Richard I and Richard's half-brother Raoul and son, Richard II. Following Dudo, later writers also supported by Rollo's heirs retold the story and reinforced the narrative of a formidable *gens Normannorum* forged from the confraternity of warriors attracted to the spring of Christian faith and Norman might. From this union came a fierce people, whose young men trained from boyhood in the arts of fighting on horseback and on foot, using the lance, javelin, bow and arrow, and sword. With these weapons and life-long exercises in their use, Normans expanded their dominion; from their distinctive castles, they controlled their lands and launched attacks on farther

---

[8] Dudo of Saint-Quentin, *De moribus et actis primorum Normanniae ducum, auctore Dudone Sancti Quintini decano*, ed. Jules Lair, Caen 1865, cap2.6; trans. in *Dudo of Saint-Quentin, History of the Normans*, trans. Eric Christiansen, Woodbridge 1998.

[9] In the notes to his translation, Eric Christiansen gives examples of the mountain as a frequent symbol of heaven, and of birds as prophetic of empire. (*Dudo of Saint-Quentin*, 188). Dudo takes care to place Rollo as high as possible above the incoming birds, at the very top of a mountain 'higher than the very highest,' and at the spring's source. With this dream, then, Rollo comes to understand that Christianity offers him a hierarchical system in which he can stand at the summit.

frontiers where they built new castles and terrified new enemies.[10]

As their own historians well understood, this Norman dominion depended upon the tight control of an unruly conglomeration of warriors. Orderic Vitalis, the most masterful of those historians, put these words into the mouth William the Conqueror as the king lay dying:

> If the Normans are governed by a good and strict rule, they are very vigorous, and they all excel unvanquished in difficult circumstances, and they fight bravely to conquer every enemy. But when no one controls them, they maul and devour one another, for they long for rebellions, hanker after seditions, and are ready for every abomination. So they should be restrained by the strong arm of the law and compelled by the reins of discipline to walk the path of justice. But if they are allowed to go at will like a wild ass, they themselves and their prince will be overwhelmed by disgraceful anarchy and poverty. This I learned long ago from ample experience. My closest friends and relatives, who ought to have protected me by all possible means against all men, frequently conspired and rose up against me, and took from me almost all my inheritance from my father.[11]

Under strict control, Normans were a nearly invincible force. Without it, their historians insist, they could turn against one another and wreak havoc among their own.

The treacherous and unruly Normans maintained a sense of Norman identity through the twelfth century at least.[12] Signs of personal affiliation with *Normanitas* may even have endured into the late Middle Ages.[13] Indeed, while Marjorie Chibnall has traced the Normans after 1204 in history and memory, that survival of Norman identity held mainly for Normandy itself.[14] As R. H. C. Davis argued in his provocative study, *The Normans and Their Myth*, Normans and Normandy were profoundly tied to one another.[15] Davis identified this unity of land and people as "a most important part of the Norman myth," beginning with Dudo's account:

[10]   For a concise account of the rise of Normandy, facilitated by martial arts and the Church, see Chibnall, *The Normans*, 9–37; a map of Norman castles built in England, 1066–71 appears on page 46.

[11]   The translation is my own, from *The Normans in Their Histories*, 204. For the Latin text of Orderic, see *The Ecclesiastical History of Orderic Vitalis*, ed. and trans. Marjorie Chibnall, 6 vols, Oxford 1969–80.

[12]   Hugh M. Thomas, *The English and the Normans: Ethnic Hostility, Assimilation, and Identity 1066–c.1220*, Oxford 2003, especially 32–45.

[13]   Philippe Contamine, 'The Norman 'Nation' and the French 'Nation' in the fourteenth and fifteenth centuries,' in *England and Normandy in the Middle Ages*, ed. David Bates and Anne Curry, London 1994, 215–34.

[14]   Chibnall, *The Normans*, 161–73.

[15]   R. H. C. Davis, *The Normans and Their Myth*, London 1976, 57.

[By Dudo's reckoning] the land of Normandy was a unity and indivisible. It was called Normandy because it belonged to the Normans, but conversely the Normans belonged to it. It was on the land of Normandy that Dudo's patriotism was centred. He insisted on its fertility, was eloquent about the blue waters (*gurgite caeruleo*) of the Seine, described how they lapped 'the odoriferous grasses of its bank' and apostrophized the city of Rouen five times in verse ... The history of the Normans was shown to be deeply rooted in the soil of Normandy.

Once Normans left Normandy, however, their common identity dissipated rather quickly.[16] This is especially true in the so-called Norman Principality of Antioch, established in 1098/99 through the ambition of Bohemond, son of Robert Guiscard, enabled by the dominant Norman presence on the First Crusade. *Normanitas*, reinforced by an influx of Normans like the chronicler Ralph of Caen in the immediate wake of that Crusade, was barely discernable a generation later.[17] Almost from its beginnings, the crusader state at Antioch held a pan-Frankish, crusader-state identity.[18] In southern Italy as well, despite the waves of Norman immigration throughout the eleventh century, Norman identity dissolved in the twelfth. Decades before Constance, the Norman heiress to the 'Norman Kingdom of Sicily' married the German Emperor Henry VI in 1186, offering Norman Sicily as her dowry to the German imperial line, descendants of Normans in Sicily had ceased to identify themselves by any pan-Norman connections. "Norman identity outside of Normandy," Hugh Thomas has concluded, "was clearly vulnerable over the long term."[19]

Thomas has pointed to a variety of factors that weakened the sense of *Normanitas* for Normans once they left Normandy. These included the broad range of non-Norman allies associated with their conquests and the absence of a common ideology that bound Normans to one another and kept them distinct from the conquered. Close reading of Norman historians writing about all the Norman conquests – from the earliest creation of Normandy itself to Norman acquisitions in southern Italy, Sicily, England, and Antioch – adds another compelling reason for the failure of Normans to retain their identity or to exercise the influence that one might expect in England or in any of the other territories they conquered and settled. Their own histories, often commissioned as celebratory records of grand

---

[16]   For summary and analysis, see Thomas, *The English and the Normans*, 42–45.

[17]   Alan V. Murray, 'How Norman was the Principality of Antioch? Prolegomena to a Study of the Origins of the Nobility of a Crusader State,' in *Family Trees and the Roots of Politics: The Prosopography of Britain and France from the Tenth to the Twelfth Century*, ed. K. S. B. Keats-Rohan, Woodbridge 1997, 349–59.

[18]   Alan V. Murray, 'Ethnic Identity in the Crusader States: The Frankish Race and the Settlement of Outremer,' in *Concepts of National Identity in the Middle Ages*, ed. Simon Forde *et al.*, Leeds 1995, 59–73.

[19]   Thomas, *The English and the Normans*, 45.

events, instead emphasize patterns of betrayal and deceit that worked against the creation of stable and strong polities.[20] Norman historians, even those with apparently strong affinities for Norman princes and people, most typically present Normans eager to shed their treacherous Norman identities for the more prestigious or cultured or stable identities of their enemies, including peoples they conquered and subdued. Tensions within the concept of *Normanitas* seem to have left Normans vulnerable to assimilation.

The Normans produced a great deal of written evidence, both for their spectacular conquests and for their fractious behavior. In England, as everywhere else they penetrated, Normans provoked and often commissioned a veritable explosion of commentary on their exploits. As Ann Williams has observed, "The past is particularly the business of historians and it is no accident that there was a renaissance in historical writing in England after the Conquest." In addition to the accounts written by or for Normans, English historians also weighed in, following a long drought since Bede's *Ecclesiastical History*. In Williams' words, "It took the trauma of conquest to make their past a matter of burning interest to the English."[21] Williams offers persuasive evidence that the Conquest shocked the English into reasserting their English identity and "preserving what was good in the English past."

But was it possible for the English to recover, having suffered such a blow at Hastings? Would the Kingdom of the English be subsumed under the Duchy of Normandy? Would the English lose their cultural identity and their system of law, along with their lands? Would the Norman French language crowd out English, relegating it to limited use in isolated backwaters?

These questions may seem absurd in retrospect. But in 1066 the future of the English lay in considerable doubt. Their best hope might well have seemed a Norman-English synthesis.[22] The revolt of English earls in 1069–70 squashed that hope. William, Norman duke and newly crowned king of England, suppressed the rebellion with "savage reprisals," and "within twenty years of the conquest the Normans had slaughtered, exiled, or dispossessed almost all of the most powerful preconquest landholders."[23] In this process, William toppled the English aristocracy from virtually all bastions of power, wealth, and authority. In their stead he placed Normans and other loyalists on the great landed estates and in positions of authority within the Church. Foreign earls, abbots, and bishops alike supplanted their English predecessors.[24]

[20] Albu, *The Normans in Their Histories*, examines these patterns.

[21] Ann Williams, *The English and the Norman Conquest*, Woodbridge 1995, 164–5.

[22] Williams recalls the precedent that they held in recent memory, the 'Anglo-Danish synthesis' of Cnut; *The English and the Norman Conquest*, 44.

[23] Thomas, *The English and the Normans*, 3. The memory of William's brutal vengeance lingered for generations. For the later Anglo-Norman view, see *Orderic* ii. 230–2.

[24] Robin Fleming, *Kings and Lords in Conquest England*, Cambridge Studies in Medieval Life and Thought Fourth Series no. 15, Cambridge 1991, 132, 143–4.

The evidence in Domesday Book seems irretrievably bleak for the English. A generation after the Conquest, Normans appear to have supplanted the English almost entirely as lords of land and church. The divide between Norman lords and English subjects was contentious, even bitter. Who could have imagined then that English identity would survive, supplanting the dominant Norman identity to define England as the firm and clear home of English language and culture? And how did that happen?

As we have seen, Normans had no ideological reason to remain Norman after leaving Normandy. As their own historians suggest, they had a deeply dysfunctional social structure and way of being, which threatened their survival as a people. Bonds of kinship, even very close ones, often dissolved in competition and treachery. Even so, as Hugh Thomas has reminded us, assimilation was never the inevitable result in medieval societies when different ethnic groups collided. "A strong and at least partly positive image of the English was also important to ensure the survival of Englishness after the conquest."[25]

Many elements converged to make this sense of Englishness sturdy enough to prevail over the identity of their Norman conquerors. Most obvious, of course, is the geographical cohesiveness of an island people. Their physical place in the world was very important. They were only 34 kilometers at the nearest point from the continent of Europe, and yet geographically distinct. Other factors, too, conspired to strengthen English identity. In recent years, we have come especially to appreciate the crucial role played by the historian Bede (672/3–735) in forging a common sense of Englishness.[26] It was Bede, Ann Williams has reminded us, who first expressed this concept of an English *gens*.[27] Centuries before the creation of Normandy, Bede promulgated a powerful myth of the origins of the English, which was essentially positive. They were a chosen people, specially protected by the God of the Old Testament. Compare the pragmatic origin myth of the Normans, which features an acquisitive pagan, drawn to accept Christianity because it promises him power atop a Christian hierarchy of diverse peoples loyal to him. Many Normans, of course, came to embrace the new faith fervently. But the English had centuries before, under the tutelage of the Venerable Bede, affirmed their bond to ancient Christianity. Their church, and the cults of English saints with unique ties to English soil, gave Bede's English a special sense of "cultural, religious, and historical unity."[28]

---

[25] Thomas, *The English and the Normans*, 13.
[26] Patrick Wormald, 'Bede, the *Bretwaldas* and the Origins of the *Gens Anglorum*,' in *Ideal and Reality in Frankish and Anglo-Saxon Society*, ed. Patrick Wormald *et al.*, Oxford 1983, 120–2; Patrick Wormald, '*Engla Lond*: The making of an allegiance,' *Journal of Historical Sociology* 7, 1994, 10–18.
[27] Williams, *The English and the Norman Conquest*, 154.
[28] Thomas, *The English and the Normans*, 22.

Contemplating Bede's influence, we need to abandon the neat textbook analysis of the English as a people requiring the firm hand of the Normans to bring order to their island community. Just as Bede had constructed or perhaps identified an English identity with strong moral and religious underpinnings, so Alfred the Great (c. 849–99) and his heirs built on that foundation to construct a robust and cohesive state, finally exercising influence on virtually all their subjects "through military power, coinage, taxation, and judicial control."[29] Immigrants continued to enter English lands – Scandinavians, French, Welsh, and Cornish – but by 1066 they had assimilated remarkably well into the English majority. The English were thus a mixed people themselves, but one with a shared conviction in their common identity. In 1066 they faced a shocking blow that tested the resilience of that Englishness.

Contrary to the textbook story that the Normans brought order and civilization to England, they first brought mayhem, then the loss of English lands and authority to the Normans, and a rancorous division that lasted into the twelfth century.[30] Yet for its part, England drew the intruders into an affection for their new home. The intertwined influence of the English church and English holy land, reinforced by the authority of Bede's English vision, almost immediately won the allegiance of some Norman conquerors.

Signs of that attraction surfaced quite soon after the Conquest, in the renaissance of monasticism in the north, which in turn, as Ann Williams has shown, contributed to the renewal of English identity.[31] The movement began when Reinfred, a knight in service to a local Norman lord at Whitby, moved by the ruins of the old monastery there, embraced a spiritual calling that soon drew him to form an English-Norman monastic alliance. In this venture, Norman monks with their powerful patrons joined English monks who taught them about the glory days of Northumbrian monasteries described by Bede in his *Historia Ecclesiastica*. Further inspired by Bede's account, English and Normans collaborated to rebuild Bede's own foundation, Wearmouth / Jarrow, and moved on to restore Whitby and others. Norman lords must have had their own political as well as religious motives. Normans were also replicating the actions of their dukes in Normandy itself. Just so, William the Conqueror followed the example of his ancestors as far back as Rollo's son, William Longsword, in restoring monasteries like Jumièges and Fécamp, which their Viking forebears had destroyed. In the north of England, a similar impulse led to a restoration of education and culture within a tradition that celebrated Bede's vision of an English people, a venerable *gens Anglorum*. The northern monastic revival nurtured that idea and kept it within the common

29 Thomas, *The English and the Normans*, 22–3.
30 On the initial shock of the conquest, see Elisabeth M. C. van Houts, 'The Trauma of 1066,' *History Today* 46 no. 10, October 1996, 9–15.
31 Williams, *The English and the Norman Conquest*, 150–4.

discourse, through copying and distributing Bede's seminal work and producing new histories influenced by Bede and repeating his idea of an old and continuing English people.

By the end of the twelfth century, the Normans elites in England had adopted that identity for themselves.[32] For yet another hundred years, they would continue to speak Norman-French and retain elements of Norman culture. But little more than a century after the Conquest, it was impossible to distinguish Norman from English in most respects.[33] Virtually all identified themselves as English.

Theirs was of course an Englishness different from pre-Conquest Englishness. After an initially hostile clash, Normans and English had amalgamated into a distinctive culture that historians today term Anglo-Norman. This is a modern coinage. The people living in that culture came to call themselves English, no matter what their blood ancestry and, increasingly, no matter what language they used to declare their Englishness. The Church used Latin, the landed classes spoke French, and everyone else spoke English. After the Conquest, that English was much in flux. When Standard Old English ceased to be the vehicle for royal writs and local court documents, the fluid tongue of English speakers replaced the conservative clerical language. English structure simplified even as the language added thousands of words from French and Latin. Though William the Conqueror never learned English, and French remained the language of the court for some time, the English language of the native peoples gradually returned to both manors and courts. By the reign of Edward I (1239–1307) the English language had significantly replaced French. The king himself spoke English.

Today we remember the Normans as a vigorous people disciplined by strong rulers and endowed with a gift for administrative structure and control. Yet in England they encountered a culture already highly developed in terms of law and administration. The Norman addition into that society produced a gradual movement to "a new streamlined lordship in England which more tightly bound together personal, jurisdictional and territorial lordship."[34] Robin Fleming's nuanced reading here, *contra* the dramatic textbook account, highlights the slow

[32]   John Gillingham has placed that development of Englishness much earlier in the twelfth century: 'Henry of Huntingdon and the Twelfth-Century Revival of the English Nation,' in *The English in the Twelfth Century: Imperialism, National Identity and Political Values*, ed. John Gillingham, Woodbridge 2000; repr. 2008, 123–44. In a seminal article, Ian Short examined the gradually evolving identity, linguistic and ethnic, of the people we call Anglo-Normans: '*Tam Angli quam Franci*: self-definition in Anglo-Norman England,' *ANS* 18, 1996, 153–75.

[33]   On the similarities between pre-Conquest England and pre-Conquest Normandy, which facilitated this assimilation, see Williams, *The English and the Norman Conquest*, 187.

[34]   Robin Fleming, *Domesday Book and the Law: Society and Legal Custom in Early Medieval England*, Cambridge 1998, 75.

emergence of laws and culture that came from the union of two peoples, a union that very soon came to validate a renewed English identity marked by adherence to English law, devotion to local saints, and loyalty to an English homeland.

Which of these views, then, is correct? Did the Normans fundamentally transform English society, or did the English reassert their own identity? The authority of my student days, Charles Homer Haskins, claimed that he and most of his contemporary scholars held a middle ground. They stood, he wrote, half way between the assessment of "a French scholar like [Émile] Boutmy" who thought that "everything begins anew in 1066, when 'the line which the whole history of political institutions has subsequently followed was traced and defined,'" and the conclusions of the English historian Edward A. Freeman, who believed that "the changes then introduced were temporary and not fundamental."[35] It is curious, isn't it, that Haskins' Frenchman assumed a lasting Norman revolution in England, while the Englishman advanced the persistence of Englishness? For his part, the American Haskins, who had studied medieval history in France, clearly betrayed continental sympathies, despite his claims to neutrality:

> The trend of present scholarly opinion lies between these extremes. It refuses to throw away the Anglo-Saxon period, whose institutions we are just beginning to read aright; but it rejects its idealization at Freeman's hands, who, it has been said, saw all things 'through a mist of moots and witans' and not as they really were, and it finds more truth in Carlyle's remark that the pot-bellied equanimity of the Anglo-Saxon needed the drilling and discipline of a century of Norman tyranny.[36]

I believe that very recent historians have arrived at a truer middle ground with the perspective that I have followed here: the Norman Conquest did change Normans and English alike. Yet from this mix of Normans and English emerged a new England that was in a very deep sense English. If he were with us today, I imagine that Haskins would accuse me of seeing that England, with Freeman, through those old "moot and witan mists." The symposium in Sendai has invited another audience – one with the clarity that comes from distance in time and space and with its own historical tradition as an island people – to reassess the impact of 1066.

---

[35] Haskins, *Normans in European History*, 101, citing Emile Boutmy, *The English Constitution* [*Développement de la constitution et de la société politique en Angleterre*] and Edward A. Freeman, *Origin of the English Constitution*.
[36] Haskins, *Normans in European History*, 101–2, citing Stubbs' critical assessment of Freeman.

'The Welsh, you know, are Welsh': the Individual, the Alien, and a Legal Tradition

BRONAGH NÍ CHONAILL

Much has been written about the highs and lows of medieval Welsh history in the pursuit of political unity between the ninth and fourteenth centuries. An overall summary sentence for this period could read as follows: Welsh-speaking Wales was politically fragmented, but culturally and socially cohesive – an interesting scenario when investigating a given people or a nation. In the case of medieval Scotland, Professpr Broun demonstrated how over time a single authority figure emerged, one capable of harnessing both internal and external influences and incorporating a variety of peoples loyal to a *Rex Scottorum* (and who in fact found definition and identity through this very office).[1] The history of Wales, however, did not follow this paradigm. In this same period, and in marked contrast to the growing strength and usage of the term *rex* in Scotland, we find not a kingly but princely flavour in the terminology applied to the rulers in Wales (*princeps, arglwydd, tywysog*); a contraction of territory which once was under the hand of native Welsh dynasties; the establishment of Norman and Anglo-Norman Marcher lordships; and finally the Edwardian conquest of Wales (1280s), which was followed by the annexation of the principality of Gwynedd to the Crown of England. Just over a century later, amidst unrest and rebellion, legislation was issued which indicated an inferior status to being Welsh, when placed alongside being English.[2] Upon this broad brushstroke synopsis, a bleak picture could indeed be painted of the political (mis)fortunes of Wales. Our attention, however, will focus on the Welsh people. For in contrast to Scotland, the existence and expression of a people who were deemed 'British' (to become 'Welsh') and located in a 'Wales' existed before our time period commences and persisted throughout the middle ages in the face of great political change.

In this paper, I wish to highlight three particular aspects (and here I should note that in this 'land of two peoples' the areas under native Welsh control will form the focus of what follows).[3] First, to undertake a brief analysis of Welsh polit-

---

[1]   See paper within this volume by Prof. Dauvit Broun, 'Becoming a nation: Scotland in the twelfth and thirteenth centuries'.

[2]   See *The Statutes of Wales*, ed. I. Bowen, London 1908.

[3]   R. R. Davies, 'The Identity of 'Wales' in the thirteenth century', in *From Medieval to*

ical fortunes, which may reveal in part why Wales and Scotland diverged in their respective political paths. Second, to turn to a particular primary source, the body of native Welsh legal writings in order to discover what in the medieval legal mind's eye constituted the average or ideal Welshman, and by extension what forged his identity and community. Third, upon entering this legal world, important questions are raised in relation to the nature of authority, the status of law and how legal identity might create, as Davies notes, an 'ideology of national unity'.[4] Once done, we might be a little closer to understanding the comment made in a correspondence to Edward I in 1296 which read, 'the Welsh, you know, are Welsh',[5] but perhaps from one internal Welsh perspective and the extant legal material.

Setting the Scene

Medieval Wales was '"a geographical expression" for a fluctuating assembly of countries' according to Dafydd Jenkins.[6] This comment could be applied in equal measure to the tenth, eleventh, twelfth, thirteenth, and even fourteenth centuries. The political landscape for the student of Welsh history reflects fluctuation between royal dynasties, where personal ability combined with the military might of individual rulers dominated the course of Welsh history (note the use of the plural *dynasties* and the existence of more than one native royal line). One will read of a medieval Welsh king/prince who *almost* united Wales, or held sway over *a vast amount* of Wales, only for his success to quickly come undone upon his downfall (at which point the re-building process would re-commence with the rise of another capable dynast). And therefore, while Professor Broun was able to plot the gradual creation of a unified Scottish entity, built on a stable political footing in the adherence to a royal line and office, the historian of medieval Wales simply cannot.[7] Wales never achieved such unification or political coherence in the middle ages. What is important to emphasise, however, is that there was an awareness and

---

    Modern Wales: Historical Essays in Honour of Kenneth O. Morgan and Ralph A. Griffiths, ed. R. R. Davies and G. H. Jenkins, Cardiff 2004, 51. For information on the Marcher areas see, R. R. Davies, *Lordship and Society in the March of Wales, 1282–1400,* Oxford 1978; *idem,* 'Kings, lords and liberties in the march of Wales, 1066–1272', *Transactions of the Royal Historical Society* 29, 1979, 41–61; *idem,* 'The law of the March', *Welsh History Review* 5:1, 1970, 1–30.

4   R. R. Davies, 'Law and national identity in thirteenth-century Wales', in *Welsh Society and Nationhood: Historical Essays Presented to Glanmor Williams,* ed. R. R. Davies, R. A. Griffiths, I. G. Jones, and K. O. Morgan, Cardiff 1984, 56.

5   R. R. Davies, 'Race relations in post-conquest Wales: confrontation and compromise', *Transactions of the Honourable Society of Cymmrodorion* (1975 for 1974), 37–8. The quotation is question was noted in 1296 by two of Edwards I's commissioners, James of St. George and Walter of Winchester.

6   D. Jenkins, ed., *Celtic Law Papers,* Studies presented to the International Commission for the History of Representative and Parliamentary Institutions 42, Brussels, 1973, 26.

7   Broun, 'Becoming a nation: Scotland in the twelfth and thirteenth centuries'.

promotion by medieval dynasts, chroniclers, lawyers and poets of the possibility of a 'Wales' to be won or united in this cyclical pattern of political consolidation and collapse.

What serves to re-enforce this territorial awareness of a Wales, was the presence of a physical demarcation or border known as Offa's Dyke (*Clawdd Offa*), attributed to Offa, king of Mercia (d. 796), and possibly constructed in the context of on-going tensions between the Mercians and the Welsh.[8] This physical boundary – one of Davies' emblems of common identity[9] – was generally accepted as the border between Wales and England throughout the medieval period. This particular earthen work leads us to another important point which must be borne in mind in relation to the people of Wales and her eastern neighbours who lay beyond it, which is how from the early middle ages Welsh rulers on occasion played a subordinate role within the workings and aspirations of the Anglo-Saxon court.[10] The expectation of overlordship, or at the very least a precedent of importance on the part of Anglo-Saxon and English kings in turn, would have a part to play in the history of a politically fragmented Wales and how she interacted with her neighbour.

Before continuing further, a brief tour of Wales is necessary. The leading territories of Wales were Gwynedd in the north-west (with its leading court at Aberffraw), Deuheubarth in the south-west (with its leading court in Dinefwr), Powys occupying a more northern central position (with its leading court at Mathrafal), and Glamorgan to the south.[11] The roots of these kingdoms stretch back into the Romano-British world and so, by the tenth and eleventh centuries, there were well established, regional, competing Welsh royal dynasties striving for dominance - a further contrast to Dr Broun's colourful palette of peoples and influences ready to be moulded into a 'Scotland' when the climate was ripe.[12]

---

[8] H. Pryce, 'British or Welsh? National identity in twelfth-century Wales', *EHR* 116, 2001, 777; D. Hill, 'Mercians: The Dwellers on the Boundary', in *Mercia: an Anglo-Saxon Kingdom in Europe*, ed. M. P. Brown and C. A. Farr, London 2001, 173–82; C. Fox, *Offa's Dyke*, London 1955; Frank Noble, *Offa's Dyke Reviewed*, ed. M. Gelling , BAR British series 114, Oxford 1983.

[9] Davies, 'The Identity of 'Wales' in the thirteenth century', 49 (law, custom, language, mythology and borders constitute the emblems noted by this author).

[10] See T. M. Charles-Edwards, 'Wales and Mercia, 613–918', in *Mercia*, ed. Brown and Farr, 89–105; R. R. Davies, "Keeping the natives in order': the English king and the 'Celtic' rulers 1066–1216', *Peritia* 10, 1996, 212–24.

[11] For maps of the medieval divisions within Wales see J. Davies, *A History of Wales*, Harmondsworth 1990, 86; D. Jenkins, *Hywel Dda: The Law,* Gomer 1986, page prior to 'Preface'; R. R. Davies, *The Age of Conquest: Wales 1063–1415,* Oxford 1991, 5, 22; W. Rees, *An Historical Atlas of Wales,* Cardiff 1951, see Plates: 23 (9th to 12th centuries), 38 (ca. 1200), 39 (ca. 1234), 45 (The Statute of Rhuddlan, 1284).

[12] Broun, 'Becoming a nation: Scotland in the twelfth and thirteenth centuries'.

What of the rulers of these territories? To illustrate the pattern of high politics in pre-Conquest Wales: the dominant figure in the twelfth century was Owain
Gwynedd (d. 1170) situated in the territory in the north/north-west. Upon his
death, however, Gwynedd was divided between his sons.[13] At this point, the pen-
dulum of power and dominance swung to the south and to Rhys ap Gruffudd (the
Lord Rhys), ruler of Deheubarth, until his death in 1197, whereupon Deheubarth
was divided between his offspring. There follows, yet again, the rise and dominance of Gwynedd in the north under Llywelyn ap Iorwerth (d. 1240), where upon
his death (as one may well suspect at this point) Gwynedd was once again divided
between two of his sons.[14] In this brief check-list of the great and good of medieval
Welsh politics, the common and core factor in a pattern of dismantlement and
shifting power was the practice of *cyfran* (gavelkind, partibility). According to
Welsh practice, *all* recognised sons (born within or outwith wedlock) were, in theory, permitted to inherit a share of the patrimony in question: 'it is right for the
youngest son to divide the whole patrimony, and for the eldest to choose and then
from the eldest to next eldest down to the youngest'.[15] This particular inheritance
practice was deeply embedded in medieval Welsh social structure - one which
stood in stark contrast to primogeniture, and in the context of high politics has
generally been perceived as a restrictive and debilitating custom.[16] It was one
which could not only result in the undoing or weakening of an individual Welsh
(ruling) family, but, as evident from the examples just noted, could also be a fundamental impediment to any possible move towards a unified Wales, or the sus-
taining of such a movement. This practice went straight to the heart of authority
and stability, with the division amongst sons capable of quickly dismantling
decades of power building and consolidation.

A further point for consideration is that although a 'Wales' finds recognition
as a territorial unit in both legal and literary sources, she was a country 'without a
centre',[17] and when combined with strong, competing regional dynasties, this
would have made the path to political unification a harder one to pursue. The
physical terrain of Wales re-enforced the regional territorial divisions. But there
can be no denying that leading Welsh princes had real ambition for a unified
politic. The terminology applied is revealing in this matter. From the 1130s
onwards there is growing consistency within documents to the terms applied to

---

[13]   Davies, *Age of Conquest*, 238–9.
[14]   Davies, *Age of Conquest*, 192–3, 249–50.
[15]   *Llyfr Iorwerth*, ed. A.R. Wiliam, Cardiff 1960, §82, trans. in Jenkins, *Hywel Dda*, 99.
[16]   T. M. Charles-Edwards, *Early Irish and Welsh Kinship*, Oxford 1993, 167–256; Davies,
       Age of Conquest, 71, 158, 239.
[17]   Davies, *Age of Conquest*, 8; Here again we have a contrast with Scotland. The eastern
       lowlands became the centre for Scotland around which grew the kingship and king-
       dom, see Prof. Broun's paper.

Wales: Latin, *Gualis/Wallia* (derived from Old English *Walas/Wealas*), and *Cymry* in the vernacular texts.[18] This reflected a shift away from a more 'British'-based terminology in the previous centuries: Latin, *Britannia* (for the territory), *Britones/Britanni* (for the people).[19] H. Pryce has noted how this development would have eliminated any confusion which might have occurred in understanding the older terms, e.g. *Britones* could refer to a 'Briton' of Roman times, a Breton, or a Welsh person.[20] Therefore, in the fast changing world of the late eleventh-/early twelfth-century Britain, Welsh rulers were content to be redefined as *Walenses*, 'Welsh', in documents of English origin, and followed suit within their own. As R. R. Davies notes, the Welsh had 'adjusted'.[21] The terminology did after all reflect a territorial reality. Therefore, Owain Gwynedd (d. 1170) of the Northern dynasty, quite ambitiously uses the term *rex Wallie*, when corresponding with Louis VII of France in 1160s.[22] On the international stage, he sought to be perceived as the King of Wales. Native Welsh legal writings purposefully buy into this ideal of a Wales, when in the Prologue to the legal corpus Hywel Dda is referred to as 'prince of all Wales'.[23] Even when the rulers of Gwynedd or Deuheubarth refer to themselves as *rex Norwallie* or *Sudwallie*, it is a north or south within *Wallia*.[24] This was a conceptual hook upon which a given ruler could hang his ambitions. It was both a territorial reality and a political ideal, but one bigger than any individual could achieve in the pre-Edwardian world.

Leaving the stage of high politics to one side for the present, let us now turn to the people. As Professor Broun noted, 'when we refer to the Irish and the Welsh in this period, everyone knows who we mean'.[25] So let us investigate a particular source, the legal corpus, to seek a more detailed explanation from one medieval perspective.

The Legal Tracts

We are fortunate to possess over 40 manuscripts of medieval Welsh legal writings, the majority of which emanate from the 13th–16th centuries (pre-1536). The content of these manuscripts reflect a long-standing, native legal tradition with highly trained legal professionals who acted not only as practitioners but also custodians

---

[18]   Pryce, 'British or Welsh? National identity in twelfth-century Wales', notes 'Old English *Walas* or *Wealas*, which, like Welsh *Cymry*, was a plural noun denoting both the people and the country', 780.

[19]   Pryce, 'British or Welsh', 775–801.

[20]   Pryce, 'British or Welsh', 790–91.

[21]   Davies, 'The identity of "Wales" in the thirteenth century', 50.

[22]   Davies, 'The identity of "Wales" in the thirteenth century', 784.

[23]   *Llyfr Iorwerth* §1 (*tywyssauc Kemry oll*); trans. Jenkins, *Hywel Dda*, 1.

[24]   Pryce, 'British or Welsh? National identity in twelfth-century Wales', 783; *The Acts of Welsh Rulers, 1120–1283*, ed. H. Pryce, Cardiff 2005, see e.g. nos 172, 199, 332.

[25]   Broun, 'Becoming a nation: Scotland in the twelfth and thirteenth centuries'.

of this system. In essence, the manuscripts we possess are law books written by lawyers for lawyers of medieval Wales.[26] Therefore, they are a gateway into a particular viewpoint and perspective on the workings of society and its people (with caution needed, as with any primary source, in how this information could or should be applied to contemporary society).[27] It is important to note how this *corpus iuris* is often described in scholarship as native, traditional or customary law, which reflects its deep roots in the community (as opposed to deriving from the legislative hand of a king).

The term applied to this entire legal corpus is/was *Cyfraith Hywel* (the Law of Hywel), but who was Hywel? The prologues to the MSS relate how Hywel ap Cadell (d. 949/50), a king who dominated most of Wales in the first half of the tenth century, assembled the relevant nobles and churchmen and reformed the law for the better.[28] Historians have accepted the probability that Hywel may have played some role in the legal sphere, but that the account in the prologues is most likely the creation of the late twelfth or early thirteenth centuries.[29] The fact that a prominent king has his name attached to this legal text is not in itself surprising (a leading example is Alfred the Great). For a king to acquire an entire legal tradition, however, is another matter. What we appear to have (both in the creation of the prologue and the hive of legal scribal activity from this period) is a direct statement on the endurance and authority of native Welsh law, made in the twelfth and thirteenth centuries at a very time when tensions were mounting within Wales both from internal and external quarters. It would appear that the legal profession, as primary custodians, were attempting to reinforce their position and responsibility in relation to *Cyfraith Hywel* in the face of the reforming power and encroachment of the native Welsh rulers into the judicial field. At the same time, such reinforcement and written expression could only benefit the native princes and enhance their status, especially in the presence of the Marcher lordships and ever-changing relationship with the King of England.

Of further importance within the prologues to the manuscripts is the mention of clerics who are noted to have played a part in the reforming of native Welsh law in conjunction with Hywel Dda, therefore implying that native Welsh law was

---

[26] See Jenkins, 'Introduction' in *Hywel Dda*, xi–xxxvii; T. M. Charles-Edwards, *The Welsh Laws*, Cardiff 1989; T. M. Charles-Edwards, Morfydd E. Owen and D. B. Walters, ed., *Lawyers and Laymen : Studies in the History of Law Presented to Professor Dafydd Jenkins on his Seventy-Fifth Birthday*, Cardiff 1986.

[27] For further discussion and cautionary comments see Davies, 'Law and national identity in thirteenth-century Wales', 54ff.

[28] Jenkins, *Hywel Dda*, 1.

[29] See Jenkins, 'Introduction' in *Hywel Dda*, xii–xx; H. Pryce, 'The prologues to the Welsh lawbooks', *Bulletin of the Board of Celtic Studies* 33, 1986, 151–87; H. Pryce, 'The context and purpose of the earliest Welsh lawbooks', *Cambrian Medieval Celtic Studies* 39, 2000, 39–63.

Christian and sanctioned by the church. As Robin Chapman Stacey has noted, 'certainly it would be impossible to overestimate the significance of Hywel's myth for Welsh politics and identity in the thirteenth century: Welsh law was royal, it was Christian, and it both derived from and pertained to all of Wales. Above all, it was native, owing nothing to English or Norman traditions'.[30]

What then do the legal texts contain? The majority of the manuscripts share a common structure and content which is as follows: a section on *the laws of court* (an important statement on royal privilege and position), a section on *the laws of country* (which deal with core issues such as land and legal procedure), and a third section referred to as the *Test Book* for judges (found within a particular family of MSS). Scholarship has generally accepted that the MSS appear to separate into three general groupings (each referred to by the name of a medieval jurist associated with that particular family of manuscripts): Iorwerth, Blegywryd, Cyfnerth, which reveal territorial affiliations to Gwynedd, Dyfed and Gwent respectively.[31] Here, once again, we find recognition of regional divisions within Wales. With this noted however, there is agreement across the MSS that *Cyfraith Hywel* was the common law for Wales.[32] Regional variations on detail, and personnel, within a given procedure were noted, and fully accepted within the texts, but the key principles of social order and justice were consistent throughout the versions. Within these texts we are indeed reading 'an ideology of national unity', a legal unity, which native Welsh princes and legal practitioners could promote and utilise. What is also noteworthy and striking is the absence of reference to the Marcher or Anglo-Norman territories within this source (further re-enforcing a particular native Welsh ideology). For native Welsh society no matter where in medieval Welsh-Wales one resided, the lawyer crafts a remarkably coherent picture.

What Made a Medieval Welshman according to 'Cyfraith Hywel'?

A person must be officially recognised and accepted by the kin (and by extension the community) to fully function and participate in everyday life; for example, to be permitted to enter into a contract, to be able to stand witness in court proceedings, or to act as a guarantor for a relative or neighbour.[33] In medieval Welsh law, everyone had a place on the social ladder with a value which reflected a person's status (*braint*). The principle of this honour-price value cannot be overesti-

---

[30] R. Chapman Stacey, 'Law and literature in medieval Ireland and Wales', in *Medieval Celtic Literature and Society,* ed. H. Fulton, Dublin 2005, 77; H. Pryce, *Native Law and the Church in Medieval Wales,* Oxford 1993.

[31] See Charles-Edwards, *The Welsh Laws,* section IV, 25–48.

[32] D. Jenkins, 'Law and Government in Wales before the Act of Union' in *Celtic Law Papers,* ed. Jenkins, 25–48; Charles-Edwards, *The Welsh Laws,* 6ff.

[33] See Charles-Edwards, *Early Irish and Welsh Kinship,* Section II, 167–256.

mated, for medieval Welsh law was restorative at its core, i.e. in theory, crime could be adequately compensated for, and once compensation was given, order in society would be restored.[34] The burden of payment fell not only on the perpetrator of the crime but could at times extend to his wider kin-group, and therefore people were woven together through financial and social obligations which could extend out into the community. This aspect of medieval Welsh justice clashed with the more retributive nature of English Law, where punishing the offender (and the role and responsibility of the individual for his actions), was the order of the day, as opposed to compensating the victim and his kin. Both systems had important implications for how justice and authority were imposed and maintained. Within the English legal system, the king retained greater control over the extent and nature of punishment permitted and could receive a greater financial return from penalties imposed.[35] By the nature of the Welsh compensatory method, the victim and his/her kin remained central to the proceedings, and therefore the kin-group retained a greater degree of influence over the proceedings, and in the legal sphere in general. The local lord may be involved, and indeed at times the lord is the dominant figure in legal matters, with the figure of the king somewhat in the background. And here once again we can see a clear difference with Scotland, where we have a common judicial system across a kingdom, but one firmly under royal control, which Broun highlighted as being a key factor in the creation of 'Scotland'. On the nature of authority and justice, we see striking differences at play within a Welsh, Scottish and English context, and for Wales, these differences would in time become a matter of contention with her eastern neighbour.

What then bestowed the status of a Welshman upon a person in the eyes of the jurist? The texts refer to the desired position of being a *bonheddig canhwynol* (an innate *bonheddig*).[36] According to a thirteenth century text, this 'is a person whose complete stock is in Wales, both from mother and father', and therefore indicating a preference for *both* bloodlines to be of Welsh descent.[37] The picture presented of the 'innate *bonheddig*' is one of stability and reliability within the commote (i.e. designated neighbourhood), one who could be called upon in legal proceedings to stand as character witness or who could act as guarantor to a contract. Through his descent and actions he could hold positions of responsibility within the community and the court; within the King's court for example 'the

---

[34] *Galanas*: 'enmity', the compensation payment needed to resolve a feud; *Sarhaed*: the term for compensation owed for injury and/or insult, which varied according to status.

[35] Jenkins, *Hywel Dda*, xxx–xxxi; R. R. Davies, 'Colonial Wales', *Past and Present* 65, 1974, 19.

[36] See Jenkins, *Hywel Dda*, 'The basic word bôn, 'stock'... gives the abstract noun *bonhedd*, 'stock'... This is turn gives the adjective *bonheddig*, used as a noun for the Welshman of full free status...', 318–19; *canhwynol*, 'innate', see p. 264; Charles-Edwards, *Early Irish and Welsh Kinship*, Glossary, 561.

[37] *Llyfr Iorwerth* §87; trans. Jenkins, *Hywel Dda*, 110.

watchman must be a *bonheddig* of the country, for trust is put in him by the King'.[38] As one may expect, bloodline was the primary factor in one's claim to land: 'whosoever wants to claim land by kindred and descent, let him show his pedigree as far as the stock from which he derives'.[39] This knowledge of birth and ancestry, could only have reaffirmed one's own identity and position within a community.

With descent providing the key to social status and inheritance in the native legal tradition, the jurists ponder various scenarios where the matter is not so straightforward. What if only the mother's bloodline is of free, recognised Welsh status? For example, what of 'the son of [Welsh] woman given as a hostage into a country of strange speech, if she becomes pregnant after being given as a hostage by her kin and her lord'?[40] Because the Welshwoman has been given with the consent of both lord and kin, the son would be eligible to claim land and position in Wales through his mother's line (*mamwys*). And so, in this time period a person's place of birth did not impact upon a person's nationality. In fact, we could take the example of Gruffydd ap Cynan (d. 1137), king of Gwynedd, who on his father's side stemmed from the Welsh royal line of Gwynedd, but on his mother's side from the ruling Hiberno-Norse kingdom of Dublin. Not only was he born in the surrounds of Dublin, but he appears to have spent much of his childhood outside of his future patrimony of Gwynedd. In this case, paternal descent was the determining factor and was Gruffydd's path to power.[41]

Medieval Welsh law as depicted in the texts was very much kin-group centred, with the lord playing his part as overseer to an established system. In the eyes of the jurist, the basic unit in which a person operated was his commote (*cwmwd*, his specified neighbourhood). By birth he gained his status, and ideally, to be an innate Welshman, both parents should be of free Welsh descent. Recourse to justice was very much in the hands of the community, supported by the local lord and overseen by practitioners of the law.

Aliens: 'Alltudion'

The existence of legal discourse on a category of people who do not belong to the community, nor are entitled to the rights of an innate Welshman, is equally revealing in this area. Such a person is referred to as an *alltud(-ion* pl.) (lit. 'from another country') and within the text it notes that he comes 'from overseas or from another country'.[42] It is a term generally translated as 'aliens' in English.[43] From the early

---

38 Jenkins, *Hywel Dda*, 36.
39 *Llyfr Iorwerth*, §85; trans. Jenkins, *Hywel* Dda, 104.
40 *Llyfr Iorwerth*, §53; trans. Jenkins, *Hywel Dda*, 58.
41 See D. Simon Evans, *A Mediaeval Prince of Wales: the Life of Gruffudd ap Cynan*, Felinfach 1990; *Vita Griffini filii Conani: the Medieval Latin Life of Gruffudd ap Cynan*, ed. and trans. Paul Russell, Cardiff 2005.
42 *Llyfr Iorwerth*, §115; trans. Jenkins, *Hywel Dda*, 167, also 116.
43 *Llyfr Iorwerth*, §89; trans. Jenkins, *Hywel Dda*, 114–19. Many of the references to aliens

middle ages Wales, as elsewhere, had experienced the presence of external peoples (Saxons, Anglo-Saxons, Vikings, Normans etc.). The establishment of the Marcher lordships, plantation boroughs, the comings and goings of migrants for work (e.g. in castle-building) or for trade, alongside the growth of urban centres, meant that more people were mobile than ever before.[44] Therefore, there appears to have been a marked increase in migration into Wales in the twelfth and thirteenth centuries, and the existence of legal discourse on the 'alien' is particularly pertinent to this period.[45] The social hierarchy of the law texts note that the *alltud*'s position was below that of the *bonheddig* (innate Welshman). Within legal proceedings it was not permitted to accept the testimony of an alien against that of a Welshman 'by reason of nature', for 'an alien cannot be a knower against a patrimonial Welshman.'[46] However, their lot is not entirely lost, for here we discover that land tenure was another possible route for one to progress to full status of Welshman. This only took the patience of four generations to achieve:

> If it happens that an alien comes and does homage to the King and the King gives him land, and that he occupies the land for his lifetime, and his son after him, and his grandson and his great-grandson and his fourth-man, the latter will be a proprietor, and it is right that he should from then on have, not the status of an alien, but the status of the land which he occupies and the status of a Welshman.[47]

To be a *priodor* (proprietor), to have a claim and right to land, was to have a position of recognition within society. Up until the fourth generation and social promotion, *alltudion* were under the rule of the local lord or king. There are restrictions noted as to their actions and behaviour; for example, an alien could not assume holy orders nor could he take a wife without the permission of his lord.[48]

In the legal texts, the recurring concern about the presence of *alltudion* in society centres on who should assume financial responsibility for any illegal activity undertaken by the *alltud* and for the consequences of such action (e.g. homicide or theft). Therefore, movement of *alltudion* between lords was prohibited. If *alltudion* did not wish to remain within the community, those from overseas

are found within the text, *Llyfr y Damweiniau*, compiled in the thirteenth century, possibly from Gwynedd, see Jenkins, xxv, 114–19.

44 Davies, 'Colonial Wales', 3–4, 7.
45 Davies, *Age of Conquest*, 158–60.
46 *Llyfr Iorwerth*, §77; trans. Jenkins, *Hywel Dda*, 89 (again at 94, 'an alien against a Welshman').
47 D. Jenkins, *Damweiniau Colan*, Aberystwyth 1973, l. 476; trans. Jenkins, *Hywel Dda*, 114.
48 Jenkins, *Damweiniau Colan*, l. 370 (orders), l. 337 (wife); trans. Jenkins, *Hywel Dda*, 117.

were permitted to stay until the next wind could take them back out to sea and those who 'come from this island, they are not entitled to stay on this side of Offa's dyke'.[49]

Reference to aliens is peppered throughout the legal texts.[50] But by their very presence, we are permitted to see the jurist grappling with placing an outsider within the medieval Welsh community and through their presence we can also assess the privilege of native Welshmen within this same social structure. First and foremost the legal texts try to protect Welsh society and social order by ensuring that responsibility for outsiders rests with someone within the community. Once established, Welsh society had a mechanism which could accommodate and ultimately incorporate incomers who could in time become as legally (and functioning) Welsh as the Welsh themselves.

A brief comment should be made about language as an obvious mark of distinction between peoples. Within the legal texts, the underlying assumption is that anyone involved in legal proceedings was Welsh-speaking. At a very basic level, the actual ability to speak was essential within proceedings - being unable to verbally answer a case or state your rights could in theory exclude you from any involvement in legal action.[51] Not only was the physical mechanism of speech important, but also the actual language spoken. One text notes how a person of 'foreign speech' was not entitled to act as a surety (a guarantor) in society, thus limiting one's participation in the locality.[52] Whereas in Scotland, Broun notes the absence of, or need for linguistic harmony in the creation of a unified Scotland, in the Wales of the legal texts language is of extreme importance. The language of the law is the vernacular, i.e. Middle Welsh, indicating the strength and acceptance of the vernacular to support important mechanisms of society.[53] Manuscripts of *Cyfraith Hywel* continue to be copied and written in Welsh well into the early modern period, during the age of the 'linguistic imperialism' of English from the later fourteenth century onwards.

It is also worth emphasising the written nature of the law as it is presented in our manuscripts, a tradition which may in fact stretch back to the time of Hywel in the tenth century. The act of committing text to vellum (conceptually, physi-

---

[49]   *Llyfr Iorwerth*, §89; trans. Jenkins, *Hywel Dda*, 116.
[50]   See entry, 'alien', within index to Jenkins, *Hywel Dda*, 399.
[51]   Jenkins, *Damweiniau Colan*, 268. See how the court justice 'purchases' his tongue upon a false judgement, 17, 141; or how the value of the tongue equals the combined value of all other members (hands, eyes, lips, feet, nose, ear, testes), 'since it defends them', 196.
[52]   *Llyfr Iorwerth*, §66; trans. Jenkins, *Hywel Dda*, 76.
[53]   There are 6 extant MSS in Latin which date between the thirteenth-sixteenth centuries, see Charles-Edwards, *The Laws*, 102; H. Emanuel, *The Latin Texts of the Welsh Laws*, History and Law Series 22, Cardiff 1967. The vast majority of surviving MSS (40+) are in the vernacular.

cally, financially), is in its own right a statement of authority and status.[54] As the machinery of administration and record keeping increased across Europe in this period, medieval Wales was following suit with an air of confidence. It is of interest to note that the only extant medieval Welsh legal manuscript with illustrations is in Latin and held to have been presented to the Archbishop of Canterbury, Archbishop Pecham, at a time when the last native Welsh prince was under mounting political pressure from Edward I.[55] Here too, we can see a statement of authority being made in the possible presentation of this manuscript, especially to an Archbishop who was a staunch opponent of *Cyfraith Hywel*.[56] The physical production of law, that a legal tradition should take a written form, played its role in shaping the legal tradition and how this tradition found expression in medieval Wales. What we possess, however, is not simply a static legal corpus, or a written form of legal thought from an earlier oral-based context. Europe in the late twelfth and early thirteenth centuries witnessed a growth in the interest in the study of law. We find a similar impressive 'flowering of legal scholarship' in Wales, especially so in the thirteenth century.[57] The creation of the *Test Book* for lawyers is linked to Iorwerth ap Madog (fl. 1230-40) a jurist in Gwynedd. New and sophisticated approaches to procedures were being developed, e.g. methods of pleading a case, which reflect a vibrant native legal system in action.[58]

The Recognition of Welsh Law

What of this *corpus iuris* outside of the legal writings? We have records belonging to the thirteenth century noting the employment by Welsh princes of *sapientes* (experts in native law) and also records of disputes being settled under native Welsh law.[59] In fact, across the thirteenth century we find a peppering of references to a 'Welsh law' appearing in the political documentation. In the earliest surviving written agreement between an English King, John, and a native Welsh ruler, Llywelyn ap Iorwerth of Gwynedd, in 1201, we read of the presence and acceptance of 'the law of England or the law of Wales'.[60] *Magna Carta* (1215, Clauses, 56-7) on the issue of land tenure within Marcher lordships notes, 'concerning holdings of

---

[54] H. Pryce, 'Lawbooks and literacy in medieval Wales', *Speculum* 75, 2000, 29–67.

[55] *Peniarth 28 darlunian lyfr Cyfraith Hywel Dda: Illustrations from a Welsh Lawbook*, ed. D. Huws, Aberystwyth 1988; see http://www.llgc.org.uk/index.php?id=lawsofhywelddda for the manuscript and its illustrations.

[56] R. R. Davies, 'The twilight of Welsh law, 1284–1536', *History* 51, 1966, 143, 158; Davies, 'Law and national identity in thirteenth-century Wales', 65–6.

[57] Jenkins, *Celtic Law Papers*, 12.

[58] T. M. Charles-Edwards, 'Cynghawsedd : counting and pleading in medieval Welsh law', *Bulletin of the Board of Celtic Studies* 33, 1986, 188–98; R. Chapman Stacey, 'Learning to Plead in Medieval Welsh Law', *Studia Celtica* 38, 2004, 107–24.

[59] Pryce, *Acts*, 158, no. 16.

[60] Pryce, *Acts*, no. 221, 371, agreement with the representatives of King John, 1201.

England according to the law of England, concerning holdings in Wales according to the law of Wales', and in another clause refers to the 'laws of the Welsh'. These examples illustrate the recognition of two distinct, functioning legal traditions.

When contention broke out between Llywelyn ap Gruffydd (Gwynedd) and Gruffydd ap Gwenwynwyn (Powys) in the 1270s, Gruffydd turned to the King of England for support. In response, Llywelyn noted how Gruffydd was 'of Welsh condition', and therefore should be compelled to employ Welsh law.[61] This is very revealing as to the overall pliability and vulnerability of native Welsh law, when another jurisdiction, i.e. in the person of the King of England, could be resorted to in the expectation of intervention or protection. But this was *realpolitik* in the middle ages, especially so in a fragmented Wales. For Llywelyn ap Gruffydd, the last native ruler of Gwynedd before the Edwardian Conquest, 'all nations under the rule of the lord king have their own laws and customs according to their own language'.[62] Though politically fragmented, Llywelyn is stating a case not only for Gwynedd, but for the Wales of *Cyfraith Hywel*.

It was this political fragmentation, however, which allowed the legal tradition to remain in the hands of the practitioners of the law (the lawyers and judges), as opposed to a central, unified authority as elsewhere. Here again we see a contrast with Scotland, where Professor Broun has illustrated how royal authority came to carry significant weight within the judicial process by the mid-thirteenth century, clearly reflected in the existence of the pleadable brieves and the power to appeal to the Crown of Scotland. Within Wales, recourse to law remained on a much more local and community footing.

Finally, I wish to briefly mention what happened next to *Cyfraith Hywel*, for with the Edwardian conquest we may expect such a royal as Edward I to act as the central authority-figure for law and justice within Wales. This, however, was not so straightforward. Post-1284, certain aspects of native Welsh practice would not to be tolerated within the newly created Principality of Wales, for example, the kin-based compensatory system for felonies (e.g. homicide, theft, larceny).[63] A criminal, therefore, was to be punished by the standards of English Law. However, other aspects of native law were to be retained: for example, the native Welsh system of land holding, 'by Welsh tenure … and according to Welsh custom', or to take a further example, the virginity-payment (*amobr*) to the local lord upon a marriage of a girl from his jurisdiction, which could be quite lucrative for the lord in question and an incentive for its retention.[64]

---

[61] Davies, 'The twilight of Welsh law, 1284–1536', 151.

[62] M. Richter, 'The political and institutional background to national consciousness in medieval Wales', in *Nationality and the Pursuit of National Independence*, ed. T. M. Moody, Historical Studies (Irish Conference of Historians) 11, Belfast 1978, 54–5.

[63] Davies, 'The twilight of Welsh law', 147–8.

[64] Davies, 'The twilight of Welsh law, 145–6, 152; R. R. Davies, 'The survival of the blood-

This simple statement of what was abolished and what was retained after 1284 masks a fundamental shift in the standing of native Welsh law within Wales, now that the leading political figure in the form of the king of England adhered to a different legal system; access to which, by the late thirteenth century, was a privilege and not an automatic right. Therefore, native Welsh law continued to be a marker of identity, but could also be one of inferiority and exclusion. When the King's free tenants of North Wales appealed to the king (Edward II) and his council for the possible extension of English law in the following words:

> they are greatly impoverished because they cannot sell their lands or give them according to the laws and customs of England, for if a gentleman of the country has a carucate of land and has five sons or more, the land will be divided up among them after the death of their father and so far from degree to degree so that they become each a beggar living on their parents ... for which grievance they pray that they may have leave to sell their lands ... they would sell according to the law and custom of the Kingdom of England; for the profit of the King.... (1320–22) [65]

the response given was, 'the King does not feel himself advised to do away with the ancient customs of Wales'. Law had become a tool which could be strategically applied or denied to maintain the status quo in an area, or to protect the established privileges of certain communities when so desired. Not everyone sought change in local practice it must be noted which once again reflects the strong regional variations and divisions within Wales. While the tenants of North Wales (above) wished for an extension of English Common Law within their community, the liegemen of West Wales sought the reverse,

> The lord the King, father of the present King, after the conquest of Wales granted them their laws and customs which they had before the conquest, which [are called] keveretz Howel (Cyfraith Hywel) and which they and their ancestors have used in all particulars until the thirteenth year of the present King [1319–20] [when Roger de] Mortimer ... introduced [the law] of England which is unfamiliar to your liege people and entirely contrary to their laws and usages, to the great loss and disinheritance of the same ... wherefore all the people of those parts feel themselves seriously aggrieved, and pray the King that they may have their laws and customs in all particulars as he had granted them after the conquest ... (1319–20). [66]

Here, English Law was too 'unfamiliar' and permission is sought to apply 'their laws and customs', i.e. native Welsh law to proceedings. Unfortunately, the record

---

feud in medieval Wales', *History* 54:182, 1969, 338–57.

[65] *Calendar of Ancient Petitions Relating to Wales: Thirteenth to Sixteenth Century*, ed. W. Rees, History and Law Series 28, Cardiff 1975, no. 3179, 16–7.

[66] *Ibid.*, no. 7288, 245–6.

does not contain an answer to the liegmen's plea.[67] The co-existence of two legal systems and in turn two communities (of Welsh/Welshries and English/Englishries) under one authority, and the thorny (but crucial) issue of jurisdiction, continued to be a great source of tension throughout the fourteenth and into the fifteenth century, to the point of rebellion. But that is for another day.[68] In both pre-Conquest and post-Conquest Wales, on the matter of being 'of Welsh condition', law and one's legal tradition is very much central to any definition.

To conclude with the texts: the legal writings are of particular importance as they allow us to ground ourselves in contemporary thought through a profession which held a position of privilege in society. By the nature of this profession, we read detailed commentary about the nuts and bolts of social order and in turn its people. From this legal standpoint, a man could be labelled or declare himself a Welshman (*Cymro*, lit. a person or member of the same locality or district) by blood, by land tenure, by language, and post-1284, by whether or not he followed native Welsh law or was permitted to do so. And we discover how patterns of loyalty remained first and foremost within his locality, to his lord and his kin-group. With medieval Scotland, a political kingdom was formed and on this foundation a community followed. With medieval Wales, a distinct community was ever present in the absence of a unified polity, and one with a shared legal tradition and identity in the fabric of its composition.

[67] For further examples see, Davies, 'The twilight of Welsh law', 150.
[68] Recent scholarship has begun to move towards investigating the more commercial and financial opportunities open to the native Welsh within the context of co-existence and race relations within medieval Wales (e.g., 'a differentiation in fiscal privilege' rather than distinction in legal status between peoples), see J. Beverley Smith, '"Distinction and Diversity" : the Common Lawyers and the Law of Wales', in *Power and Identity in the Middle Ages: Essays in Memory of Rees Davies*, ed. H. Pryce and J. L. Watts, Oxford 2007, 143; also M. Stevens, 'Wealth, status and "race" in the Ruthin of Edward II', *Urban History* 32:1, 2005, 17–32.

Becoming a Nation: Scotland in the Twelfth and Thirteenth Centuries

DAUVIT BROUN

Of all the nations of Britain and Ireland, the Scots in the twelfth and thirteenth century are particularly difficult to talk about.[1] The problem is one of basic terminology. When we refer to the Irish and the Welsh in this period, everyone knows who we mean. The English in the aftermath of the Norman Conquest are a little more difficult. The obvious question here is: when did the conquerors become 'English'? Although it is a challenge to answer this, the question itself is readily understandable. The situation of a conquering élite eventually assuming the identity of the people they conquered is a recognised phenomenon that has occurred in other places and times. What makes Scotland especially difficult is that the way Scottish identity developed in the twelfth and thirteenth centuries does not conform to any familiar pattern. In the twelfth century the term 'Scots' referred particularly to the native inhabitants of only a small part of what is now Scotland. This original 'Scottish' region was only part of the kingdom, and did not include the area from Stirling to Berwick (including Edinburgh) which was where nearly all the most important royal centres were situated. By around 1300, however, 'Scots' meant what it means today: all the inhabitants of Scotland. The situation is further complicated by significant immigration from England in the twelfth century, particularly by members of what may be called the Anglo-Norman or English-French élite (who in the twelfth century came to regard themselves as English).[2] This English élite regarded the Welsh and Irish with disdain as barbarians, so it would be easy to assume that they regarded native Scots in the same way: the original Scots

[1] I would like to thank Professor Hirokazu Tsurushima for the invitation to give the lecture on which this paper is based, and for his exceptional hospitality. I would also like to acknowledge the AHRC for funding the project, the 'Paradox of Medieval Scotland', under whose auspices this article has been completed, as well as its sister article, 'A second England? Scotland and the monarchy of Britain in *The First English Empire*', in *The First English Empire*, ed. Seán Duffy and Susan Foran, Dublin forthcoming. These two articles belong to a group on Scottish identity in the twelfth and thirteenth centuries (others are cited in nn. 10, 23 and 28) between which there is some overlap.
[2] See, for example, John Gillingham, *The English in the Twelfth Century: Imperialism, National Identity, and Political Values*, Woodbridge 2000, 123–42, and Prof. M. T. Flanagan's article in this volume.

spoke Gaelic, a Celtic language very close to Irish.[3] Nevertheless, by around 1300 the descendants of these English incomers identified themselves as 'Scots' like everyone else in Scotland. The striking change in who were the Scots in this period is a particular puzzle, therefore, not only because, on the face of it, everyone eventually adopted the identity of what may be seen as a minority, who lived beyond the area most closely associated with royal government in this period, but also because it was adopted by an élite who once regarded Scots as uncivilised savages. In this paper I will attempt to explain this change. I will begin by giving more detail about Scottish history before 1300, and then look more closely at when Scottish identity began to be applied to all the kingdom's inhabitants. This will provide the key to a possible solution to the puzzle of how Scottish identity was adopted by the king's subjects at large. The basis of my approach is to try to discern what being a Scot meant to those living in the kingdom in the twelfth and thirteenth centuries.[4] The limited sources make it possible, of course, to access the identity and thinking of only a very few in this period. What is at stake is explaining the emergence of what can readily be recognised as the most basic elements of Scottish identity today. It is only in this limited sense that my paper is about Scotland 'becoming a nation'.

Scotland's early development in most books is usually described as a gradual process of unification involving Gaels (*Scoti* in Latin) and Picts, Norse and Britons, and also the English in the north of the old kingdom of Northumbria. This process was largely completed, it is said, when the kingdom of Scotland reached its current southern boundary after the battle of Carham on the River Tweed in 1018. Unfortunately it is possible to challenge almost every aspect of this account, but that is not my purpose on this occasion.[5] I will confine myself to one of the main objections, which is that no attention is paid in this standard narrative to what 'Scotland' or 'Scots' meant to people *at that time*. In particular, the typical textbook account is written on the assumption that there was no distinction between the country, 'Scotland', and the territory ruled by the king of Scots. This is not a surprise: it seems very natural to our modern way of thinking to regard 'kingdom' and 'country' as identical. How could it be otherwise: was not Scotland a kingdom? When we look at any source written in the Scottish kingdom before the thirteenth century, however, it is apparent that 'Scotland' (in any language) typically referred to only part of the kingdom. It was sometimes used as the name of the entire landmass north of the Firth of Forth, or more commonly to denote the region north

[3]   Gillingham, *The English in the Twelfth Century*, 3–18, 145–60.
[4]   For a wider discussion of being a Scot, particularly in a foreign context, see Matthew H. Hammond, 'The use of the name Scot in the central middle ages. Part 1: Scot as a byname', *Journal of Scottish Names Studies* 1, 2007, 37–60.
[5]   This is discussed in Dauvit Broun, 'Scotland before 1100: writing Scotland's origins', in *Scotland: The Making and Unmaking of the Nation c.1100–1707*, ed. Bob Harris and Alan R. MacDonald, vol.i, *The Scottish Nation: Origins to c.1500*, Dundee 2006, 1–16.

of the Firth of Forth, east of Argyll and south of Moray. Either way, it was almost unheard of for 'Scotland' to be thought of as stretching south of the Forth. This is despite the fact that, for nearly 250 years before 1200, the area around Edinburgh had been controlled by kings of Scots; they eventually extended their domain to the River Tweed in the early eleventh century. In other words, the king of Scots had loyal subjects south of the Forth who did *not* think that they lived in Scotland, although they were firmly part of the kingdom.

What country did they think they lived in? There are only a couple of surviving texts which can offer an answer. In one of these, written about 1180, Adam, prior of Dryburgh Abbey on the north bank of the River Tweed, described himself as living 'in the land of England and the kingdom of the Scots'.[6] On the south bank of the Tweed opposite Dryburgh began the diocese of Glasgow, which stretched west to the Firth of Clyde. By the beginning of the twelfth century this region was under the control of the Scottish king or a member of his immediate family. The diocese of Glasgow was referred to in some contexts in Latin as *Cambria* or *Cumbria*, a name derived from the Welsh word for Wales, *Cymry*. Another Latin word for Wales, *Wallia*, was used in the special celebration of Glasgow's patron saint, Kentigern, composed in the late twelfth century or thirteenth century. It was announced at the very beginning of the church-service, in song, that 'Kentigern's holy church dwells in northern Wales not far from Scotland'.[7] Kentigern's holy church was Glasgow cathedral. What was being proclaimed here was that Glasgow was in 'Wales', rather than in Scotland proper.[8]

If we put all this together, it can be seen that, even in the late twelfth century the king of Scots was thought of as ruler of a realm which consisted not only of 'Scotland' (that is, the country north of the Forth), but included part of England in the south-east and also, in the south-west, a country corresponding to the diocese of Glasgow called Cumbria or northern Wales. There were also areas in the twelfth century which acknowledged the authority of the king of Scots only occasionally and more loosely, and which only became more regularly and firmly part of the realm as a result of military force. One of these was Galloway in the south-west, a country which had its own ruler and its own bishop who did not belong to the Scottish church, but owed obedience to the archbishop of York in England. Another was Moray in the north, whose last king was killed in battle in 1130, but which remained a theatre of war against the kings of Scots for another century. In the west was Argyll which also had its own king who, by the thirteenth century,

---

6   Adam of Dryburgh, *De tripartito tabernaculo*, in J.-P. Migne, ed., *Patrologiæ cursus completus ... series Latina*, 221 vols, Paris 1844–64, vol.198, cols 609–792, at col. 723.

7   Dauvit Broun, *Scottish Independence and the Idea of Britain from the Picts to Alexander III*, Edinburgh 2007, 126. The word used for 'Scotland' here is *Albania* (derived from Gaelic *Alba*, 'Scotland'): for a discussion of its significance in this context, see *ibid.*, 164.

8   The ecclesiastical context for this is explored in *ibid.*, chapter V.

belonged to the same family as the kings of the Isles further west. Overlordship of the Western Isles was claimed by the king of Norway, who finally surrendered this to the king of Scots in the Treaty of Perth in 1266. The Northern Isles, in contrast, remained Norwegian (and later Danish) for another two centuries.

Not only did the king of Scots in the twelfth century rule directly over more than one 'country', with 'Scotland' denoting only the historic core of his realm, but his subjects were not all 'Scots'. Before the thirteenth century the 'Scots' were, it seems, chiefly the inhabitants of the region north of the Forth: in short, the Scots were first-and-foremost the people of 'Scotland' in its most restricted sense. There is also some indication that the king's subjects south of the Forth, in what were regarded as parts of England and Wales, saw themselves as 'English' and (in an ecclesiastical context, at least) 'Welsh'. The people of Galloway, for their part, were Galwegians. (In their native language, Gaelic, they were *Gall Gaídel*, which literally means 'foreign Gaels', i.e., Gaelic-speakers of Norse ancestry).[9] The mix of peoples ruled by the king of Scots in the twelfth century was, however, made even more complex by immigrants from England, France and Flanders, who came to the Scottish kingdom either as leading members of society, such as knights, bishops and monastic superiors, or as merchants, monks and retainers. They all arrived, not as conquerors, but as friends and supporters of the king of Scots, or as associates and followers of the king's friends and supporters, or as traders operating under the king's protection. This was in stark contrast to Ireland and Wales, where such immigration was at the expense of native rulers, and was soon harnessed by the king of England as a means of extending and maintaining his power beyond England itself. In what is now Scotland a similar experience of aggressive immigration was only felt in those areas, such as Galloway in the south-west and Moray in the north, where the king of Scots sought to use knights and burgesses to increase his grip on regions that in the early twelfth century had had kings of their own. In the English south-east of the Scottish kingdom and the Welsh or Cumbrian south-west, as well as in 'Scotland' north of the Forth, the English, French and Flemish incomers served to strengthen native power, not diminish it. The leaders of native society who benefited from this included not only the king of Scots himself, but also the earls, who were rulers of regions that typically corresponded roughly to a modern (pre-1975) county (e.g., Angus or Fife) or under half one of the bigger counties (e.g., Buchan and Mar in Aberdeenshire).

At the beginning of the thirteenth century, therefore, the Scottish kingdom was a realm consisting of a number of countries, and the inhabitants of each of these countries, particularly those in positions of power, were of diverse ethnic origin. On the face of it the Scots were simply the predominant native population in 'Scotland', that is, in the ancient core of the kingdom north of the Forth. By the

---

[9] See most recently Thomas Owen Clancy, 'The Gall-Ghàidhel and Galloway', *Journal of Scottish Name Studies* 2, 2008, 19–50.

end of the thirteenth century, however, when King Edward I of England attempted to destroy the Scottish kingdom, the situation had been transformed. Although the evidence is patchy, it appears that all these different peoples identified themselves as Scots. Certainly those, like the monks of Melrose on the banks of the River Tweed who had identified themselves as English subjects of the Scottish king, now regarded themselves as Scots (without necessarily losing the ethnicity of their native language, which for two more centuries was known as *Inglis*, 'English'). They also regarded knights of English and ultimately French origin, like their neighbour Guy de Balliol, as Scots as well.[10] Also, not only were all the king's subjects 'Scots', but his realm was seen as a single country, 'Scotland'. There was no more talk of the kingdom including parts of England or Wales. The entire kingdom was simply 'Scotland'.

In this change we can recognise in a Scottish context the emergence of the modern European ideal that kingdom (or state), country and people should typically coincide.[11] What it meant to be Scottish for the descendants of immigrants may be gauged in the Declaration of Arbroath (1320).[12] This famous document is a letter sent to the pope in the name of 39 nobles 'and the whole community of the realm of Scotland' justifying Scottish independence from the king of England and Robert Bruce's legitimacy as king of Scots. Here the Scots were imagined as an ancient people who, it was stated, had been ruled by an uninterrupted succession of 113 kings, 'all of our own native and royal stock, without the intervention of any foreigner'. It did not seem to matter that King Robert Bruce's surname betrayed his family's origins in Brix in Normandy in France, and that the impressive list of Scottish nobles named as sponsors of the letter included many of French, Flemish and English extraction. Of the 39 who were named, not much more than five might readily have been reckoned a century earlier as 'Scots' (i.e., as natives of the kingdom's historic core north of the Forth).[13] Yet in the Declaration of Arbroath all 39 nobles identified themselves as Scots, regardless of their

---

[10]   Dauvit Broun, 'Becoming Scottish in the thirteenth century: the evidence of the Chronicle of Melrose', in *West over Sea: Studies in Scandinavian Sea-Borne Expansion and Settlement before 1300. A Festschrift in Honour of Dr Barbara E. Crawford*, ed. Beverley Ballin Smith, Simon Taylor and Gareth Williams, Leiden 2007, 19–32, at 25–7.

[11]   The seminal discussion of the emergence of an expectation that kingdoms and people formed two sides of the same coin is Susan Reynolds, 'Medieval *origines gentium* and the community of the realm', *History* 68, 1983, 375–90. See also Susan Reynolds, *Kingdoms and Communities in Western Europe*, Oxford 1984.

[12]   Variant texts are discussed in Grant G. Simpson, 'The Declaration of Arbroath revitalised', *SHR* 56, 1977, 11–33. There are numerous translations: the one that has become best established is in A. A. M. Duncan, ed. and trans., *John Barbour. The Bruce*, Edinburgh 1997, 779–82.

[13]   That is, reckoned as 'Scots' by the kingdom's inhabitants, rather than in a foreign context. For the latter, see the article by Matthew Hammond cited in note 4.

family origins, and all saw the Scottish past as *their* history. It is clear that what it meant to be 'Scots' – as far as the king's subjects were concerned – had expanded dramatically.

A very similar view of what it meant to be Scottish is also found in a much less well known text, a verse history written c. 1305, about fifteen years earlier than the Declaration of Arbroath.[14] Unlike the Declaration, this text is not pro-Bruce: it includes comments that are critical of Robert Bruce and argues that John Balliol, not the Bruces, had the best claim to be king. In it the Scots, including Bruces and Balliols and the rest, are also imagined as an ancient people and kingdom. It is claimed that the kings of Scots 'had all been Scots like their people', and it is explained graphically that 'a people is defiled when a foreigner becomes king'. It has recently been argued that this was written by someone who regarded John Comyn as the best person to restore Scotland's independence as king when the aged King Edward I of England would eventually die.[15] If so, it plainly did not matter that John Comyn was descended in the male line from an English incomer (apparently of French ancestry) in the reign of David I (1124–53), and was head of a family who were prominent landholders in England in the thirteenth century as well as in Scotland.[16]

When and how did this unification into a single people, the Scots, happen? In the twelfth century an awareness that the kingdom comprised different peoples is found most obviously in the address of royal charters.[17] The peoples named in this way included French, English, Scots and Galwegians, and very occasionally

---

[14]   This text is found in an 'additional book' (*liber extravangans*) appended to Bower's *Scotichronicon*: Dauvit Broun with A. B. Scott, ed. and trans., 'Liber Extravagans', in *Scotichronicon by Walter Bower in Latin and English*, ed. D. E. R. Watt, 9 vols (Aberdeen/Edinburgh 1987–98), vol. ix, 54–127.

[15]   Alexander Grant, 'The death of John Comyn: what was going on?', *SHR* 86, 2007, 176–224, at 205–7, 211–19. John Comyn was killed by Robert Bruce on 10 February 1306, and Bruce took the throne on 25 March, more than a year before Edward I's death.

[16]   Alan Young, *Robert the Bruce's Rivals: The Comyns, 1212–1314*, East Linton 1997, 80–2; the family's position in Scotland began with William Cumin, a clerk of Henry I of England and later archdeacon of Worcester, who became chancellor of David I; his nephew Richard, ancestor of the Comyns of the thirteenth century, was a major landholder in northern England who was granted estates in the Scottish borders: see *ibid.*, 15–17. For the family's possible origins in Normandy see G. W. S. Barrow, *The Anglo-Norman Era in Scottish History*, Oxford 1980, 175 (citing Alan Young, *William Cumin: Border Politics and the Bishopric of Durham, 1141–1144*, York 1978, 5).

[17]   In Scotland it is rare apart from royal charters. There are examples in the charters of David, earl of Huntingdon (King William's brother), Countess Ada (King William's mother), Donnchad II earl of Fife, and Waldef earl of Dunbar. The only example outside the royal family and premier earls that I am aware of is in a charter of Henry Lovel, lord of Hawick: Thomas Thomson, ed., *Liber Cartarum Prioratus Sancti Andree in Scotia. E registro ipso in archivis baronum de Panmure hodie asservato*, Bannatyne Club, Edinburgh 1841, 261.

Welsh and Flemings. This was not a regular feature of royal charters, and disappeared sometime after 1179 (except the odd instance where the text of an earlier charter was reproduced).[18] Did the king no longer refer to the peoples he ruled by name because he now regarded them as a single people? Unfortunately an occasional feature like this could simply go out of fashion.[19] Certainly the Galwegians, even after their lordship had been divided among heiresses, were still regarded as a people with distinct laws which meant that they were excluded from provisions for bringing criminals to justice that were enacted in 1245.[20]

One source that is often referred to as indicating ethnic divisions in Scottish society is the Barnwell Chronicle, which runs as a contemporary witness of events from 1202 to 1225. This was written in eastern England, and is a particularly acute observer of English affairs during the reign of King John (1199–1216). Occasionally its gaze moves north to Scotland when King John is involved, for example in its reference to the uprising in Moray in 1212 when King John paid for a force of mercenary soldiers to support the king of Scots against his dynastic rival, Gofraid Mac Uilleim. The Barnwell Chronicle added a comment at this point which has been quoted repeatedly: 'the most recent kings of Scots', explained the Chronicle, 'profess themselves to be rather Frenchmen in race, manners, language and culture; and, having reduced the Scots to utter servitude, admit only Frenchmen to their service and following'.[21] This graphic image may have held some truth for the way the native nobles and freemen of Moray were treated by William I, king of Scots (1165–1214), but is hardly applicable to other regions, especially the historic core of the kingdom south of Moray. We cannot blame the Barnwell chronicler for

[18] For example, it is found in about 10 per cent of the extant charters of William in the first fifteen years of his reign: G. W. S. Barrow (ed.), in collaboration with W. W. Scott, *Regesta Regum Scottorum* vol ii, *The Acts of William I, King of Scots 1165–1214*, Edinburgh 1971, 77. The last (except a repeat of an earlier charter) could be as late as 1190 (*ibid.*, no.218). The fullest discussion of this type of address is in Kenji Nishioka, 'Scots and Galwegians in the 'peoples address' of Scottish royal charters', *SHR* 87, 2008, 206–32.

[19] It continued in some other contexts: see Hideyuki Arimitsu, 'Migration and assimilation seen from the 'nation address' in post-1066 Britain', in *Migration and Identity in British History. Proceedings of the Fifth Anglo-Japanese Conference of Historians*, ed. David Bates and Kazuhiko Kondo, Tokyo 2006, 7–13.

[20] Thomas Thomson and Cosmo Innes, ed., *Acts of the Parliament of Scotland,* vol.i, part 1, *A.D. MCXXIV–A.D. MCCCCXXIII*, Edinburgh 1844, 403.

[21] *Memoriale Fratris Walteri de Coventria: the Historical Collection of Walter of Coventry*, ed. William Stubbs, Rolls Series, 2 vols, London 1872–3, vol. ii, 206. The Barnwell Chronicle is the contemporary source used for the early thirteenth century by the compilation that was abridged by Walter of Coventry 1293×1307. See *ibid.*, vol. i, xix–xxii, xxxi–xxxii, xxxvii–xxxviii; see also xlv–xlvii. For a nuanced (and different) discussion of this passage see David Carpenter, *The Struggle for Mastery: Britain 1066–1284*, London 2003, 12–13, 258.

assuming that all the king's native subjects were 'Scots', and for failing to make a distinction between the indigenous population of the historic core ('Scots') and the native population of Moray. He was writing many hundreds of kilometres away, and cannot be expected to have appreciated the ethnic and regional situation in the north of the Scottish realm.[22] If we take a Scottish source from very near this time as our guide (a versified king-list composed in or soon after William I's death in December 1214), we find that the king and those close to him did, indeed, have a bitter hatred of Moravians (the natives of Moray), who are decried as a treacherous and apostate people.[23] The target of this invective is unambiguous: it is not the king's native subjects in general, but the men of Moray in particular.

The truth is that native Scots from north of the Forth and south of Moray remained a prominent (although certainly not predominant) presence in the witness-lists of royal charters throughout the twelfth century. During the reign of King William (1165–1214) there was Donnchad earl of Fife, who was also justiciar, and as such was second to the king in the administration of justice. Another justiciar was Gilbert or Gille Brigte, earl of Strathearn.[24] More generally, Matthew Hammond has emphasised the extent to which incomers and natives operated together as leaders of local society.[25] For example, when the king, around 1200, granted to the Cistercian abbey of Coupar the moorland belonging to an estate

---

[22] He may also have had a specifically English agenda in mind when making his famous comments about kings of Scots admitting only Frenchmen to their service. Who were these Frenchmen? The Barnwell Chronicle must mean the English knights and churchmen who had been given lordships and royal offices by kings of Scots. It may be significant, therefore, that the Chronicle has referred to them as *French* rather than English (especially since the same élite in England now identified themselves as English, despite retaining the French language, manners and culture of their conquering ancestors). Perhaps the chronicler's comments should therefore be taken in the context of his criticism of King John's tendency to depend on foreigners (and particularly Frenchmen) at court and in government. There is at least a suspicion, therefore, that the Barnwell Chronicle's vision of a king who admitted only *Frenchmen* to his service and following and reduced the native population to utter servitude may have been written with King John's England specifically in mind. I am indebted for this perspective on the Barnwell Chronicler's comment on Scottish kings to my recollection of a paper given by Professor John Gillingham at a conference on *National Identities in Medieval Europe* sponsored by the European Union Raphael project, held at St George's House, Windsor Castle, and the University of Kent at Canterbury, in April 1998.

[23] Dauvit Broun, 'Contemporary perspectives on Alexander II's succession: the evidence of king-lists', in *The Reign of Alexander II, 1214–49*, ed. Richard D. Oram, Leiden 2005, 79–98, at 84–91.

[24] G. W. S. Barrow, *The Kingdom of the Scots. Government, Church and Society from the Eleventh to the Fourteenth Century*, 2nd edn, Edinburgh 2003, 84–5.

[25] Matthew H. Hammond, 'A prosopographical analysis of society in east central Scotland with special reference to ethnicity, *c.* 1100–*c.* 1260', Ph.D. thesis, University of Glasgow 2005, chapters IV and V.

directly under royal management, possession of the moorland was formally transferred to the abbey by five named individuals on the king's command.[26] These
included an English knight who was lord of another estate in the region, a person
with a Gaelic name who held the native position of judge of the region, and an
obscure individual with a Gaelic name and patronymic who was presumably a
native Scot of local significance. There was no distinction between native and
incomer. The authority of the king of Scots was the same for all freemen regardless of their culture or origin.

It is also true, however, that in the thirteenth century Gaelic gave way increasingly not to French but to English. Those who abandoned Gaelic for English did
not, however, simply 'become English'. This is indicated by a number of places
called *Ingliston*, which have been discussed briefly by Professor Barrow and
Alexander Grant.[27] *Ingliston* is an English name: *ton* is an old form of modern English 'town', and in this context meant an estate, farm or settlement; *Inglis* is simply an old cognate form of the modern word 'English'. *Ingliston* must therefore
denote a settlement of English people. Now, there would be no point in calling a
particular place 'settlement of the English' if everyone in the area thought of themselves as English, because all settlements would be settlements of the English!
There would be nothing distinctive about Ingliston at all. But Ingliston is itself a
place-name in the English language. If the name was created by people in the locality (which I would argue was the usual pattern), rather than by the inhabitants
themselves, then the people in the locality must have been English-speakers who
did *not* think of themselves as English. These English-speakers presumably identified themselves as Scots, and north of the Forth belonged to communities
descended from Scots who had once spoken Gaelic. (In Galloway they may, of
course, have identified themselves as Galwegians.) The places called Ingliston
must therefore refer to small communities of settlers from England, and presumably date to the twelfth or thirteenth century, before the wars of independence.

---

[26]   G. W. S. Barrow, ed., in collaboration with W. W. Scott, *Regesta Regum Scottorum*, vol.
ii, *The Acts of William I, King of Scots 1165–1214*, Edinburgh 1971, no. 420.

[27]   G. W. S. Barrow, 'The Anglo-Scottish border: growth and structure in the middle ages',
in *Grenzen und Grenzregionen/Frontières et régions frontalières/Borders and Border Regions*, ed. Wolfgang Haubrichs and Reinhard Schneider, Saarbrücken 1993, 197–
212, at 210–12; Alexander Grant, 'Aspects of national consciousness in medieval
Scotland', in *Nations, Nationalism and Patriotism in the European Past*, ed. C. Bjørn,
A. Grant and K. J. Stringer, Copenhagen 1994, 68–95, at 78. I follow Alexander Grant's
interpretation, rather than Professor Barrow's. Barrow argued that Ingliston denoted
'a permanent settlement of a distinctively 'English' (we might say Anglo-Norman) character', i.e. mottes (a type of defensive earthwork topped with a castle). Inglistons are
certainly associated with mottes, but they are not identical with them (otherwise Inglistons might be expected to be typically much closer physically to the mottes in question, rather than 'within one kilometre').

When did those who at one stage would have regarded themselves as English start to see themselves as Scots? The best case-study for the adoption of Scottish identity by people who previously considered themselves to be English is the Chronicle of Melrose. Melrose was the premier Cistercian monastery in Scotland and counted the king of Scots as its chief patron. It was located near the border with England, and was therefore in the area which Adam of Dryburgh in 1180 identified as 'in the land of England and the kingdom of the Scots'. As late as the 1250s, the monks of Melrose still regarded Scots as 'others', as a people different from themselves. For example, in the account of events in 1258 (written into the chronicle probably in 1259) the Scots are paired with the people of Galloway as distinct elements in the king's army who were clearly not at home in Roxburghshire, the county where Melrose was situated, and who behaved like unchristian savages.[28] A similar view of the Scots as belonging to some other part of the kingdom is found in the *Miracles of St Margaret*, a text written in the thirteenth century by monks of Dunfermline just a few miles north of the Firth of Forth. On one occasion a Scot is contrasted with a 'local girl', which suggests, as Professor Bartlett has pointed out, that 'clearly the monks of thirteenth-century Dunfermline did not see themselves unequivocally as 'Scots''.[29]

Presumably in each of these examples the Scots were the native population north of the Forth, and did not include incomers such as the predominantly English monks and merchants of Dunfermline. For the Chronicle of Melrose, moreover, 'Scots' was a term loaded with cultural significance, conjuring up an image of people who lived beyond common Christian decency. Nevertheless, a generation after 1259, the monks of Melrose were prepared to identify themselves as Scots. The first indication of this in the chronicle is when events in the mid-1260s were belatedly added sometime between Easter 1286 and (probably) May 1291. When a monk of Melrose called Reginald of Roxburgh (who was presumably of local origin) successfully negotiated the king of Norway's surrender of the Western Isles to the king of Scots in 1266, it was boasted in the chronicle (in a rather flowery style typical of this section) that 'none out of the sons of the Scots has ever been able to accomplish this mission except for the aforesaid monk'. On another occasion a local English knight was described as 'by nation a Scot'.[30] On this evi-

---

28 Broun, 'Becoming Scottish in the thirteenth century: the evidence of the Chronicle of Melrose', 24–5; Dauvit Broun, 'Attitudes of *Gall* to *Gaedhel* in Scotland before John of Fordun', in *Miorun Mòr nan Gall, 'The Great Ill-Will of the Lowlander'? Lowland Perceptions of the Highlands, Medieval and Modern*, ed. Dauvit Broun and Martin MacGregor, Glasgow 2009, 49–82, at 64, 66–7 (originally published in 2007 as an e-book: http://www.arts.gla.ac.uk/scottishstudies/ebooks/miorunmor.htm).

29 *The Miracles of St Æbbe of Coldingham and St Margaret of Scotland*, ed. and trans. Robert Bartlett, Oxford 2003, xli; 84–5 (chap. 6).

30 Broun, 'Attitudes of *Gall* to *Gaedhel* in Scotland before John of Fordun', 73; Broun, 'Becoming Scottish in the thirteenth century: the evidence of the Chronicle of Melrose', 25–7.

dence, slender though it is, it would seem that the critical period when all the king's subjects started to think of themselves as Scots was during Alexander III's personal rule, between about 1260 and his death in 1286. This would mean that, when Edward I led his army to conquer Scotland in 1296, a whole generation had grown up with the idea that all the king's subjects were Scots.

How is this to be explained? In general terms, the adoption of Scottish identity by the different peoples who inhabited the Scottish realm has been interpreted as a result of their shared allegiance to a king whose title was *rex Scottorum*, king of Scots. As Archie Duncan has put it, 'it was as kingdom and then as community that Scotland was put together'.[31] Why, though, did it take until the 1260s, or even later, for monks of Melrose to become Scots – to develop this sense of 'community'? It will be recalled that this area had been controlled by kings of Scots since the eleventh century. This question is even more insistent in the light of another important change. The Chronicle of Melrose, in its account of events in 1216 (written into the chronicle a few years later), refers to the south-east of the kingdom and also Galloway as parts of 'Scotland'.[32] This may seem obvious to us, but it was not so at the time. For example, an account of William I's movements in the months before his death in December 1214 refers to how he 'went into Moray', and, 'returning from Moray to Scotland, went from Scotland into Lothian'.[33] It will be recalled that 'Scotland' up to this time had (for those inside the kingdom) typically meant the region north of the Forth.[34] For the chroniclers at Melrose writing

---

[31] A. A. M. Duncan, 'The making of Scotland', in *Who are the Scots?*, ed. Gordon Menzies, London 1971, 13. See also, for example, G. W. S. Barrow, *Kingship and Unity: Scotland 1000–1306*, London 1981, 153; Barrow, *The Anglo-Norman Era in Scottish History*, 155.

[32] Stratum 9, entered probably in 1218 or not long thereafter: *The Chronicle of Melrose Abbey: a Stratigraphic Edition*, vol.i, *Introduction and Facsimile Edition*, ed. Dauvit Broun and Julian Harrison, Scottish History Society, Woodbridge 2007, 134; *The Chronicle of Melrose from the Cottonian Manuscript, Faustina B. IX in the British Museum*, ed. A. O. and M. O. Anderson with an index by W. Croft Dickinson, London 1936, 62 (where towns in the Merse are described as 'in the southern part of Scotland' when King John of England wasted them in 1216), and at 64 (where Galloway is described as 'in the western part of Scotland' in an account of a supernatural event witnessed there in 1216).

[33] *Johannis de Fordun Chronica Gentis Scotorum*, ed. W. F. Skene, Historians of Scotland vol. i, Edinburgh 1871, 279.

[34] Exceptions are rare: a unique instance among the charters of Mael Coluim IV is an original charter for Walter the Steward which refers to lands south of the Forth as being held on the same terms 'as any earl of baron in the kingdom of Scotland' (*sicut aliquis comes vel baro in regno Scotie*): *Regesta Regum Scottorum*, vol. i, *The Acts of Malcolm IV King of Scots*, ed. G. W. S. Barrow, Edinburgh 1960, no.183, dated by Barrow to 'probably 24 June 1161'. Barrow observes that this is the earliest use of the phrase *regnum Scotie* referring to land south of the Forth (Barrow, *The Anglo-Norman Era in Scottish History*, 153–4, where he also points out that circumlocutions, like 'kingdom of the

not long after 1216, however, it seems that 'Scotland' denoted the name of the whole territory of the kingdom. This means that, from about 1220 until at least 1259, the monks of Melrose thought of themselves as living in Scotland but *not* as Scots. They were happy to call their country 'Scotland', rather than part of England, but still thought of the Scots as wild folk from elsewhere. When they finally began to think of themselves as Scots, it was not simply because they were subjects of the king of Scots, or even because they identified their country as Scotland. There must have been other factors that inspired them to become Scots. One of these, it can be argued, was in the sphere of what may (a little anachronistically) be called property law.[35]

An important initial clue is the extension of the term 'Scotland' to mean the whole kingdom. This can be traced in a distinctive feature in the drafting of charters.[36] It was not uncommon for it to be said that the subject of a donation (be it land or a church or something else) was to be held as freely, peacefully (and so on) as any other similar property was held. (By 'property' here I mean a possession that was conceived of as having the capacity to be held permanently because it was heritable or because it belonged to the Church.) What is particularly interesting is how, in non-royal charters, it became increasingly common to specify that the land or church (or what-have-you) was to be held as freely as any other in the 'kingdom of Scotland' or 'kingdom of the Scots'. Professor Barrow commented that this became common from the end of the twelfth century.[37] As Keith Stringer has pointed out, this phraseology shows that people thought in terms of standard legal customs existing throughout the realm.[38] It is not difficult to see how an expectation that law and custom in relation to property should be the same throughout the king's territory could engender a sense of the kingdom as a single country. This would have become more concrete with the creation of a judicial system across most of the kingdom: by the early thirteenth century there were sher-

---

king of Scots', are more common in charters until the end of the twelfth century). In the charter Mael Coluim states that the lands were given 'after I had received arms', i.e., after he had been knighted by Henry II of England at Tours in 1159. Could there be a connection between the use of *regnum Scotie* – which would not be unusual of someone referring to the kingdom from abroad – and the recollection of the king's achievements while in Henry II's entourage?

35   For brief discussion of another factor – the growth of a money economy – see Dauvit Broun, 'A second England? Scotland and the monarchy of Britain in *The First English Empire*', in *The First English Empire*, ed. Seán Duffy and Susan Foran, Dublin forthcoming.

36   For what follows see Broun, *Scottish Independence and the Idea of Britain*, 9–10.

37   Barrow, *The Anglo-Norman Era in Scottish History*, 153–4: for the earliest example, see note 31, above.

38   Keith J. Stringer, 'The charters of David, earl of Huntingdon and lord of Garioch: a study of Anglo-Scottish diplomatic', in *Essays on the Nobility of Medieval Scotland*, ed. K. J. Stringer, Edinburgh 1985, 72–101, at 90.

iff courts in all regions securely under royal control, and, above the sheriffs, there were justiciars who were each responsible for the administration of the king's justice in 'Scotland' (north of the Forth), in Lothian and in Galloway.

In order to understand how this might, by about 1260, have engendered a heightened sense that all the king's subjects were one people (the 'Scots'), regardless of origin or ethnicity, it is important to consider what practical effect the emerging system of royal courts may have had for anyone who 'counted for something' in Scottish society. It was not only knights and prelates who 'counted', but also those who were referred to, in the catch-all phrase at the end of royal charter-addresses, as *probi homines*, 'men of standing'. At the very least this must have referred to men and women who held property (in the sense outlined above). It is significant, therefore, that royal authority became increasingly important in the sphere of landholding from the mid-thirteenth century.[39] From about 1260 a number of records survive of inquests in sheriff courts initiated by a royal brieve to determine facts relating to a particular landholding. These include the confirmation in a court held by a justiciar-depute in Dumbarton that Richard, a priest, was entitled to hold a named piece of land (1259); the establishing in the sheriff court of Lanark of the terms on which a named land was held of the king by a certain Adam 'of the livery'[40] (1259?); a confirmation in the sheriff court of Forfar that the heirs of Simon the gatekeeper of Montrose Castle were his five daughters, and that Simon owed nothing for his lands except the performance of his duties as gatekeeper (1261); the establishing in the sheriff court of Elgin of Robert the crossbowman's rights to the garden of Elgin Castle (1261); confirmation in the sheriff court of Inverness that a named piece of land ought to be held by Eógan son of Óengus son of Eógan (1262); and confirmation in the sheriff court of Dumbarton of the heirs of Dubgall, brother of Mael Domnaich earl of Lennox (1271).[41] The significance of all this activity is that, by the middle of the thirteenth century, they

[39]   Ian Douglas Willock, *The Origins and Development of the Jury in Scotland*, Stair Society, Edinburgh 1966, 8–14, 32–4. Willock shows that an important early stage was royal involvement in perambulations (especially the establishing of the boundary between pieces of land) which, by the early thirteenth century, was registered in a central record. For a brief overview of the development of royal authority and Scots law in this period, see Hector L. MacQueen, *Common Law and Feudal Society in Medieval Scotland*, Edinburgh 1993, 47–50, and Hector MacQueen, 'Scotland: politics, government and law', in *A Companion to Britain in the Later Middle Ages*, ed. S. H. Rigby Oxford 2003, 283–308, at 293–5.
[40]   'Livery' (or 'Liverance') suggests that Adam or his ancestors were responsible for organising the provisions of an important household.
[41]   *Select Cases of the Thirteenth Century*, ed. T. M. (Lord) Cooper, London 1944, 72–4, 76–8, 81, 85; *Acts of the Parliament of Scotland*, ed. Thomas Thomson and Cosmo Innes, vol.i, part 1, *A.D. MCXXIV–A.D. MCCCCXXIII*, Edinburgh 1844, 98–101 (red pagination); *Registrum Monasterii de Passelet*, ed. Cosmo Innes, Maitland Club, Edinburgh 1832, no. 191.

show that the justiciar's court and the sheriff court had together evolved into a system with the capacity to safeguard property with the force of royal authority. An inquest could be completed in is little as a fortnight of the date of the brieve.[42] It is also noticeable that the cases I have listed involved small landowners, women as well as men, and also people from Moray in the north and the Lennox in the west who must still have been Gaelic-speakers.

This capacity to guarantee property by invoking royal authority was especially important when someone claimed that they had been dispossessed. The brieve of inquest – which was designed simply to establish facts in response to specific questions rather than to initiate a process of argument and counter-argument – could, it seems, be used by a party in a dispute. In 1262 the burgesses of Peebles, for example, obtained a brieve instructing the sheriff and bailies of Peebles to inquire whether a named individual had dispossessed the burgesses of a peat-moss: a month later a narrative of the dispute in support of the claim of the burgesses was duly returned to the king. It is not known what action the king then took. Another mechanism was to obtain a 'pleadable brieve' – that is, a royal brieve instructing the justiciar or sheriff to initiate a different process in which the emphasis was on argument and counter-argument (hence the term 'pleadable').[43] This type of brieve was borrowed from English legal practice, and first appears in Scotland in the 1230s.[44] In England it lay at the heart of royal protection of 'private' property because of a rule that nobody could be subjected to a legal challenge to their heritable land without a royal brieve (or 'writ' in English parlance). Hector MacQueen has therefore argued persuasively that the borrowing of pleadable brieves from England is the most likely explanation of the origins of this rule (known as the 'brieve rule') in Scotland.[45] If so, this would have created an explicit and direct bond between royal authority and property in land (and thereby status).

[42]   Cooper, *Select Cases of the Thirteenth Century*, 77–8.
[43]   See Hector L. MacQueen, 'Pleadable brieves, pleading and the development of Scots law', *Law and History Review* 4, 1986, 403–22. The other class of brieve (discussed above), which required a 'return' of information in response to specific questions, is known as 'retourable' rather than 'pleadable'. After the thirteenth century pleadable brieves were only heard before the justiciar.
[44]   MacQueen, *Common Law and Feudal Society in Medieval Scotland*, 137–8. For an early case before a sheriff see Cooper, *Select Cases of the Thirteenth Century*, 40–1, discussed in Hector L. MacQueen, 'The brieve of right in Scots law', *Journal of Legal History* 3, 1982, 52–70, at 52–3, 55.
[45]   MacQueen, *Common Law and Feudal Society in Medieval Scotland*, 106–11. The doubt which MacQueen detects in the reference to this rule by Alexander MacDonald of Islay in 1296 might be explained by the special circumstances of the West Highlands and Islands, which had only in 1293 come under the jurisdiction of a local sheriff. It is likely that, in reality, the 'brieve rule' had been meaningless in the region because it had been unenforceable.

Experience of these procedures was not confined to the parties who were immediately involved in cases heard before the sheriff or justiciar. It is also significant that the outcomes were decided upon by men of social standing in the locality acting as the jury. Unfortunately the evidence is patchy, making it very difficult to assess how regularly such cases may have occurred. If these brieves did become a frequent occurrence in sheriff courts across the realm during the personal rule of Alexander III, then it would be possible to envisage how all those with property could have experienced royal authority not simply as something notionally or occasionally available to safeguard their lands (however small), but now as something with the capacity to be routine and effective.[46] Even if these cases arose only occasionally, it could still be argued that the 'brieve rule' of itself would have been sufficient to foster a bond between royal authority and heritable land in the consciousness of those obliged to attend the courts of sheriff and justiciar. Being a subject of the king of Scots would now have had practical force that related directly to who you were in your world. An indication of this more explicit sense that all the king's subjects were Scots bound together by royal justice is to be found in the treaty of Perth in 1266 in which (it will be recalled) the Western Isles were surrendered by the king of Norway to the king of Scots. As Hector MacQueen has pointed out, the idea of the kingdom as a single jurisdiction applicable to all its inhabitants was articulated for the first time in this document.[47] This seems to match very well with seeing the kingdom not only as a single country, 'Scotland', but also a single people, 'the Scots'.[48]

If this, in essence, was a key element in how the king's subjects as a whole came to regard themselves as Scots, then it was not based on family origins, language or culture. This is consistent with the image of Scottishness projected in the Declaration of Arbroath in 1320 and in the slightly earlier verse history. What was emphasised in each text was the Scots as a people ruled by a conspicuously long and unbroken line of their own kings. According to this definition, the origins and culture of the thirty-nine nobles named as the Declaration's sponsors were irrelevant to their sense of being Scottish. They could be as French or English or Flemish in culture or ancestry as it was possible to be: what made them Scottish was not language or a native pedigree, but their obedience to the king of Scots. This idea of Scottishness was not peculiar to those who drafted the Declaration of Arbroath.[49] It is found, for example, in the celebration of Robert Bruce's career as

46 See the comment in MacQueen, *Common Law and Feudal Society in Medieval Scotland*, 109. There is some evidence that, as early as the twelfth century, procedures in non-royal courts could be supervised by royal officials (see *ibid.*, 42).

47 Hector L. MacQueen, '*Regiam Majestatem*, Scots law and national identity', SHR 74, 1995, 1–25, at 10.

48 Broun, 'Becoming Scottish in the thirteenth century: the evidence of the Chronicle of Melrose', 30–1.

49 For what follows see Dauvit Broun, 'The Declaration of Arbroath: pedigree of a

king which was written by John Barbour in 1375 or 1376. Barbour tells us, for example, that Laurence of Abernethy, when he rode with his men to help King Edward II of England at Bannockburn, 'was at that time still an Englishman'.[50] Laurence of Abernethy's ancestors in the male line in the twelfth century were native, Gaelicspeaking lords north of the Forth. But this was irrelevant: in Barbour's eyes Laurence's allegiance to the king of England made him an Englishman. To take another case from Barbour's work: when Sir Ingram de Umfraville appeared in King Robert Bruce's court just before defecting to England, it is reported by Barbour that he, Sir Ingram, 'was then with the king as a Scotsman'.[51] Sir Ingram's English credentials were impeccable, but again this was irrelevant: he was a Scot as long as he was in the Scottish king's allegiance.

There is one nagging question about this extension of Scottish identity to all the king's subjects. It will be recalled that, as late as 1259, the monks of Melrose regarded Scots as sacrilegious savages. Yet within a generation they were prepared to identify themselves as Scots. Could their deeply negative view of Scots have disappeared so quickly? The answer is that it need not have disappeared at all. The key to this puzzle is an important change in terminology which can be detected during the personal rule of Alexander III, between about 1260 and 1286.[52] It is during this period that the first mention of 'highland Scots' can be traced. The evidence for this has only recently come to light. It was generally believed by scholars that the earliest account of the division of Scotland into Gaelic-speaking 'Highlanders' and English-speaking 'Lowlanders' was in John of Fordun's *Chronicle of the Scottish People*, datable to the 1380s. It is now clear, however, that Fordun's *Chronicle* is based almost entirely on an earlier work, datable to 1285, of which only a fragment survives (known to scholars as *Gesta Annalia* I). This, in turn, had an earlier history at its core that may be dated to the 1260s.[53] There is a good chance that this earlier work is the ultimate source of Fordun's account of the division of Scotland into Highlanders and Lowlanders. Certainly the definition of a 'highland Scot' is the same as what is found in *Gesta Annalia* I of 1285. In both cases 'highland Scot' refers specifically to Gaelic-speaking native Scots. The adoption of this term was important because it allowed a clear distinction to be drawn between Scots of the kind denigrated in the Chronicle of Melrose, who were now classified as highlanders, and other Scots, who could be seen as naturally 'civi-

---

nation?', in *The Declaration of Arbroath: History, Significance, Setting*, Society of Antiquaries Monograph Series, ed. Geoffrey Barrow, Edinburgh 2003, 1–12.

[50] *John Barbour. The Bruce*, ed. and trans. A.A.M. Duncan, Edinburgh 1997, 509 (bk. XIII, line 560/556).

[51] *Ibid.*, 703 (bk. XIX, lines 73–74).

[52] For what follows, see Broun, 'Attitudes of *Gall* to *Gaedhel* in Scotland before John of Fordun', 73–7.

[53] Broun, *Scottish Independence and the Idea of Britain*, chapters VIII and IX.

lized'. It was possible to be a Scot and to see yourself as quite different from Scots you might regard as barbarians, who in your mind (if not in reality) were located away in the mountains. In this way monks of Melrose could become Scots while still retaining their prejudice against Gaelic-speaking Scots. Finally, it is notable that, if we look further at *Gesta Annalia* I and at the account of the Highland/Lowland divide that survives in Fordun's *Chronicle*, both share the same idea of what makes a Scot a Scot. In *Gesta Annalia* I a 'true Scot' is represented as someone who was loyal to the king, even though it would cost him his life. The example of a 'true Scot' given in the text is of a lord of Galloway who was killed by his brother. In Fordun's *Chronicle* it is explained that Highlanders, for all their shortcomings, are loyal and obedient to the king and kingdom if they are governed properly. The key to being a Scot in their eyes, therefore, is allegiance to the king of Scots. This clearly coincides with the vision of the Scots in the Declaration of Arbroath as a people obedient to their king since ancient times. It was possible for all the king's subjects to be Scots and, at the same time, have different languages, cultures and family origins.

Professor Donaldson has observed that 'it is remarkable that a separate state, with its frontier at the Tweed and the Solway, ever came into existence and preserved its identity', and that 'the full explanation remains mysterious'.[54] In this paper I can only claim to have sketched how the puzzling change in Scottish identity in the twelfth and thirteenth centuries, and the origins of Scotland as we know it today, might be understood, at least in part. A much fuller explanation is, happily, a real possibility in the near future because of the work of a number of scholars. I will name only those who have completed their doctorates in the past couple of years, or who are still Ph.D. students. The very beginning of the process of uniting the diverse peoples ruled by the king of Scots in the twelfth century is being made clear in the work of Kenji Nishioka.[55] The next stage in this process, looking particularly at changing patterns of governance in the late twelfth and early thirteenth century, has been researched by Alice Taylor with seminal work on the collections of royal laws and on charter diplomatic.[56] Matthew Hammond has used the techniques of prosopography to challenge the deep-rooted habit of discussing this period of Scottish history in terms of Anglo-Normans/English versus Celts.[57] He has argued convincingly that Scottish society in the thirteenth century func-

[54]   Gordon Donaldson, *Scotland: The Shaping of a Nation*, 2nd edn, London 1980, 23.
[55]   For example, Kenji Nishioka, 'Scots and Galwegians in the 'peoples address' of Scottish royal charters', *SHR* 87, 2008, 206–32.
[56]   Alice Taylor, 'Aspects of Law, Kingship and Government in Scotland *c.*1100–1230', D.Phil. thesis, University of Oxford 2009.
[57]   Matthew H. Hammond, 'A prosopographical analysis of society in east central Scotland with special reference to ethnicity, *c.*1100–*c.*1260', Ph.D. thesis, University of Glasgow 2005.

tioned in the localities as a single entity. The way this society began to engage increasingly with the king as guarantor of their property has also been illuminated by the research of Akihiro Takamori.[58] A deeper and fuller understanding of strategies for consolidating property-rights is being achieved in the work of Andrew Smith.[59] There is also a very significant project in the Celtic Department of Glasgow University researching place-names as a source for understanding where Gaelic was spoken and when.[60] This may show, for example, whether the critical stage of identifying Gaelic-speaking Scots as Highlanders, which I have suggested might be datable to the 1260s, may be linked to a retreat of Gaelic from the Lowlands. Another approach to this question would be to study the history of stereotypes of Highlanders not just in Scotland but elsewhere, and in different periods.[61] An interdisciplinary collection of essays along these lines has recently been published on the website of the Centre of Scottish and Celtic Studies at Glasgow University. Last, but not least, is the AHRC-funded project, the 'Paradox of Medieval Scotland', involving the Universities of Glasgow and Edinburgh and King's College, London, which (among other things) will result in a web resource with everything that can be extracted from just over 6,000 documents about people and interrelationships in Scotland 1093–1286. There can be little doubt that, in the light of all this work, our understanding of this pivotal period of Scottish history will be deepened considerably, and much of what I have sketched here will need to be modified.

---

[58] Akihiro Takamori, 'Regnal consolidation and regional networks: charters and religious benefactions in the diocese of Glasgow, c. 1120 to 1270', Ph.D. thesis, University of Glasgow 2009.

[59] Andrew Smith, 'Kelso Abbey as a focus of social interactions in the 12th and 13th centuries', current Ph.D. thesis, University of Glasgow.

[60] 'The Expansion and Contraction of Gaelic in Medieval Scotland: the Onomastic Evidence', funded by the Arts and Humanities Research Council. The Principal Investigator is Professor Thomas Owen Clancy; the Lead Researcher is Dr Simon Taylor; the Research Assistant is Gilbert Márkus and the PhD student is Peter McNiven. A pioneering series by the same team is *The Place-Names of Fife*, 5 vols (Donington, from 2006, of which 3 vols are already published). See http://www.gla.ac.uk/departments/celtic/place-names/placenameshome.htm.

[61] *Mìorun Mòr nan Gall, 'The Great Ill-Will of the Lowlander'? Lowland Perceptions of the Highlands, Medieval and Modern*, ed. Dauvit Broun and Martin MacGregor, Glasgow 2009 (originally published as an e-book: http://www.arts.gla.ac.uk/scottishstudies/ebooks/miorunmor.htm in 2007).

Strategies of Distinction: Defining Nations in Medieval Ireland

MARIE THERESE FLANAGAN

The term nation presents difficulties of definition for a medieval historian, but especially for historians of medieval Ireland. The Latin usage of *natio* does not necessarily translate into what is understood today in English by the term 'nation'. In medieval Ireland the Latin *natio* frequently equated with *familia*, signifying a particular descent group. Such a familial usage survived in Ireland into the sixteenth century when there can still be found instances of the term *suae nationis capitaneus*, 'captain of his nation', deployed to describe simply a head of a family; and it might be used in that sense to refer to families both of native Irish origin as well as those from the settler population that moved into Ireland from the late twelfth century onwards, drawn predominantly from South Wales and England. In 1500, for example, the death of William Barry, *suae nationis capitaneus*, was reported.[1] William Barry was a descendant of one of the very earliest newcomer families into late twelfth-century Ireland.[2] *Natio* therefore might simply connote the family into which a particular individual had been born.

An alternative usage of *natio* is to be found in the document known as the Remonstrance addressed around 1317 to Pope John XXII by the Irish people (*populus Hiberniacus*) under the leadership of Domnall Ó Néill, styled king of Ulster.[3] The purpose of the Remonstrance was to justify Irish support for the involvement in Ireland at that time of the king of Scots, and to argue a case against the legality of the rule of the king of England in Ireland. As a result of a colonising movement that began in the late twelfth century, Ireland had become a land of two nations, the Irish and the English. The Remonstrance referred to the Irish and to the 'English of Ireland' as distinct nations. Furthermore, in a memorable phrase, the Remonstrance claimed that 'the English inhabitants of our land of Ireland, who say that they belong to a middle nation (*media natio*) are so different in behaviour

---

[1] 'The Annals of Nenagh', ed. D. F. Gleeson, *Analecta Hibernica* 12, 1943, 163.

[2] For the earliest Barrys in Ireland, see Giraldus Cambrensis, *Expugnatio Hibernica*, ed. A. B. Scott and F. X. Martin, Dublin 1978, 32–9, 116–17, 156–7, 188–9, 192–3.

[3] The most accurate Latin version with English translation is in Walter Bower, *Scotichronicon*, vi, ed. D. E. R. Watt, Aberdeen 1991, 384–403 (= *Scotichronicon*, XII, cc.26–32). The reference to the 'middle nation' is on pp. 392–3.

from the English of England, or from other nations, that they can most properly be called a nation not of middling but of extreme perfidy'.

The Remonstrance therefore asserts that the English of Ireland themselves claimed to be 'a middle nation'. This is the only known occurrence of the term 'middle nation' applied to the English in Ireland.[4] What it suggests is that the English settlers in Ireland were a self-consciously distinct grouping, distinguishable not only from the native Irish but also within the wider English nation; in short that there was a distinctive settler identity in Ireland. The description, 'middle nation', illustrates in an acute way just how difficult the settler population in Ireland sometimes found it to define its own identity: there was a continual interplay not only between the native Irish and the incomers, but also between the English colony in Ireland, which produced its own variety of Englishness, and its original English homeland.

In the 1317 Remonstrance the sense of the term *natio* approximates to its more modern usage of *natio* as a group of people with a sense of some kind of common unity, such as a common ethnicity or political identity, a common language, or a common sense of history or shared historical experience. That is what was claimed in the Remonstrance for the Irish nation. From an alternative perspective – that of the English settler community in Ireland – the nation was an isolated entity, defined oppositionally in relation to the indigenous population, and occasionally even in relation to the English of England. Strategies of distinction are already apparent among the first generation of colonists on the evidence of Gerald of Wales (also known as Giraldus Cambrensis and Gerald, archdeacon of Brecon), who wrote his *History and Topography of Ireland* and the *Expugnatio Hibernica*, 'Conquest of Ireland', around 1189 as an apologist for English intervention in Ireland. Gerald's writings reveal that from the outset the settler population sought to define itself as distinctively different from, and superior to, the native Irish,[5] but that the settler community also early identified a sense of difference from the English of England which resulted from the specific circumstances in which it found itself in Ireland. In the *Expugnatio Hibernica*, Gerald puts into the mouth of his kinsman, Maurice fitz Gerald, the following rhetorical speech:

> Surely we do not look to our own people for succour? We are now constrained in our actions by this circumstance, that just as we are English as far as the Irish are concerned, likewise to the English we are Irish, and the

---

[4]   See discussion by James Lydon, 'The middle nation' in James Lydon, *The English in Medieval Ireland*, Dublin 1984, 1–26.

[5]   See John Gillingham, 'Conquering the barbarians: war and chivalry in twelfth-century Britain', *Haskins Society Journal* 4, 1993, 67–84, reprinted in John Gillingham, *The English in the Twelfth Century: Imperialism, National Identity and Political Values*, Woodbridge 2000, 41–58.

inhabitants of this island and the other assail us with an equal degree of hatred.[6]

Tensions and rivalries between the English colonists established in Ireland and subsequent incomers from England were identified by Gerald of Wales as problematic as early as around 1189. Although the English colony in Ireland did not produce substantial historical narratives or political discourses, enough survives to show that the settlers knew how and why they had arrived in Ireland and from where they had come. As a founding story, the narrative related by Gerald of Wales remained the most important source for ideas of identity for the settler community down to the sixteenth century.[7]

However, before exploring further the distinction between the Irish and the English of Ireland that emerged in the context of English conquest and settlement from the late twelfth century onwards, let us begin with the first identifiable nation in medieval Ireland. Although the historic period (that is, the period from which written evidence is extant) was inaugurated in Ireland when the island was converted to Christianity in the course of the fifth century, and a written culture introduced as a concomitant of the adoption of the Christian religion, it is only from the seventh century that written evidence survives in sufficient quantity for historians to be able meaningfully to analyse Irish society and its notions of identity. Irish society, as it appears around AD 700, was a politically fragmented society with a multiplicity of kings and kingdoms of varying power and size. Nevertheless, those localised polities shared unifying features, such as a common language (with no evidence in the extant sources of dialectal variations), and common legal traditions, exemplified in the *Senchas Már*, the principal compilation of customary Irish law committed to writing around AD 700.[8] Most important of all was the contribution made by the Christian religion in forging a developing sense of a common Irish identity. The first identifiable conception of the island of Ireland as constituting *one* people was as a 'Christian nation', an idea that derived from the Bible: it was modelled on a belief that the Christian church comprised the peoples that had been baptised in response to Christ's command to his apostles to go forth and to make disciples of all nations (*omnes gentes*) – 'Go out therefore, making disciples of all nations, baptising them in the name of the Father, the son and the Holy Spirit' (Gospel of Matthew 28.19). The notion that there was an Irish *gens* that was greater than the individual dynastic, or political, groupings in early Ireland is graphically evidenced in the hagiographical life of the fifth-century British missionary, Patrick, written about AD 690 by the Christian scholar, Muirchú. In his

6   Giraldus, *Expugnatio Hibernica*, 80–1.
7   Hiram Morgan, 'Giraldus Cambrensis and the Tudor conquest of Ireland' in *Political Ideology in Ireland*, ed. Hiram Morgan, Dublin 1999, 22–44.
8   *Corpus Iuris Hibernici*, ed. D. A. Binchy, 6 vols, Dublin 1978.

imaginative reconstruction of Patrick's evangelising mission in fifth-century Ireland, Muirchú depicted the Irish as a people who, by virtue of their baptism, had gained a place among *omnes gentes*. On the basis of what he had read in Scripture, Muirchú believed that Christ had commanded his apostles to go out to the ends of the earth and to baptise the nations (*gentes*), and that it was Patrick who had fulfilled that command in relation to the people of the whole island of Ireland.[9]

Muirchú's concern with the status of the Irish as a Christian people is analogous with that of Gregory of Tours in his *History of the Franks*, written about AD 590 or Bede's *Ecclesiastical history of the English people*, written about AD 730. In the case of Muirchú, however, it took the form, not of a narrative history of the Irish people, but of a hagiographical re-telling of the evangelising mission of Patrick who converted the Irish to christianity. In Muirchú's presentation of Patrick's mission, everyone on the island of Ireland belonged to a single *gens*. And there was but one baptiser, Patrick, the apostle of the *gens*, and that apostle, Patrick, was also the heavenly protector of the Irish, such that on the last day of judgement the Irish would be met at the gates of heaven, not by the apostle Peter, but by their own apostle, Patrick. Muirchú elaborated the notion of Patrick as the apostle of Irish, but he also concomitantly promoted the notion of the Irish as a Christian nation. Muirchú therefore fashioned a unifying Christian identity that could operate in the secular world as an alternative to competing dynasties and population groups, and even offered the Irish a collective destiny in the Afterlife.

Under the influence of Christian learning, the Irish came increasingly to see themselves in Old Testament terms as a chosen nation. Elaborated alongside that perception was the emergence of the notion of the Irish as a descent group from

---

[9] The most recent edition is *Muirchú moccu Machténi's 'Vita Sancti Patricii': Life of Saint Patrick*, ed. David Howlett, Dublin 2006. For the view that Patrick was to judge *omnes Hibernenses* on the Last Day, see pp. 120–1. For Muirchú's alternative usage of *Scotti* for the Irish people, see his description of Tara as *caput Scotorum*, pp. 58–9. Muirchú was not the first to articulate the view of the Irish as a Christian people, or that Patrick would judge them on the Last Day; the concept is already found in the anonymous Book of the Angel, *c*. AD 675: *The Patrician Texts in the Book of Armagh*; ed. Ludwig Bieler, Scriptores Latini Hiberniae, 10, Dublin 1979, 184–91. It is also evident in the hymn, *Audite omnes amantes*, where Patrick is depicted as apostle of the *Hibernae gentes;* see Andy Orchard, '*Audite omnes amantes*: a hymn in Patrick's praise' in *St Patrick, AD 493–1993*, ed. David Dumville, Woodbridge 1993, 153–73. The earliest vernacular use of *Fir hÉrend*, 'men of Ireland', occurs in *Annals of Inisfallen*, ed. S. Mac Airt, Dublin Institute for Advanced Studies, Dublin 1951, *s.a.* 838 (hereafter *AI*); cf. *Annals of Ulster (to A.D. 1131)*, ed. Gearóid Mac Niocaill, Dublin Institute for Advanced Studies, Dublin 1983, *s.a.* 858.4 (hereafter *AU*). It should be noted that the term *gens* was also used by Hiberno-Latin authors, such as Adomnán, to signify a more restricted ruling group designated in Irish by the terms *dál, corcu*, and names with the suffixes –*rige* and –*acht*. For discussion of *gens* in this usage, see T. M. Charles-Edwards, *Early Irish and Welsh Kinship*, Oxford 1993, 141–65.

a common set of ancestors: an artificial genealogical scheme was forged, presenting the Irish as one huge kindred going back to a remote common ancestor, Míl Espáine, 'Míl of Spain', a borrowing from the Latin phrase, *miles Hispaniae*, 'the Spanish soldier'. Míl was a character fictitiously invented by borrowing from the first Christian universal history, the fourth-century Christian author, Orosius's, 'History against the pagans' (Historiarum adversus paganos libri VII). An emerging discipline of Christian historiography resulted in the creation of an Irish national origin-legend, a synthetic pseudo-history that set out to create a national myth which endeavoured to place the Irish on the same footing as both the people of Israel and the citizens of Rome. The Irish national origin legend was to find its most elaborate expression in *Lebor Gabála hÉrenn*, 'the Book of the Taking of Ireland', now extant in a version dating from the twelfth century, but the archetype of which may go back to the ninth century.[10] *Lebar Gabála hÉrenn* sought to provide the Irish with a common identity by way of descent and to harmonise the origin-legend of the Irish people with that of the Book of Genesis and the Jewish people as a chosen race.

A developing common Christian identity was to be further sharpened under the impact of a group of pagan intruders, known to modern scholarship as Vikings, who began attacks on the Irish coastline from the late eighth century onwards. Because the monasteries were the targets of so many raids and burnings, the records of Viking attacks are particularly well recorded in the monastic annals. Having fully absorbed the idea of the Irish as a Christian nation, a chosen people, the Irish annalists referred to the Vikings in Latin as *gentiles* (first occurrence, 794),[11] and in Irish as *gennti* (first occurrence, 795),[12] that is, pagans. The contrast between Christians and gentiles, or pagans, was modelled on that between the Jews and the gentiles: since the Irish regarded themselves as a chosen Christian people, the pagan Scandinavians were gentiles.

An alternative term *Gaill* (plural), to refer to the Scandinavian intruders, first occurs in 828.[13] It may be assumed that *Gall* (singular) originally had been used in Irish to refer to an inhabitant of Gaul (early medieval Frankia) because these were for a long period the most common foreigners to visit Ireland, but it subsequently came to be used in a more general sense for a foreigner from overseas; and it was transferred with that meaning to the Scandinavians from the ninth century onwards. Less common, but also attested in the Irish annals as a descriptor of

[10] An excellent brief discussion is that by John Carey, *The Irish National Origin-legend: Synthetic Pseudohistory*, Quiggin Pamphlets on the Sources of Medieval Gaelic History 1, Cambridge 1994; also Vincent Comerford, *Inventing the Nation: Ireland*, London 2003, 51–5.

[11] *AU, s.a.* 794.7.

[12] *AU, s.a.* 795.3. The vernacular *gennti*, derived from Latin *gentes* but was used in the sense of non-Christian, that is, pagans or heathens.

[13] *AU, s.a.* 828.3.

Vikings is the vernacular term *Norddmannaibh* and the Latinised *Nordmanni*, literally 'Northmen'.[14]

By the twelfth century the Scandinavians who had established restricted coastal settlements and founded the first commercial trading centres, especially along the east coast of Ireland, and who constituted a very small minority of the population in Ireland by comparison, for example, with the more extensive Scandinavian settlements that led to the formation of the Danelaw in Anglo-Saxon England, had become Christianised and were absorbed into native Irish society. There was no longer a contrast between Christian and pagan. The term *Gaill* was therefore free to be applied to the next influx of foreigners, namely the English colonists who began arriving in Ireland from 1167 onwards: Irish annalists transferred the use of the term *Gaill* from the Scandinavians to these twelfth-century incomers. Irish annalists also deployed a number of other descriptions. In the very early stages the terms 'Overseas men' and 'Grey Foreigners' occur.[15] Quite quickly, however, there was a shift to *Saxain*, literally 'Saxons', which translates as English.[16] Whilst the Venerable Bede in his *Ecclesiastical History of the English People* was chiefly responsible for popularising a preference for the use of the term English – rather than Saxon – among the English themselves, the Irish preferred *Saxain* which is still used among Gaelic (the Celtic language of Ireland and Scotland) speakers, both Irish and Scottish, to refer to the people of England. Modern Irish and Scottish *Sassanach* translates literally as 'Saxon'.

The twelfth-century incomers into Ireland are most commonly referred to by modern historians as the 'Normans', or the 'Anglo-Normans', though a range of other terms, such as Anglo-French, Cambro-Normans and Cambro-French are also deployed.[17] Such terms are artificial scholarly constructs. There are serious methodological difficulties with the myriad definitions that have been used to describe the incomers into Ireland in the late twelfth century, which have been deployed by scholars without chronological circumscription and usually also with-

---

[14] *AU, s.a.* 837.3; cf. 842.8, 856.4, 859.4, 870.6, 871.4, 873.3, 875.4, 934.1. The hybrid term, *Gallgoídel*, 'Foreign Irish', first occurs in 856: *AU, s.a.* 856.3.

[15] *Allmarchaib* in *AI, s.a.* 1170.3; *AU; Gaill glassa* in *AI, s.a.* 1173.4. The term *Frainc* was used in the same annals from the late eleventh and early twelfth centuries to refer to Normans intruding into Wales and Scotland: *AI, s.a.* 1093.5, 1093.13, 1102.6.

[16] 'Three defeats inflicted by Mac Carthaig on the Saxons'; see 'The annals of Tigernach', ed. Whitley Stokes, *Revue Celtique* 18, 1897, 278, *s.a.* 1170; reprinted in *The Annals of Tigernach* ii, ed. Whitley Stokes, Felinfach 1993, 424.

[17] Cf. J. A. Watt, *The Church and the Two Nations in Medieval Ireland*, Cambridge 1970, x–xi, who makes the case for 'Anglo-French'; K. W. Nicholls, 'Anglo-French Ireland and after', *Peritia*, 1, 1982, 370–403, who proposed Anglo-French as a means of breaking loose from 'some of the old Anglo-centric constraints' (p. 371). See also H. B. Clarke', '1066, 1169 and all that' in *European Encounters*, ed. Judith Devlin and H. B. Clarke, Dublin 2003, 25, 28–30.

out explanatory justification, since very few of those terms are warranted by the contemporary sources.

The earliest charters issued by the incomers into late twelfth-century Ireland did distinguish different ethnic groupings. Thus, a charter of the most important of the colonists, Richard fitz Gilbert, lord of Strigoil (d. 1176), more popularly known as Strongbow (and used hereafter), the first non-Irish lord of Leinster,[18] issued in favour of one of his associates, was addressed to *Franci, Anglici, Walenses et Hibernenses*, 'Franks, English, Welsh and Irish'.[19] Similarly, a charter issued by Strongbow's constable, Raymond le Gros, was addressed to *Francigeni, Anglici, Flandrenses, Walenses et Hibernenses*, 'French, English, Flemish, Welsh, and Irish.[20] The specificity of that charter-address, with the inclusion of Flemings, is warranted by the fact that Raymond's charter was witnessed by Richard fitz Godebert, who was of Flemish origin,[21] drawn from the colony of Flemings that had been established by King Henry I of England (1100-35) on the Rhos peninsula in south Wales.[22] Notably absent, however, from the address clauses in charters issued by the incomers into Ireland is the term 'Norman'.

Only a very limited number of contemporary examples of the use of the term 'Norman' may be found. Thus, towards the end of his narrative in the *Expugnatio Hibernica*, Gerald of Wales detailed a series of reasons why the English conquest of Ireland had not been completed, singling out in particular the failure of the expedition of the Lord John, son of Henry II, to Ireland in 1185. In describing the composition of John's entourage, Gerald described it as comprising three distinct groups, *Normanni, Angli, nostri in Hibernia reperti*, 'Normans, English, and those of us now based in Ireland'.[23] This is one of the very few instances in a contemporary source of the use of the term 'Normans'. Gerald was arguing that the Lord John foolishly had paid most attention to the *Normanni*, those in his entourage who were drawn from Normandy, had paid less attention to a second group, the *Angli*, and had paid no attention to the third group, *nostri*, Gerald's relatives and the earliest adventurer-settlers, despite the fact that they were longest

[18] See M. T. Flanagan, 'Richard fitz Gilbert de Clare', *ODNB*.
[19] Original extant charter in favour of Gilbert de Angulo: National Library of Ireland, D.3; English summary in *Calendar of Ormond Deeds, 1172–1350*, ed. Edmund Curtis, Dublin 1932, no. 2.
[20] Eric St J. Brooks, 'An unpublished charter of Raymond le Gros', *Journal of the Royal Society of Antiquaries of Ireland* 69, 1939, 167–9.
[21] He is described as a 'knight of Pembrokeshire' in the near contemporary French rhyming history: *The Deeds of the Normans in Ireland: La geste des Engleis en Yrlande,* ed. Evelyn Mullally, Dublin 2002, lines 409–10; cf. G. H. Orpen, *Song of Dermot and the Earl*, Oxford 1892, 33.
[22] R. R. Davies, *Domination and Conquest: The Experience of Ireland, Scotland and Wales*, Cambridge 1999, 11–12.
[23] Giraldus, *Expugnatio Hibernica*, 244–5.

established in Ireland and therefore had the most experience of conditions in the country.[24] Here again, as in the speech, already quoted, that he attributed to his uncle, Maurice fitz Gerald, Gerald appeared to be arguing for an emergent separate identity among the settlers, an intermediate status, not dissimilar to the claim later made in the Remonstrance of around 1317 that the English of Ireland regarded themselves as a 'middle nation'.

Gerald's isolated use of the term 'Norman' in this passage is far outweighed by his much more common description of the colonists as 'English'. Similarly, the other principal narrative source produced among the colonist community, the French rhyming history known as the *Song of Dermot and the Earl*, dating from around 1190, overwhelmingly referred to the newcomers as *Engleis*.[25] The *Song of Dermot and the Earl* was the title coined in 1892 for the untitled anonymous text by its first modern editor, Goddard Henry Orpen. It is unfortunate that the most recent edition in 2002 has invented another wholly anachronistic title, namely 'The deeds of the Normans in Ireland', with an inconsistent French subtitle *La geste des Engleis en Yrlande*.[26] Confusing and fluctuating terminology therefore endures into the twenty-first century.

There are some few occurrences of 'Flemings' in twelfth-century documentary and narrative sources, but the modern scholarly construct, Cambro-Norman, is non contemporary. Either term – the contemporary Flemings and the non-contemporary Cambro-Normans – might be said to have some validity for the very earliest group of newcomers into Ireland between 1167 and 1170, those overseas mercenaries recruited by the exiled Leinster king, Diarmait Mac Murchada (died 1171), who were drawn exclusively from the region of south Wales (Cambria) – hence Cambro-Norman. However, already by August 1170 with the arrival of Strongbow, and his associates, the English element among the newcomers became politically more predominant than the Flemish or Cambro-Norman element. Strongbow's substantial landholdings were located in England, and, to a lesser extent, in Normandy and south Wales. He was a tenant-in-chief of the English king; and the associates, whom he brought with him to Ireland to settle on his newly won lands in Leinster, were drawn primarily from his English landholdings.[27]

---

[24] For interpretation of this passage, see John Gillingham, 'The English invasion of Ireland', in *Representing Ireland: Literature and the Origins of Conflict, 1534–1660,* ed. Brendan Bradshaw, Andrew Harfield and Willy Maley, Cambridge 1993, 24–42, reprinted in Gillingham, *The English in the Twelfth Century,* 145–60.

[25] In the poem of 3457 lines there is only one occurrence each of 'Normans' and of 'Flemings': *The Deeds of the Normans in Ireland*, ed. Mullally, l. 2646; there is one reference to a Richard Fleming and one to a Thomas Fleming: ll. 3110, 3173. There are at least 33 references to 'English'.

[26] See above, notes 21, 25.

[27] M. T. Flanagan, *Irish Society, Anglo-Norman Settlers, Angevin Kingship: Interactions in Ireland in the Late Twelfth Century,* Oxford 1989, 156–60.

The English element received additional reinforcement as a result of the personal expedition to Ireland of Henry II, king of England, in the autumn of 1171. Henry stayed for a period of six months in Ireland, a momentous visit which was to inaugurate a constitutional link between Ireland and the English crown that has continued so problematically to the present day in Northern Ireland. The intervention of Henry II ensured the participation of a more diverse range of settlers, drawn from a wider geographical area, not only from the southern English counties, but as far east as East Anglia and as far north as Yorkshire. From 1170 onwards therefore, 'Cambro-Normans' were augmented by 'Anglo-Normans'.

It could be argued that, since Strongbow, when he came to Ireland in 1170, also held some lands in Normandy, the term 'Anglo-Norman', although unattested in contemporary sources, might nonetheless have some validity for him and his associates. Yet historians of twelfth-century England have argued that by 1171 the descendants of those continental Normans, who had first gone to England with William the Conqueror in 1066, had already lost much of their Norman identity and had begun to regard themselves as English. This was to be even more decisively so following the loss of the duchy of Normandy by King John in 1204 to Philip Augustus, king of France. The continental ties of the Normans of England with Normandy were so weakened after 1204 that they rapidly became English; and scholars have no qualms about referring to them as English from the thirteenth century, notwithstanding the fact that the polite language of the elite in England may have continued to be French until the triumph of the English language in the fourteenth century. Studies of contemporary sources written in England in the second quarter of the twelfth century have shown that, whether authors were writing in Latin – like William of Malmesbury or Henry of Huntingdon – or in French – like Geoffrey Gaimar – they felt themselves to be English. Therefore, there is a convincing case to be made that by the time of their intervention in Ireland, the incomers already perceived themselves to be English and so described themselves in their own contemporary sources. That constitutes another persuasive argument against the use by modern scholars of such terms as 'Norman' and 'Anglo-Norman' for those who began to colonise parts of Ireland in the late twelfth century. In any case, even if the earliest incomers may have been multi-ethnic polyglots from south Wales, that is, of mixed Norman, native Welsh, and Flemish origins, and may have spoken French and/or English, the extension of English law to those settlers under the overlordship of the English crown from 1171 was rapidly to corral them all together and to invest them with an overriding English legal identity.[28]

[28] For the importance of legal identity, see Robin Frame, '"Les Engleys nées en Irlande": the English political identity in medieval Ireland' in Robin Frame, *Ireland and Britain, 1170–1540*, London 1998, 130–5; idem, 'Exporting state and nation: being English in medieval Ireland' in *Power and the Nation in European History*, ed. Len Scales and Oliver Zimmer, Cambridge 2005, 143–65.

Apart from the fact that such descriptions as 'Norman' and 'Anglo-Norman' are anachronistic and conflict with the contemporary sources, there is a further methodological criticism that can be advanced, namely that such terms preference one particular social stratum of newcomer – the aristocratic elite who may have been in the minority – at the expense of what may have been the non-aristocratic, largely silent but numerically greater, accompanying peasant settlers.[29] The frequently unexplained shift by scholars to the term 'English' from the thirteenth century onwards implicitly reflects a change of perspective to the activities of the rank and file colonising movement, as well as the incorporation of economic and archaeological dimensions into a hitherto dominant political narrative that focused exclusively on the activities of the aristocratic elite. It assuredly is inappropriate to label the rank and file settlers 'Norman' or 'Anglo-Norman'. The accompanying peasant migrants were unlikely to have been of mixed Anglo-Norman origins; they were more likely to have been predominantly English, more occasionally Welsh. They would have spoken English, although the argument has been advanced that even the aristocratic elite by the late twelfth century was already speaking more English rather than French. That would also negate the term 'Anglo-French' used by a minority of historians, focusing on linguistic particularities (rather than ethnicity), namely that the two languages spoken by the incomers were English and French. Surreptitious shifts in terminology, that is rarely explained or justified by scholars, are bound up with a further question of just how many settlers came to Ireland.

The earliest incomers were identified as English in both contemporary Irish and newcomer sources. Subsequently, additional explanatory emendations were to develop, such as 'the English of Ireland', 'the English born in Ireland', and the 'English by blood' as opposed to the 'English by birth' or, as expressed in The Remonstrance of around 1317, 'the English inhabiting our land'. Such terms highlight the enduringly separate identity of the colonists. It might have been expected that the passage of time would produce a distancing of the colonists from England and an increased identification with Ireland. Yet far from that being the case, a distinctive settler identity persisted within Ireland and was indeed reinforced from the mid-thirteenth century onwards by the special experience of belonging to communities that were increasingly under threat from a militarily resurgent Irish population, whose leaders were encroaching on the colony and recovering portions of its territory. The colonists' vulnerability produced a heightened sense of dependency on England and a parading of, and emphasis on, English identity. A mentality of encirclement developed in the eroded colonial settlements and

[29]   Davies, *Domination and Conquest*, 12. H. B. Clarke has warned against overestimating the numerical strength of peasant migration into Ireland: 'Decolonization and the dynamics of urban decline in Ireland, 1300–1550' in *Towns in Decline, AD 100–1600*, ed. T. R. Slater, Aldershot 2000, 157–92.

caused the colonists to emphasise their shared allegiance, shared culture, and common privileges with the English on the other side of the Irish sea. Frontier interactions with the Irish were perceived as threatening. Far from acculturation, public expressions of Englishness therefore intensified in the fourteenth century, that is, roughly six generations after the arrival of the first English in Ireland. The triumphalist tone of cultural superiority of the colonists, so apparent in the writings of their twelfth-century historian, Gerald of Wales, changed to that of shrill voices insisting that they – the king's loyal subjects in Ireland – were every bit as truly English as the English born in England and were entitled to parity of esteem. Such protestations occurred especially on occasions when the colonists were seeking help from England. Ironically, they might intensify even more when that English help arrived, for assistance took the form of English governors with their retinues, who were then seen as competitors for lands and patronage with the local settler community.

The lowest common denominator of identity among the colonists was consciousness that they were not Irish. From the late thirteenth century onwards, however, as the colony began to shrink, division among the colonists themselves emerged: recurring complaints were voiced that certain English within the colony had become *degeneres*,[30] that is, that they were abandoning the customs of their own people and adopting those of the native Irish. Those described by their compatriots as 'degenerate' were pilloried as unreliable and disloyal because of their supposed contamination by Irish customs and culture. Complaints focused on such issues as language and dress, alliance with Irish families through intermarriage, fosterage or godparenthood, and patronage of Irish poets and musicians. From 1297 onwards, attempts were made to redress such 'degeneracy' by legislation. In 1297, for example, legislation was passed against English settlers having Irish haircuts, one particularly obvious marker of a whole range of ethnic differences that cumulatively created a deep divide, and more practically, because an Englishman with an Irish-style haircut could mistakenly be killed as an Irishman.[31] Such legislation has been interpreted as less a practical programme than 'a declaration of identity through law'.[32] The most comprehensive body of legislation was the Statutes of Kilkenny, passed in 1366, which reveal the acute anxieties among the colonists about a resurgent Irish population that was perceived as not only a military but also a cultural threat. The Statutes of Kilkenny aimed at halting and

---

[30] This description is first attested in 1297. The sense is that such people had abandoned, or were in the process of losing, the characteristic traits of their nation; they were *de genere*, out of their *genus* or proper national descent.

[31] Text in Philomena Connolly, 'The enactments of the 1297 parliament', in *Law and Disorder in Thirteenth-Century Ireland: The Dublin Parliament of 1297,* ed. James Lydon, Dublin 1997, 158–60.

[32] Brendan Smith, 'Keeping the peace', in *Law and Disorder*, ed. Lydon, 65.

reversing a trend towards Irishisation; among its 36 clauses were prescriptions that all those living within the colony were to use the English language and English personal names, to ride their horses in the English manner and to use only English methods of dispute settlement.

The Statutes of Kilkenny also highlight the complexities of national identity in fourteenth-century Ireland since the colonists defined themselves, not only in opposition to the native Irish, but also in contrast with those degenerates among them who had adopted Irish customs. The Statutes expose the reality that there was not a homogeneous 'English' people in Ireland. The Statutes also reveal the related problem of cultural tensions between the English of Ireland and the English of England. Thus, one statute declared that the long-term settlers in Ireland were forbidden from denigrating those whom they viewed as more recent interlopers with the label 'English hobbes' (fools or clowns), while the new arrivals, in turn, were ordered not to describe the established colonists as 'Irish dogs'. Instead, all the English king's subjects, wherever born, were to be called 'the English lieges of our lord, the king'.

> And that no difference of allegiance shall henceforth be made between the English born in Ireland, and the English born in England, by calling them English hob, or Irish dog, but that all be called by one name, the English lieges of our Lord the king; and he who shall be found doing to the contrary, shall be punished by imprisonment for a year, and afterwards fined, at the king's pleasure (statute 4).[33]

If, as we have seen, there is little support in contemporary sources for the deployment by modern historians of such terms as 'Norman', 'Anglo-Norman', or 'Anglo-French', how and when did those terms come to be adopted by scholars to refer to Ireland's new settlers from the late twelfth century onwards? In fact, until the mid-nineteenth century historians writing on both sides of the Irish sea had generally referred to the *English* invasion of Ireland. Numerous examples across a broad chronological time-span could be given, but as an instance of colonialist historiography Richard Cox's *Hibernia Anglicana* ('English Ireland'), published in 1692, can serve as representative of newcomer historiography.[34] Representative of the native Irish historiographical tradition was the Abbé James Geogeghan's account of Irish history, *Histoire d'Irlande ancienne et moderne*, first published

---

[33] Text and translation (the language of the original is Norman French) in [Ordinances of Kilkenny] in *Statutes and Ordinances, and Acts of the Parliament of Ireland. King John to Henry V*, ed. H. F. Berry, Dublin 1907, 374–397; also available at http://www.ucc.ie/celt/published/T300001–001/index.html. See also Peter Crooks, '"Hobbes", "Dogs" and politics in the Ireland of Lionel of Antwerp, c. 1361–6', *Haskins Society Journal*, 16 (2005), 117–48.

[34] Richard Cox, *Hibernia Anglicana: Or the History Thereof from the Conquest of England to this Present Time*, 2 vols, London, 1689–90. On Cox, see S. J. Connolly, 'Richard Cox', *ODNB*.

in French in Paris in 1758, and dedicated to the emigrant Irish soldiers fighting on the European mainland to whom Geoghegan acted as a chaplain for a time. Geoghegan divided his history into three distinct periods, pagan Ireland, Christian Ireland, and 'From the English invasions'. It is not perverse to choose a work on Irish history written in French as representative of the native historiographical tradition, since the English translation of Geoghegan's work was one of the most widely read books in nineteenth-century Ireland.[35]

Insofar as the term 'Norman' was used by native Irish writers, it referred to the Scandinavian 'Northmen' who had intruded into Ireland from AD 795 onwards and remained active as raiders until about the 980s, after which they settled as peaceful traders and were gradually absorbed into native Irish society. By way of example, Charles O'Conor's *Dissertations on the History of Ireland* (1753), a work written by a direct descendant of the last native Irish high-king of Ireland (Ruaidrí Ua Conchobair, king of Connacht, died 1198), affords an example of the usage of 'Norman' as referring to the Scandinavian Northmen.[36]

The term 'English' rather than 'Norman', and its variants to refer to the twelfth-century incomers into Ireland therefore remained conventional into the mid-nineteenth century in conformity with the predominant usage in the contemporary sources. It was only from the second half of the nineteenth century that the term 'Norman' and its hybrid forms, such as 'Anglo-Norman', gained wide currency in historical writing. The shift in nomenclature from English to Norman may be traced to the Regius professor of history at Oxford, Goldwin Smith who in 1861, in a lecture titled *Irish History and Irish Character* wrote, 'It is not the Saxon that is responsible for the conquest of Ireland, but the Norman'.[37] In presenting the twelfth-century invasion of Ireland as Norman rather than English, Goldwin Smith,

---

[35] James MacGeoghegan, *History of Ireland, Ancient and Modern ... translated from the French by P. O'Kelly*, 3 vols, Dublin 1831–2; reprinted Dublin, Glasgow, New York, 1844, 1849, 1868, 1884, 1898; John Pope Hennessy, 'What do the Irish read?', *The Nineteenth Century*, 15, 1884, 926–7.

[36] Thus, O'Conor described the Viking intrusion as the 'commencement of the Norman war': Charles O'Conor, *Dissertations on the History of Ireland*, Dublin 1766, 194, 229.

[37] Goldwin Smith, *Irish History and Irish Character*, Oxford 1868, 47. Its agenda is reflected in the preface which stated that the work would serve its purpose if it should be read by 'the popular writer on Irish history, and induce him ... to cultivate the charities of history'. Cf. his later *Irish History and the Irish Question*, Toronto 1905, 12–24, where the same stance is maintained. During the summer of 1861 Smith had stayed as a guest of the Chief Secretary in the Vice-regal Lodge in Phoenix Park, Dublin, where he discussed 'the Irish Question' with a number of parties, as a result of which he wrote his *Irish History and Irish Character*, as he described in *Irish History and the Irish Question*, iii–vi. He maintained a pro-Unionist and anti-Home Rule stance. On Smith's career, see C. A. Kent, 'Goldwin Smith', *ODNB*. For earlier though less influential usages, see John Gillingham, 'Normanizing the English invaders of Ireland' in *Power and Identity in the Middle Ages: Essays in Memory of Rees Davies*, ed. Huw Pryce and John Watts, Oxford 2007, 85–97.

by his own admission, aimed to take the heat out of contemporary political debate, to foreshorten the portrayal of seven hundred years of English misrule and oppression that was so prevalent in nineteenth-century Irish nationalist discourse. As Smith stated, he hoped 'to transfer the question to a calmer realm of discussion and disarm special resentment in reasonable minds'.

A simplistic Whig-nationalist interpretation of Irish history was that the central – if not the only – theme to be studied over the seven or eight centuries from the first arrival of the English in twelfth-century Ireland was the Irish attempt to secure freedom from English domination. It was in the heated contemporary political context of growing nationalist sentiment that Goldwin Smith first deployed the term 'Norman' to refer to the English colonists infiltrating into Ireland from the late twelfth century onwards. One effect of Goldwin Smith's shift in terminology was to defer the 'English' conquest and Anglicisation of Ireland until the sixteenth and seventeenth centuries. By avoidance of the term 'English' and substitution of 'Norman', the medieval period between 1200 and 1500 could be distinguished and distanced from the English reconquest that began with King Henry VIII (1509-47). The nationalist view of seven hundred years of English oppression was thereby foreshortened and undermined.

Goldwin Smith's substitution of 'Norman' for 'English' to refer to the colonists in Ireland was adopted most influentially from an Irish perspective, by Goddard Henry Orpen, the first modern historian of the medieval English colony in Ireland. Orpen titled his magisterial four-volume work, published between 1911 and 1922 at the height of the Home Rule Crisis, *Ireland under the Normans*. It remains the classic exposition and best narrative account of the English advance into Ireland and consequent settlement up to the early fourteenth century, as evidenced by its most recent reissue in 2005.[38] Already in 1892, however, in his edition of the *Song of Dermot and the Earl*, Orpen had referred to the 'coming of the Normans' and the 'Norman invasion of Ireland'.[39]

[38]   G. H. Orpen, *Ireland under the Normans, 1169–1333*, 4 vols, Oxford, 1911–1920; reprinted 1968 (4 vols), Dublin 2005 (1 vol.). Orpen terminated his narrative with the death of Walter de Burgh, earl of Ulster in 1333, after which it would have been difficult to sustain the view of a *pax Normannica*. Orpen's title was influenced by Richard Bagwell's *Ireland under the Tudors*, 3 vols, London 1885–90, and *Ireland under the Stuarts*, 3 vols, London, 1909–1916. Orpen, whose sympathies, like those of Gerald of Wales, lay with the colonists rather than royal government or English administrators in Ireland, did not choose as a title Ireland under the Angevins or Plantagenets. Cf. Kate Norgate, *England under the Angevin Kings*, 2 vols, London 1907.

[39]   Orpen, *Song of Dermot*, v, vii, xvi (but he also referred to the beginnings of 'how the English first got a foothold in Ireland' and the 'English occupation'). In 1889 G. T. Stokes had published his *Ireland and the Anglo-Norman Church: A History of Ireland and Irish Christianity from the Anglo-Norman Conquest to the Dawn of the Reformation*, London 1909. Stokes, in similar vein to Goldwin Smith, had expressed the aspiration that 'the present work may be as fruitful, and tend in some small degree to

Orpen's history of the English colony in Ireland was to generate considerable controversy in nationalist Irish circles. A key element of debate at the beginning of the twentieth century between nationalists, who sought Home Rule and self-determination, and Unionists, who sought the retention of a permanent constitutional link with the English crown, was whether or not Ireland had benefited from English rule. In historical terms, that argument began with the arrival of the first colonists in 1167. Orpen, writing as a proponent of the retention of the constitutional Union between Ireland and England, advanced the view that, as he termed it, the 'Norman' invasion of Ireland had brought an era of unparalleled peace and progress to Ireland. Indeed, Orpen coined the term *pax Normannica* (invoking an analogy with the *pax Romana* of the Roman empire)[40] to refer to the enduringly positive influence that he believed the colonists to have had on political and legal institutions in Ireland. The shift away from the term 'English' and the substitution of 'Norman' to describe the incomers who began settling in late twelfth-century Ireland was conditioned by late nineteenth-century Irish nationalism and the conflictual relations between Ireland as a colony and England as the colonial power, as Irish nationalists sought first to gain Home Rule, and, after the 1916 Rising, full independence. Goldwin Smith took the initial step, but it was Orpen who secured its embedding in twentieth-century historical writing.

The most prominent nationalist critic of Orpen's *Ireland under the Normans* was the politician and historian, Eoin MacNeill, founder of the Gaelic League in 1893, the first professor of early Irish history in University College, Dublin, leader of the Irish Volunteers, and the first Minister for Education in the Irish Free State government.[41] Although a trenchant critic of Orpen's *Ireland under the Normans*, MacNeill was nonetheless prepared to follow Orpen in referring to the 'Norman' conquest.[42] MacNeill described the leaders of the invasion as 'so-called Normans' and Franks who spoke French, while he identified the rank and file as 'Welshmen and Flemings'. Indeed, MacNeill claimed that 'the colonists had no nationality until in the course of time they became Irelandmen'.[43] MacNeill's use of 'Irelandmen' is a particularly clumsy circumlocution, since he was determined not to concede to them any nationality. MacNeill drew a distinction between nationalism and nationality. Nationalism he described as 'a political doctrine meaning localised statism'.[44] On the other hand, nationality 'was the type of civil-

a better understanding and a more kindly feeling among the various races, Norman, Saxon, Scandinavian, and Celtic, inhabiting England, Ireland, and Scotland': ibid., p. x.
40 Orpen, *Ireland under the Normans*, ii, 323, iv, 262.
41 See F. X. Martin and F. J. Byrne, ed., *The Scholar Revolutionary: Eoin MacNeill, 1867–1945 and the Making of the New Ireland*, Dublin 1973; P. Maume, 'Eoin MacNeill', *ODNB*.
42 Eoin MacNeill, *Phases of Irish History*, Dublin 1919, repr. 1968, 300–2.
43 Ibid., 308.

isation which a people has developed, which has become the people's tradition and is distinctive of that tradition'. Writing of Irish independence, he wrote 'our claims to political autonomy, to have a state of our own, have never been based and could not have been based on Ireland's having existed in former times as a state. They were based and rightly based on the existence of an Irish nation throughout the ages of history'.[45]

Taking their cue from Orpen and MacNeill, subsequent authors either followed them in referring to the settlers as 'Norman', or coined hybrid designations, such as 'Anglo-Norman', 'Cambro-Norman', 'Anglo-French'. There is no doubt that professional historians writing on medieval Ireland are now acutely aware of the ambivalences and anachronisms in their continued usage of such terms and would accept that 'English' most accurately describes the overwhelming number of the late twelfth-century colonists.[46] Many scholars, most especially those writing in Ireland, nonetheless remain hesitant about reinstating the more accurate term 'English'. This is because the terminology continues to have contemporary political implications that resonate beyond the circles of academic discourse. In the context of the prolonged period of political unrest that erupted in Northern Ireland in 1968, professional historians have been reluctant to be thought either to contribute to heightening political tensions, or to be seen as supporting one particular political perspective – that viewed as the final phase of the historical process of ridding Ireland of English rule. In short, the continued use by academic historians of the terms 'Norman' and its variant, 'Anglo-Norman', is less politically charged. As someone who teaches medieval Irish history at Queen's University, Belfast, I plead guilty to the continued use of 'Anglo-Norman' as politically neutral and less problematic in that, unlike 'English', it has fewer contemporary political resonances. In doing so, I have followed Goldwin Smith, and for the very same reasons, long before I became aware that it was he who was chiefly responsible for the promotion of 'Norman' rather than 'English' to describe the newcomers into twelfth-century Ireland.

In conclusion, one overriding fact that emerges inescapably from even the most superficial reflection on the course of Irish history is that it has been profoundly conditioned by a fundamental ethnic and cultural duality resulting from a process of English colonisation set in train by twelfth-century adventurers who were drawn to Ireland from different parts of Britain. That colonisation divided Ireland between two nations, Irish and English, each with its own language, legal cus-

[44] See Art Cosgrove, 'The writing of Irish medieval history', *Irish Historical Studies*, 27, 1990, 100.
[45] Donal McCartney, 'MacNeill and Irish-Ireland' in Martin and Byrne, *The Scholar Revolutionary*, 84–5.
[46] For my acknowledgement of this dichotomy, see M. T. Flanagan, 'The Normans in Ireland' in *Irish History in the Classroom*, Belfast 1987, p. 23.

toms, and social institutions. By contrast with the Norman conquest of England in 1066, a complete conquest of Ireland was never achieved in the medieval period. The English colony in Ireland was established and expanded in a series of unco-ordinated initiatives, resulting in a piecemeal conquest. English settlement was unevenly distributed, both in territorial breadth and in numerical depth. Inces-sant, localised and usually indecisive warfare perpetuated distinctions between the native Irish and the English colonists. Up until the fourteenth century it was still possible to hypothesise that the colonists might eventually gain political con-trol over the entire island, but thereafter, a pronounced shift in the equilibrium in favour of the native Irish occurred, conventionally labelled the 'Irish recovery', or the 'Gaelic resurgence', or 'Gaelic revival'. A heightened tension resulted between an English colony in decline and a native Irish Ireland in resurgence. It is nonethe-less important to note that the two nations did not merely collide perennially, they also interpenetrated: each nation in different degrees, at different times and to unequal extents was affected and changed by the other. Labels such as 'native Irish' or Anglo-Irish'[47] cannot adequately describe the complexities of accultura-tion, of anglicised Irish and of hibernicised English.[48] Notwithstanding a degree of acculturation, however, the two remained sufficiently distinctive to perpetuate two nations and two distinct historiographical traditions, native and newcomer historiographies of Ireland: histories that were written from the perspective of either the native Irish or the English colonists. That dichotomous historiography, re-ignited by recurrent periods of heightened political tensions, accounts for the confusing and inconsistent terminology coined in the medieval period and by modern scholars to describe the two nations of medieval Ireland.

[47] 'Anglo-Irish', a term as problematic as 'Anglo-Norman', is often used without explana-tion or justification as a convenient label for those of English origin from the fourteenth century onwards who were born in Ireland, by contrast with the English born in Eng-land. Cf. the shift from Anglo-Norman to Anglo-Irish in *A New History of Ireland II: Medieval Ireland, 1169–1534*, ed. Art Cosgrove, Oxford 1987, p. x and passim. The term *Anglo-Hiberni* was first used by Richard Stanihurst (1547–1618): Comerford, *Inventing the Nation*, 59.

[48] Cf. Thomas Finan, *A Nation in Medieval Ireland? Perspectives on Gaelic National Identity in the Middle Ages*, BAR British Series, 367, Oxford 2004.

BIBLIOGRAPHY OF WORKS CITED

Primary

Acts of the Parliament of Scotland, vol. i, part 1, *A.D. MCXXIV–A.D. MCCCCXXIII*, eds Thomas Thompson and Cosmo Innes, Edinburgh 1844

The Acts of Welsh Rulers, 1120–1283, ed. H. Pryce, Cardiff 2005

Adam of Dryburgh, *De tripartito tabernaculo*, in J.-P. Migne, ed., *Patrologiæ cursus completus ... series Latina*, 221 vols, Paris 1844–64, vol. 198, cols 609–792

The Anglo-Saxon Chronicle, ed. M. J. Swanton, London 1996

The Anglo-Saxon Chronicle: a Revised Translation, eds D. Whitelock, D. C. Douglas, and S. I. Tucker, 2nd edn London 1963

Annales Cambriae, ed. J.Williams ab Ithel, Rolls Series, London 1860

'The Annals of Nenagh', ed. D. F. Gleeson, *Analecta Hibernica* 12, 1943, 155–64

Annals of Inisfallen, ed. S. Mac Airt, Dublin Institute for Advanced Studies, Dublin 1951

'The Annals of Tigernach', ed. Whitley Stokes, *Revue Celtique* 16, 1895, 375–419; 17, 1896, 6–33, 119–263, 337–420; 18, 1897, 9–59, 150–97, 267–303; reprinted in *The Annals of Tigernach* ii, ed. W. Stokes, Felinfach 1993

Annals of Ulster (to A.D. 1131), ed. Gearóid Mac Niocaill, Dublin Institute for Advanced Studies, Dublin 1983

Armes Prydein, ed. Ifor Williams, translated by Rachel Bronwich, Dublin 1972

Bede's Ecclesiastical History of the English People, eds B. Colgrave and R. A. B. Mynors, Oxford 1969

Calendar of Ancient Petitions Relating to Wales: Thirteenth to Sixteenth Century, ed. W. Rees, History and Law Series 28, Cardiff 1975

Calendar of Ormond Deeds, 1170–1350, ed. Edmund Curtis, Dublin 1932

The Chronicle of Æthelweard, ed. A. Campbell, London 1962

The Chronicle of John of Worcester ii–iii, eds R. R. Darlington and P. McGurk, Oxford 1995–8

The Chronicle of Melrose from the Cottonian Manuscript, Faustina B. IX in the British Museum, ed. A. O. and M. O. Anderson with an index by W. Croft Dickinson, London 1936

The Chronicle of Melrose Abbey: a Stratigraphic Edition, Introduction and Facsimile Edition, ed. Dauvit Broun and Julian Harrison, Scottish History Society, Woodbridge 2007

Corpus Iuris Hibernici, ed. D. A. Binchy, 6 vols, Dublin 1978

Damweiniau Colan, ed. D. Jenkins, Aberystwyth 1973

The Deeds of the Normans in Ireland: La geste des Engleis en Yrlande, ed. Evelyn Mullally, Dublin 2002

Dudo of Saint-Quentin, *De moribus et actis primorum Normanniae ducum, auctore Dudone Sancti Quintini decano*, ed. Jules Lair, Caen 1865

Dudo of Saint-Quentin, *History of the Normans*, trans. Eric Christiansen, Woodbridge 1998.

The Ecclesiastical History of Orderic Vitalis, ed. and trans. Majorie Chibnall, 6 vols, Oxford 1969

English Historical Documents i, *500–1042,* ed. D. Whitelock, London 1979–81

Gildas: The Ruin of Britain and Other Works, ed. and trans. Michael Winterbottom, Chichester 1978

Giraldus Cambrensis, Expugnatio Hibernica, eds A. B. Scott and F. X. Martin, Dublin 1978

Great Domesday Book: County Edition, eds Ann Williams, R. W. H. Erskine and G. H. Martin, 30 vols, London 1986–92

Great Domesday Book: Library Edition, eds Ann Williams, R. W. H. Erskine and G. H. Martin, 6 vols, London 1986–92

Historia de Sancto Cuthberto. A History of Saint Cuthbert and a Record of his Patrimony, ed. Ted Johnson South, Woodbridge 2002

Johannis de Fordun Chronica Gentis Scotorum, ed. W. F. Skene, Historians of Scotland vol. i, Edinburgh 1871.

John Barbour. The Bruce, ed. and trans. A. A. M. Duncan, Edinburgh 1997

The Kalendar of Abbot Samson of Bury St Edmund's and Related Documents, ed. R. H. C. Davis, Camden Society, 3rd series 84, 1954

The Latin Texts of the Welsh Laws, ed. H. Emmanuel, History and Law Series 22, Cardiff 1967

The Laws of the Earliest English Kings, ed. F. L. Attenborough, Cambridge 1922

The Laws of the Kings of England from Edmund to Henry I, ed. A. J. Robertson, Cambridge 1925

Liber Eliensis, ed. E. O. Blake, Camden Society 3rd ser. 92, 1962

'Liber Extravagans', ed. and trans. Dauvit Broun with A. B. Scott, in *Scotichronicon by Walter Bower in Latin and English*, ed. D. E. R. Watt, 9 vols Aberdeen/Edinburgh 1987–98, vol. ix, 54–127

The Life of Bishop Wilfrid by Eddius Stephanus, ed. Bertram Colgrave, Cambridge 1927

Little Domesday, eds Ann Williams and G. H. Martin, 6 vols, London 2000

Llyfr Iorwerth, ed. A. R. Wiliam, Cardiff 1960

Memoriale Fratris Walteri de Coventria: the Historical Collection of Walter of Coventry, ed. William Stubbs, Rolls Series, 2 vols, London 1872–3

The Miracles of St Æbbe of Coldingham and St Margaret of Scotland, ed. and trans. Robert Bartlett, Oxford 2003

Muirchú moccu Machthéni's 'Vita Sancti Patricii': Life of Saint Patrick, ed. David Howlett, Dublin 2006

The Patrician Texts in the Book of Armagh, ed. Ludwig Bieler, Scriptores Latini Hiberniae, 10, Dublin 1979

Peniarth 28 darlunian lyfr Cyfraith Hywel Dda: Illustrations from a Welsh Lawbook, ed. D. Huws, Aberystwyth 1988

Regesta Regum Scottorum, vol. i, *The Acts of Malcolm IV King of Scots*, ed. G. W. S. Barrow, Edinburgh 1960

Regesta Regum Scottorum vol ii, *The Acts of William I, King of Scots 1165–1214*, ed. G. W. S. Barrow in collaboration with W. W. Scott, Edinburgh 1971

Registrum Monasterii de Passelet, ed. Cosmo Innes, Maitland Club, Edinburgh 1832

Scotichronicon by Walter Bower in Latin and English, ed. D. E. R. Watt, 9 vols, Aberdeen/Edinburgh 1987–98

Scottish Annals from English Chroniclers, AD500 to 1286, ed. A. O. Anderson, London 1908, corrected edition, Stamford 1991

Select Cases of the Thirteenth Century, ed. T. M. (Lord) Cooper, London 1944

Sermo Lupi ad Anglos, ed. Dorothy Whitelock, London 1939

Song of Dermot and the Earl, ed. G. H. Orpen, Oxford 1892

Sources for York History to AD 1100, eds D. W. Rollason with D. Gore and G. Fellows-Jensen, York 1998

Statutes and Ordinances, and Acts of the Parliament of Ireland. King John to Henry V, ed. H. F. Berry, Dublin 1907

The Statutes of Wales, ed. I. Bowen, London 1908

Symeon of Durham, Libellus de Exordio atque procursu istius, hoc est Dunhelmensis ecclesie. Tract on the Origins and Progress of this the Church of Durham, ed. D. Rollason, Oxford 2000

Symeonis monachi opera omnia, ed. T. Arnold, Rolls Series, 2 vols, London 1882–85

Vita Griffini filii Conani: the Medieval Latin Life of Gruffudd ap Cynan, ed. and trans. Paul Russell, Cardiff 2005

William of Malmesbury, Gesta Regum Anglorum, the History of the English Kings, eds R. M. Thomson and M. Winterbottom, 2 vols, Oxford 1988–89

Unpublished Ph.D. Theses

Matthew H. Hammond, 'A prosopographical analysis of society in east central Scotland with special reference to ethnicity, *c.* 1100–*c.* 1260', Ph.D. thesis, University of Glasgow 2005

D. R. Roffe, 'Nottinghamshire and the North: a Domesday Study', PhD thesis, Leicester 1987 (http://www.roffe.co.uk/phdframe.htm)

Andrew Smith, 'Kelso Abbey as a focus of social interactions in the twelfth and thirteenth centuries', current Ph.D. thesis, University of Glasgow

Akihiro Takamori, 'Regnal consolidation and regional networks: charters and religious benefactions in the diocese of Glasgow, *c.* 1120 to 1270', Ph.D. thesis, University of Glasgow 2009

Alice Taylor, 'Aspects of law, kingship and government in Scotland *c.* 1100–1230', D.Phil. thesis, University of Oxford 2009

Secondary

Abels, R. P., *Lordship and Military Obligation in Anglo-Saxon England,* London 1988

Abrams, Lesley, 'The conversion of the Danelaw', in *Vikings and the Danelaw,* ed. Graham-Campbell *et al.*, 31–44

Abrams, Lesley, 'Edward the Elder's Danelaw', in *Edward the Elder, 899–924,* ed. N. J. Higham and D. H. Hill, London 2001, 128–43

Aird, W. M., *St Cuthbert and the Normans. The Church of Durham, 1071–1153,* Woodbridge 1998

Aird, W. M., 'Copsi, earl of Northumbria (d. 1067)' *ODNB,* Oxford 2004

Aird, W. M., 'Osulf, earl of Bamburgh (d. 1067)', *ODNB,* Oxford 2004

Aird, W. M., 'Siward, earl of Northumbria (d. 1055)', *ODNB,* Oxford 2004

Alavosus, Laura *et al.,* ed., *History Alive! The Medieval World and Beyond (Student Edition),* Palo Alto, CA 2005

Albu, Emily, *The Normans in Their Histories: Propaganda, Myth, and Subversion,* Woodbridge 2001

Albu, Emily, 'Scandinavians in Byzantium and Normandy,' in *Peace and War in Byzantium: Essays in Honor of George T. Dennis, S. J.,* eds Timothy S. Miller and John Nesbitt, Washington, D.C. 1995, 114–22

Arimitsu, Hideyuki, 'Migration and assimilation seen from the 'nation address' in post-1066 Britain', in *Migration and Identity in British History. Proceedings of the Fifth Anglo-Japanese Conference of Historians,* eds David Bates and Kazuhiko Kondo, Tokyo 2006, 7–13

Barlow, F., *Edward the Confessor*, London 1970

Barlow, F., *The Godwins*, London 2002

Barrow, G. W. S., *The Anglo-Norman Era in Scottish History*, Oxford 1980.

Barrow, G. W. S., 'The Anglo-Scottish border: growth and structure in the middle ages', in *Grenzen und Grenzregionen/Frontières et régions frontalières/Borders and Border Regions*, eds Wolfgang Haubrichs and Reinhard Schneider, Saarbrücken 1993, 197–212

Barrow, G. W. S., *The Kingdom of the Scots. Government, Church and Society from the Eleventh to the Fourteenth Century*, 2nd edn, Edinburgh 2003

Barrow, G. W. S., *Kingship and Unity: Scotland 1000–1306*, London 1981

Barrow, G. W. S., 'Scots in the Durham Liber Vitæ', in *The Durham Liber Vitæ and Its Context*, eds D. Rollason, A. J. Piper, Margaret Harvey and Margaret Lynda Rollason, Woodbridge 2004, 109–116

Bartlett, Robert, *The Making of Europe*, London 1993

Bassett, Steven, ed., *The Origins of Anglo-Saxon Kingdoms*, Leicester 1989

Bradbury, J., *The Battle of Hastings*, Stroud 1998

Brooks, Eric St J., 'An unpublished charter of Raymond le Gros', *Journal of the Royal Society of Antiquaries of Ireland* 69, 1939, 167–9

Brooks, Nicholas, 'The creation and early structure of the kingdom of Kent', in *Origins of Anglo-Saxon Kingdoms*, ed. Bassett, 55–74

Brooks, Nicholas, 'The formation of the Mercian kingdom', in *Origins of Anglo-Saxon Kingdoms*, ed. Bassett, 159–70

Broun, Dauvit, 'Attitudes of *Gall* to *Gaedhel* in Scotland before John of Fordun', in *Mìorun Mòr nan Gall, 'The Great Ill-Will of the Lowlander'? Lowland Perceptions of the Highlands, Medieval and Modern*, eds Dauvit Broun and Martin MacGregor, Glasgow 2009, 49–82 (originally published in 2007 as an e-book: http://www.arts.gla.ac.uk/scottish-studies/ebooks/miorunmor.htm)

Broun, Dauvit, 'Becoming Scottish in the thirteenth century: the evidence of the Chronicle of Melrose', in *West over Sea: Studies in Scandinavian Sea-Borne Expansion and Settlement before 1300. A Festschrift in Honour of Dr Barbara E. Crawford*, eds Beverley Ballin Smith, Simon Taylor and Gareth Williams, Leiden 2007, 19–32

Broun, Dauvit, 'Contemporary perspectives on Alexander II's succession: the evidence of king-lists', in *The Reign of Alexander II, 1214–49*, ed. Richard D. Oram, Leiden 2005, 79–98

Broun, Dauvit, 'The Declaration of Arbroath: pedigree of a nation?', in *The Declaration of Arbroath: History, Significance, Setting*, Society of Antiquaries Monograph Series, ed. Geoffrey Barrow, Edinburgh 2003, 1–12

Broun, Dauvit, 'Scotland before 1100: writing Scotland's origins', in *Scotland: The Making and Unmaking of the Nation c.1100–1707*, eds Bob Harris and Alan R. MacDonald, vol. i, *The Scottish Nation: Origins to c.1500*, Dundee 2006, 1–16

Broun, Dauvit, *Scottish Independence and the Idea of Britain from the Picts to Alexander III*, Edinburgh 2007

Broun, Dauvit, 'A second England? Scotland and the monarchy of Britain', in *The First English Empire*', eds Seán Duffy and Susan Foran, Dublin forthcoming

Brown, Michelle and C. A. Farr, *Mercia: an Anglo-Saxon Kingdom in Europe*, London 2001

Cam, H. M., '*Manerium cum Hundredo*: the hundred and the hundred manor', *EHR* 47, 1932, 355–76

Cameron, K., 'Scandinavian settlement in the territory of the Five Boroughs: the place-Name Evidence', in *Place-name Evidence for the Anglo-Saxon Invasion and Scandi-*

navian Settlements: Eight Studies, ed. K. Cameron, English Place-Name Society Occasional Publications, Nottingham 1975, 115–71

Carey, John, *The Irish National Origin-Legend: Synthetic Pseudohistory*, Quiggin Pamphlets on the Sources of Medieval Gaelic History 1, Cambridge 1994

Carpenter, David *The Struggle for Mastery: Britain 1066–1284*, London 2003

Charles-Edwards, T. M., 'Cynghawsedd : counting and pleading in medieval Welsh law', *Bulletin of the Board of Celtic Studies* 33, 1986, 188–98

Charles-Edwards, T. M., *Early Irish and Welsh Kinship*, Oxford 1993

Charles-Edwards, T. M., 'Wales and Mercia, 613–918', in *Mercia*, eds Brown and Farr, 89–105

Charles-Edwards, T. M., *The Welsh Laws*, Cardiff 1989

Charles-Edwards, T. M., Morfydd E. Owen and D. B. Walters, eds, *Lawyers and Laymen: Studies in the History of Law Presented to Professor Dafydd Jenkins on his Seventy-Fifth Birthday*, Cardiff 1986

Chibnall, Marjorie, 'Feudalism and lordship', in *A Companion to the Anglo-Norman World*, eds Christopher Harper-Bill and Elisabeth van Houts, Woodbridge 2002, 123–34.

Chibnall, Marjorie, *The Normans*, Oxford 2000

Clancy, Thomas Owen, 'The Gall-Ghàidhel and Galloway', *Journal of Scottish Name Studies* 2, 2008, 19–50

Clarke', H. B., '1066, 1169 and all that' in *European Encounters*, ed. Judith Devlin and H.B. Clarke, Dublin 2003, 11–36

Comerford, Vincent, *Inventing the Nation: Ireland*, London 2003

Connolly, Philomena, 'The enactments of the 1297 parliament', in *Law and Disorder in Thirteenth-Century Ireland*, ed. Lydon, 139–62

Contamine, Philippe 'The Norman 'Nation' and the French 'Nation' in the fourteenth and fifteenth Centuries,' in *England and Normandy in the Middle Ages*, eds David Bates and Anne Curry, London 1994, 215–34

Cosgrove, Art, ed., *A New History of Ireland II: Medieval Ireland, 1169–1534*, Oxford 1987

Cosgrove, Art, 'The writing of Irish medieval history', *Irish Historical Studies*, 27, 1990, 97–111

Coupland, S., 'From poachers to gamekeepers: Scandinavian warlords and Carolingian kings', *Early Medieval Europe* 7, 1998, 85–114

Richard Cox, *Hibernia Anglicana: Or the History Thereof from the Conquest of England to this Present Time*, 2 vols, London, 1689–90

Craster, H. H. E., 'The Red Book of Durham', *EHR* 40, 1925, 504–35

Crooks, Peter, '"Hobbes", "dogs" and politics in the Ireland of Lionel of Antwerp, c. 1361–6', *Haskins Society Journal*, 16 (2005), 117–48

Dalton, P., *Conquest, Anarchy and Lordship: Yorkshire, 1066–1154*, Cambridge 1994

Dark, Ken, *Britain and the End of the Roman Empire*, Stroud 2000

Davies, J., *A History of Wales*, Harmondsworth 1990

Davies, R. R., *The Age of Conquest: Wales 1063–1415*, Oxford 1991

Davies, R. R., 'Colonial Wales', *Past and Present* 65, 1974

Davies, R. R., *Domination and Conquest: The Experience of Ireland, Scotland and Wales*, Cambridge 1999

Davies, R. R., 'The Identity of "Wales" in the thirteenth century', in *From Medieval to Modern Wales: Historical Essays in Honour of Kenneth O. Morgan and Ralph A. Griffiths*, eds R. R. Davies and G. H. Jenkins, Cardiff 2004, 43–63

Davies, R. R., '"Keeping the natives in order": the English king and the "Celtic" rulers 1066–

1216', *Peritia* 10, 1996, 212–224

Davies, R. R.,'Kings, lords and liberties in the march of Wales, 1066–1272', *Transactions of the Royal Historical Society* 29, 1979, 41–61

Davies, R. R., 'Law and national identity in thirteenth-century Wales', in *Welsh Society and Nationhood: Historical Essays Presented to Glanmor Williams,* eds R. R. Davies, R. A. Griffiths, I. G. Jones, and K. O. Morgan, Cardiff 1984, 51–69

Davies, R. R., 'The law of the March', *Welsh History Review* 5:1, 1970, 1–30

Davies, R. R., *Lordship and Society in the March of Wales, 1282–1400*, Oxford 1978

Davies, R. R., 'Race relations in post-conquest Wales: confrontation and compromise', *Transactions of the Honourable Society of Cymmrodorion* (1975 for 1974), 32–56

Davies, R. R., 'The survival of the bloodfeud in medieval Wales', *History* 54:182, 1969, 338–57

Davies, R. R., 'The twilight of Welsh law, 1284–1536', *History* 51, 1966, 143–64

Davies, Wendy, *Wales in the Early Middle Ages*, Leicester 1982

Davis, R. H. C., 'Alfred and Guthrum's Frontier', *EHR* 97, 1982, 803–10

Davis, R. H. C., 'Alfred the Great: propaganda and truth', *History* 55, 1971, 169–82, reprinted in idem., *From Alfred the Great to Stephen*, London 1991, 33–46 Davis, R. H. C., *The Normans and Their Myth*, London 1976

Donaldson, Gordon, *Scotland: The Shaping of a Nation*, 2nd edn, London 1980

Douglas, D. C., *The Social Structure of Medieval East Anglia*, Oxford 1927

Dumville, D., *Wessex and England from Alfred to Edgar,* Woodbridge 1992

Duncan, A. A. M.,'The making of Scotland', in *Who are the Scots?*, ed. Gordon Menzies, London 1971

Duncan, A. A. M., *The Kingship of the Scots, 842–1292. Succession and Independence,* Edinburgh 2002

Esmond Cleary, A. S., *The Ending of Roman Britain,* London 1989

Evans, D. Simon, *A Mediaeval Prince of Wales: the Life of Gruffudd ap Cynan,* Felinfach 1990

Evison, Martin, 'Lo, the conquering hero comes (or not)', *British Archaeology* no 23, April 1997, at www.britarch.ac.uk/ba/ba23/ba23feat.html.

Fellows Jensen, G., *Scandinavian Settlement Names in the East Midlands*, Copenhagen 1978

Finan, Thomas, *A Nation in Medieval Ireland? Perspectives on Gaelic National Identity in the Middle Ages*, BAR British Series, 367, Oxford 2004

Forte, A., Oram, R. & Pedersen, F., eds, *Viking Empires*, Oxford 2005

Flanagan, M. T., 'The Normans in Ireland' in *Irish History in the Classroom*, Belfast 1987, 23–32

Flanagan, M. T., *Irish Society, Anglo-Norman Settlers, Angevin Kingship: Interactions in Ireland in the Late Twelfth Century,* Oxford 1989

Flanagan, M. T., 'Richard fitz Gilbert de Clare', *Oxford Dictionary of National Biography* Oxford, 2004

Fleming, Robin, *Domesday Book and the Law: Society and Legal Custom in Early Medieval England*, Cambridge 1998

Fleming, Robin, *Kings and Lords in Conquest England,* Cambridge Studies in Medieval Life and Thought: Fourth Series no. 15, Cambridge 1991

Fletcher, R. A., *Bloodfeud. Murder and Revenge in Anglo-Saxon England*, London 2002

Foot, Sarah, 'The historiography of the Anglo-Saxon "nation-state"', in *Power and the Nation in European History,* eds L. Scales and O Zimmer, Cambridge 2004, 125–42

Fox, C., *Offa's Dyke*, London 1955

Frame, Robin, 'Exporting state and nation: being English in medieval Ireland' in *Power and the Nation in European History*, eds Len Scales and Oliver Zimmer, Cambridge 2005, 143–65

Frame, Robin, '"Les Engleys nées en Irlande": the English political identity in medieval Ireland' in Robin Frame, *Ireland and Britain, 1170–1540*, London 1998, 131–50

Fraser, James E., *The Battle of Dunnichen, 685*, Stroud 2002

Freeman, E. A., *The History of the Norman Conquest of England*, 6 vols, Oxford 1870–79

Gay, Tim, 'Rural dialects and surviving Britons', *British Archaeology* no. 46, July, 1999, available at www.britarch.ac.uk/ba/ba46/

Gelling, Margaret, *Signposts to the Past*, 3rd edn, Chichester 1997

Gelling, Margaret, *The West Midlands in the Early Middle Ages*, Leicester 1992

Gillingham, John 'Conquering the barbarians: war and chivalry in twelfth-century Britain', *Haskins Society Journal* 4, 1993, 67–84, reprinted in *The English in the Twelfth Century*, ed. Gillingham, 41–58

Gillingham, John, 'Henry of Huntingdon and the twelfth-century revival of the English nation,' in *The English in the Twelfth Century*, ed. Gillingham, 123–44

Gillingham, John, *The English in the Twelfth Century: Imperialism, National Identity, and Political Values*, Woodbridge 2000, repr. 2008

Gillingham, John, 'The English invasion of Ireland', in *Representing Ireland: literature and the origins of conflict, 1534–1660*, eds Brendan Bradshaw, Andrew Harfield and Willy Maley, Cambridge 1993, 24–42, reprinted in *The English in the Twelfth Century*, ed. Gillingham, 145–60

Gillingham, John, 'Normanizing the English invaders of Ireland,' in *Power and Identity in the Middle Ages: Essays in Memory of Rees Davies*, eds Huw Pryce and John Watts, Oxford 2007, 85–97

Graham-Campbell, James, C. Batey, H. Clarke, R. I. Page and N. S. Price, eds, *Cultural Atlas of the Viking World*, London 1994

Graham-Campbell, James, R. Hall, J. Jesch, and D. Parsons, eds, *Vikings and the Danelaw: Select Papers from the Proceedings of the Thirteenth Viking Congress, Nottingham and York, 21–30 August 1997*, Oxford 2001

Gransden, Antonia, *Historical Writing in England, c.550 to c. 1307*, London 1974

Grant, Alexander, 'Aspects of national consciousness in medieval Scotland', in *Nations, Nationalism and Patriotism in the European Past*, eds C. Bjørn, A. Grant and K. J. Stringer, Copenhagen 1994, 68–95

Grant, Alexander, 'The death of John Comyn: what was going on?', *SHR* 86, 2007, 176–224

Hadley, Dawn M., 'In search of the Vikings: the problems and the possibilities of interdisciplinary approaches', in *Vikings and the Danelaw*, ed. Graham-Campbell *et al.*, 13–30

Hadley, Dawn M., *The Northern Danelaw: its Social Structure, c.800–1100*, London 2000

Hadley, Dawn M., 'Viking and native: re-thinking identity in the Danelaw', *Early Medieval Europe* 11:1, 2002, 45–70

Hadley, Dawn M., *The Vikings in England: Settlement, Society, and Culture*, Manchester 2006

Dawn Hadley and J. Richards, eds, *Cultures in Contact: Scandinavian Settlement in England in the Ninth and Tenth Centuries*, Turnhout 2000

Hall, D., 'The sanctuary of St Cuthbert', in *St Cuthbert, his Cult and Community to AD 1200*, eds G. Bonner, D. Rollason and Clare Stancliffe, Woodbridge 1989, 425–36

Hall, K. Mary, 'Pre-Conquest estates in Yorkshire' in *Yorkshire Boundaries*, eds H. E. J. Le

Patourel, Moira H. Long and May F. Pickles, Leeds 1993, 25–38

Hall, R. A., 'The Five Boroughs of the Danelaw: a review of present knowledge', *ASE* 18, 1989, 149–206

Hammond, Matthew H., 'The use of the name Scot in the central middle ages. Part 1: Scot as a by-name', *Journal of Scottish Names Studies* 1, 2007, 37–60.

Hart, C. R., *The Danelaw,* London 1992

Hart, C. R., *The Early Charters of Northern England and the North Midlands,* Leicester 1975

Hart, C. R., 'Wulfstan (d. 955/6)', *ODNB*, Oxford 2004

Hennessy, John Pope, 'What do the Irish read?', *The Nineteenth Century*, 15, 1884, 920–32

Hill, D., *An Atlas of Anglo-Saxon England*, Oxford 1991

Hill, D., 'Mercians: the dwellers on the boundary', in *Mercia,* ed. Brown and Farr, 173–82

Hill, D., 'The shiring of Mercia – again', in *Edward the Elder, 899–924,* eds N. J. Higham and D. H. Hill, London 2001, 144–59

Hill, D. and A. R. Rumble, eds, *The Defence of Wessex: the Burghal Hidage and Anglo-Saxon Fortifications*, Manchester 1996

Holman, K., 'Defining the Danelaw', in *Vikings and the Danelaw*, ed. Graham-Campbell *et al.,* 1–12

Hudson, B. T., 'Cnut and the Scottish Kings,' *EHR* 107, 1992, 350–60

Jackson, Kenneth, 'On the northern British section in Nennius', in *Celt and Saxon*, ed. N. K. Chadwick, Cambridge 1963, 20–62

Jenkins, D., *Hywel Dda: The Law,* Gomer 1986

Jenkins, D., ed., *Celtic Law Papers,* Studies Presented to the International Commission for the History of Representative Institutions 42, Brussels 1973

Jenkins, D., 'Law and Government in Wales before the Act of Union,' in *Celtic Law Papers*, ed. Jenkins, 25–48

John, E., 'The West Saxon conquest of England' in *Reassessing Anglo-Saxon England,* Manchester 1996, 83–98

Jones, G. R. J., 'Early territorial organization in Northern England and its bearing on the Scandinavian settlement', in *The Fourth Viking Congress*, ed. A. Small, 1965, 67–84

Jones, G. R. J., 'Multiple estate and early settlement', in *Medieval Settlement*, ed. P. H. Sawyer, London 1976, 15–40

Kapelle, W. E., *The Norman Conquest of the North: the Region and its Transformation, 1000–1135*, London 1979

Kent, C.A., 'Goldwin Smith', in *ODNB*, Oxford 2004

Keynes, S., 'The Vikings in England', in *The Oxford Illustrated History of the Vikings,* ed. Sawyer, 48–82

Keynes, S., 'Wulfstan I, archbishop of York (931–56)', in *The Blackwell Encyclopaedia of Anglo-Saxon England*, eds M. Lapidge, J. Blair, S. Keynes and D. Scragg, Oxford 1999, 492–93

Kirby, D. P. *The Earliest English Kings*, London 1991

Krag, C., 'Harald Hardrada (1015–1066)', *ODNB*, Oxford 2004

Lawson, M. K., *Cnut. The Danes in England in the Early Eleventh Century*, London 1993

Lawson, M. K., *The Battle of Hastings, 1066*, Stroud 2002

Lawson, M. K., 'Cnut (d. 1035)', *ODNB*, Oxford 2004

Leaver, R. A., 'Five hides in ten counties: a contribution to the Domesday regression debate,' *Economic History Review* 41, 1988, 525–42

Lewis, C. P., 'Waltheof, earl of Northumbria (c. 1050–1076)', *ODNB*, Oxford 2004

Leyser, Henrietta, 'Walcher, earl of Northumbria (*d.* 1080)', *ODNB*, Oxford 2004

Lönnroth, L., 'The Vikings in history and legend', in *The Oxford Illustrated History of the Vikings*, ed. Sawyer, 229–30

Loyn, H. R., *The Governance of Anglo-Saxon England, 500–1087*, London 1984

Loyn, H. R., *The Vikings in England*, London 1977

Lydon, James, 'The middle nation' in James Lydon, *The English in Medieval Ireland*, Dublin 1984, 1–26

Lydon, James, ed., *Law and Disorder in Thirteenth-century Ireland: the Dublin Parliament of 1297*, Dublin 1997

MacGeoghegan, James, *History of Ireland, Ancient and Modern ... Translated from the French by P. O'Kelly*, 3 vols, Dublin 1831–2; reprinted Dublin, Glasgow, New York, 1844, 1849, 1868, 1884, 1898

MacNeill, Eoin, *Phases of Irish History*, Dublin 1919, repr. 1968

MacQueen, Hector L., *Common Law and Feudal Society in Medieval Scotland*, Edinburgh 1993

MacQueen, Hector L., 'Pleadable brieves, pleading and the development of Scots law', *Law and History Review* 4, 1986, 403–22

MacQueen, Hector L., '*Regiam Majestatem*, Scots law and national identity', *SHR* 74, 1995, 1–25

MacQueen, Hector L., 'Scotland: politics, government and law', in *A Companion to Britain in the Later Middle Ages*, ed. S. H. Rigby, Oxford 2003, 283–308

MacQueen, Hector L., 'The brieve of right in Scots law', *Journal of Legal History* 3, 1982, 52–70

Mahany, C. M. and D. R. Roffe, eds, *Sleaford*, South Lincolnshire Archaeology 3, Stamford 1979

Mahany, C. M. and D. R. Roffe, 'Stamford: the development of an Anglo-Scandinavian borough', *ANS* 5, 1983, 199–219

Marten, L., 'The shiring of East Anglia: an alternative hypothesis', *Historical Research* 81, 2008, available online at http://www.blackwell-synergy.com/toc/hisr/0/0

Martin, F. X. and F. J. Byrne, eds, *The Scholar Revolutionary: Eoin MacNeill, 1867–1945 and the Making of the New Ireland*, Dublin 1973

Mason, Emma, *The House of Godwine. History of a Dynasty*, London 2004

Maume, P., 'Eoin MacNeill,' in *ODNB*, Oxford 2004

McCartney, Donal, 'MacNeill and Irish-Ireland,' in Martin and Byrne, *The Scholar Revolutionary*, 77–97

McDonald, J. and G. D. Snooks, 'Were the tax assessments of Domesday England artificial? The case of Essex', *EHR* 38, 1985, 353–73

Meehan, B., 'The Siege of Durham, the battle of Carham and the Cession of Lothian', *SHR* 55, 1976, 1–19

Metcalf, D. M., 'Monetary circulation in the Danelaw, 973–1083', in *Anglo-Saxons: Studies Presented to Cyril Roy Hart*, eds Simon Keynes and A. P. Smyth, Dublin 2006, 159–85

Mills, A.D., *A Dictionary of English Place-Names*, Oxford 1998

Morgan, Hiram, 'Giraldus Cambrensis and the Tudor conquest of Ireland' in *Political Ideology in Ireland*, ed. Hiram Morgan, Dublin 1999, 22–44

Morris, C.J., *Marriage and Murder in Eleventh-Century Northumbria: a Study of the 'De Obsessione Dunelmi'*, University of York Borthwick Paper no.82, York 1992

Murray, Alan V., 'Ethnic identity in the Crusader States: the Frankish race and the settlement of Outremer,' in *Concepts of National Identity in the Middle Ages*, eds Simon Forde,

Lesley Johnson and Alan V. Murray, Leeds Texts and Monographs 14, Leeds 1995, 59–73

Murray, Alan V.,'How Norman was the Principality of Antioch? Prolegomena to a study of the origins of the nobility of a Crusader state,' in *Family Trees and the Roots of Politics: the Prosopography of Britain and France from the Tenth to the Twelfth Century*, ed. K. S. B. Keats-Rohan, Woodbridge 1997, 349–59

Nicholls, K. W., 'Anglo-French Ireland and after', *Peritia*, 1, 1982, 370–403

Nishioka, Kenji, 'Scots and Galwegians in the 'peoples address' of Scottish royal charters', *SHR* 87, 2008, 206–32

Noble, Frank, *Offa's Dyke Reviewed*, ed. M. Gelling , BAR British series 114, Oxford 1983

O'Conor, Charles, *Dissertations on the History of Ireland*, Dublin, 1766

Orchard, Andy, '*Audite omnes amantes*: a hymn in Patrick's praise,' in *St Patrick, AD 493–1993*, ed. David Dumville, Woodbridge 1993, 153–73

Orpen, G. H., *Ireland under the Normans, 1169–1333*, 4 vols, Oxford 1911–1920, reprinted Dublin 2005 (1 vol.)

Palliser, D. M., 'An introduction to the Yorkshire Domesday', in *The Yorkshire Domesday*, eds Ann Williams and G. H. Martin, 2 vols, London 1992

Palliser, D. M., 'Domesday Book and the "Harrying of the North"', *Northern History* 29 1993, 1–23

Pryce, H., 'British or Welsh? National identity in twelfth-century Wales', *EHR* 116, 2001, 775–801

Pryce, H., 'The context and purpose of the earliest Welsh lawbooks', *Cambrian Medieval Celtic Studies* 39, 2000, 39–63

Pryce, H., 'Lawbooks and literacy in medieval Wales', *Speculum* 75, 2000, 29–67

Pryce, H., *Native Law and the Church in Medieval Wales*, Oxford 1993

Pryce, H. 'The prologues to the Welsh lawbooks', *Bulletin of the Board of Celtic Studies* 33, 1986, 151–87

Pythian Adams, Charles, *Land of the Cumbrians: a Study in British Provincial Origins, AD 400–1120*, Aldershot 1996

Rees, W., *An Historical Atlas of Wales*, Cardiff 1951

Richter, M., 'The political and institutional background to national consciousness in medieval Wales', in *Nationality and the Pursuit of National Independence*, ed. T. M. Moody, Historical Studies (Irish Conference of Historians) 11, Belfast 1978, 37–55

Rivet, A. L. F. and Colin Smith, *The Place-Names of Roman Britain*, London 1979

Roffe, D. R., *Decoding Domesday*, Woodbridge 2007

Roffe, D. R., *Domesday: the Inquest and the Book*, Oxford 2000

Roffe, D. R., 'The hide and local government in Anglo-Saxon England', National Museum of Japanese History, forthcoming

Roffe, D.R., 'The Historical Context', *Anglo-Saxon Settlement on the Siltland of Eastern England*, Lincolnshire Archaeology and Heritage Reports Series 7, 2005, 264–88

Roffe, D. R., 'The Lincolnshire hundred', *Landscape History* 3, 1981, 27–36

Roffe, D. R., 'The origins of Derbyshire,' *The Derbyshire Archaeological Journal* 106, 1986, 102–22

Roffe, D. R., 'Hundreds and wapentakes,' *The Lincolnshire Domesday*, eds A. Williams and G. H. Martin, 2 vols, London 1992, 33–9

Rollason, D. W., *Northumbria, 500–1100. Creation and Destruction of a Kingdom*, Cambridge 2003

Rollason, D. W. (1987), 'The Wanderings of St Cuthbert,' in *Cuthbert: Saint and Patron*, ed.

D. W. Rollason, Durham 1987, 45–61

Sawyer, P. H., *The Charters of Burton Abbey*, London 1979

Sawyer, P. H., ed., *The Oxford Illustrated History of the Vikings*, Oxford 1997

Short, Ian, '*Tam Angli quam Franci*: self-definition in Anglo-Norman England,' *ANS* 18, 1996, 153–75

Sims Williams, Patrick, *Religion and Literature in Western England, 600–800*, Cambridge 1990

Simpson, Luisella, 'The Alfred/St Cuthbert episode in the Historia de Sancto Cuthberto: its significance for mid-tenth century history,' in *St Cuthbert, his Cult and Community to AD1200*, eds G. Bonner, D. Rollason and Clare Stancliffe, Woodbridge 1989, 397–412

Simpson, Grant G., 'The Declaration of Arbroath revitalised', *Scottish Historical Review* 56, 1977, 11–33

Smith, Brendan, 'Keeping the peace', in *Law and Disorder in Thirteenth-Century Ireland*, ed. Lydon, 57–65

Smith, Goldwin, *Irish History and Irish Character*, Oxford 1868

Smith, Goldwin, *Irish History and the Irish Question,* Toronto 1905

Smith, J. Beverley, '"Distinction and Diversity": the Common Lawyers and the Law of Wales', in *Power and Identity in the Middle Ages: Essays in Memory of Rees Davies*, eds H. Pryce and J. L. Watts, Oxford 2007, 139–52

Smyth, A. P., *Scandinavian York and Dublin,* 2 vols, Dublin 1975–9, republ. in 1 vol., Dublin 1987

Snyder, Christopher, *An Age of Tyrants: Britain and the Britons, AD 499–600,* Stroud 1998

Stacey, R. Chapman, 'Law and literature in medieval Ireland and Wales', in *Medieval Celtic Literature and Society,* ed. H. Fulton, Dublin 2005, 65–82

Stacey, R. Chapman, 'Learning to plead in Medieval Welsh Law', *Studia Celtica* 38, 2004, 107–24

Stafford, Pauline, *The East Midlands in the Early Middle Ages,* Leicester 1985

Stafford, Pauline, 'Kings, kingship and kingdoms,' in *From the Vikings to The Normans*, ed. Wendy Davies, Oxford 2003, 11–39

Stenton, F. M., *Anglo-Saxon England*, 3rd edn, Oxford 1971

Stenton, F. M., 'The Danes in England', *Proceedings of the British Academy* 13, 1927, 203–46

Stenton, F. M., *Types of Manorial Structure in the Northern Danelaw,* Oxford 1910

Stevens, M., 'Wealth, status and "race" in the Ruthin of Edward II', *Urban History* 32:1, 2005, 17–32

Stewart-Brown, R., *The Serjeants of the Peace in Medieval England and Wales,* Manchester 1936

Stocker, D., 'Monuments and merchants: irregularities in the distribution of stone sculpture in Lincolnshire and Yorkshire in the tenth century', in *Cultures in Contact*, eds Hadley and Richards, 179–212

Stocker, D. and P. Everson, 'Five town funerals: decoding diversity in Danelaw stone sculpture,' in *Vikings and the Danelaw*, ed. Graham-Campbell *et al.,* 223–43

Stokes, G. T., *Ireland and the Anglo-Norman Church: A History of Ireland and Irish Christianity from the Anglo-Norman Conquest to the Dawn of the Reformation*, London 1909

Stringer, Keith J., 'The charters of David, earl of Huntingdon and lord of Garioch: a study of Anglo-Scottish diplomatic', in *Essays on the Nobility of Medieval Scotland*, ed. K. J. Stringer, Edinburgh 1985, 72–101

Studd, Helen, 'How the Old English put all their Basques in one exit', in *The Times*, July 1 2002

Thomas, Hugh M., *The English and the Normans: Ethnic Hostility, Assimilation, and Identity 1066–c.1220*, Oxford 2003

Thomas, Mark, 'England's apartheid roots' in *The Times*, July 29 2006

Tolkien, J. R. R., 'English and Welsh', in *idem, Angles and Britons*, Cardiff 1963

Townend, M., 'Viking Age England as a bilingual society', in *Cultures in Contact*, eds Hadley and Richards, 89–105

Van Houts, Elisabeth M. C., 'The trauma of 1066,' *History Today* 46 no. 10, October 1996, 9–15

Ward-Perkins, Bryan , 'Why did the Anglo-Saxons not become more British?', *EHR* 115, 2000, 513–33

Watt, J. A., *The Church and the Two Nations in Medieval Ireland*, Cambridge 1970

Weale, Michael E., Deborah A. Weiss, Rolf F. Jager, Neil Bradman and Mark G. Thomas, 'Y Chromosome evidence for Anglo-Saxon mass migration,' *Molecular Biology and Evolution* 19, 2002, 1008–21

Werner, K. F., 'Quelques observations au sujet des débuts du 'duché' de Normandie,' in *Droit privé et institutions régionales: Études historiques offertes à Jean Yver*, Paris 1976, 691–709

Whitelock, Dorothy, 'Archbishop Wulfstan, homilist and statesman', in *Essays in Medieval History*, ed. R. W. Southern, London 1968, 42–60

Whitelock, Dorothy, 'The dealings of the kings of England with Northumbria in the tenth and eleventh centuries', in *The Anglo-Saxons: Studies in Some Aspects of the History Presented to Bruce Dickens*, ed. P. Clemoes, London 1959, 70–88; reprinted in Whitelock, *History, Law and Literature in Tenth- to Eleventh-Century England*, London 1981

Wilkinson, B., 'Northumbrian separatism in 1065–66', *Bulletin of the John Rylands Library* 23, 1939, 504–26

Williams, Ann, *The English and the Norman Conquest*, Woodbridge 1995

Williams, Ann, '*Princeps Merciorum Gentis*: the family, career and connections of Ælfhere, Ealdorman of Mercia 956–83', *ASE* 10, 1982, 143–72

Williams, Ann, A. P. Smyth, and D. P. Kirby, *A Biographical Dictionary of Dark Age Britain: England, Scotland and Wales, c.500–c.1050*, London 1991

Willock, Ian Douglas, *The Origins and Development of the Jury in Scotland*, Stair Society, Edinburgh 1966

Wormald, Patrick 'Bede, the *Bretwaldas* and the origins of the *Gens Anglorum*,' in *Ideal and Reality in Frankish and Anglo-Saxon Society*, eds Patrick Wormald, Donald Bullough and Roger Collins, Oxford 1983, 99–129

Wormald, Patrick, '*Engla Lond*: The making of an allegiance,' *Journal of Historical Sociology* 7, 1994, 10–18

Wormald, Patrick, 'The making of England', *History Today* 45:2, 1995, 26–32

Wormald, Patrick, *The Making of English Law: King Alfred to the Twelfth Century*, Oxford 1999

Wormald, Patrick, 'Wulfstan (d. 1023)', in *ODNB*, Oxford 2004

Yorke, Barbara, *Kings and Kingdoms of Early Anglo-Saxon England*, London 1990

Young, Alan, *Robert the Bruce's Rivals: The Comyns, 1212–1314*, East Linton 1997

Young, Alan, *William Cumin: Border Politics and the Bishopric of Durham, 1141–1144*, York 1978

INDEX